How To Save Your Business

Winning Ways to Put Any Financially
Troubled Business Together Again

Arnold S. Goldstein

Copyright 1983 by Enterprise Publishing, Inc.

All rights reserved. No part of this book may be reproduced, stored in a retrieval system, or transmitted in any form by an electronic, mechanical, photocopying, recording means or otherwise without prior written permission of the publisher.

ISBN: 0-913864-74-9

Library of Congress Catalog Card No. 82-83243

This publication is designed to provide accurate and authoritative information in regard to the subject covered. It is sold with the understanding that neither the author nor the publisher is engaged in rendering legal, accounting, or other professional service. If legal advice or other expert assistance is required, the services of a competent professional should be sought.

From a Declaration of Principles jointly adopted by a Committee of the American Bar Association and a Committee of Publishers and Associations.

To my wife Marlene for the encouragement she gave me to write this book and her tireless efforts in helping me to create it.

Author's Note

Every case and example in this book is true. To preserve confidentiality and privacy, most of the names of individuals and organizations have been changed. Any resemblance of fictional names to actual persons or organizations is purely coincidental.

Acknowledgments

I express my sincere appreciation to those who have made valuable contributions to this book. Special thanks to my associate, Barry R. Levine, for his critical reviews, to Helen Siegal for her diligent clerical assistance, to my good friend and literary mentor, H. Michael Snell, for assistance with the manuscript; and particularly to my wife, Marlene, who worked tirelessly to bring this book about.

A special acknowledgment is extended to the countless individuals, attorneys, accountants, consultants and bankruptcy judges who made it their careers to assist honest men and women to overcome their business problems and achieve a fresh start so they could realize their dreams in our free enterprise system.

Perhaps I am most indebted to my many clients who have proven that the will and desire to survive in the business arena can overcome any obstacle.

Table of Contents

Introduction

Chapter 1: Starting Smart

    Playing "What If?".. 1
    Hope for the Best—Prepare for the Worst..................... 3
    Why a Corporation is a Must 4
    Make Uncle Sam Share Your Losses 5
    Small Investments Mean Small Losses....................... 6
    How to Invest Safely... 7
    Assets You Never Have to Lose 8
    Create Your Own Mini-Holding Company 10
    Side-Stepping Dangerous Guarantees......................... 11
    How Deep are Your Pockets? 13
    Your "Starting Smart" Self-Exam............................ 15

Chapter 2: Taking Charge

    You Come First... 17
    Define Your Objectives...................................... 19
    Fight or Flight! 21
    Will the Real You, Please Stand Up......................... 25
    Assess Your Management Mentality......................... 30
    The Moment of Truth 36

Chapter 3: Putting Together Your Winning Team

What Your Team Will Do For You 39
Finding the Right Attorney 39
Wanted: An Accountant Who Can Keep Score 43
Consultants Who Mean Business 45
Free Help—Yours For the Asking 52
Ask Your Key Employees to Help 53
Partners For Your Winning Team 55
Check Your Starting Line-Up 57

Chapter 4: Profits: The Name of the Game

Face the Facts 59
Five Early Warning Signals 60
Take a Quick Trip Through Your Financial Statements 63
Why Is Your Business in Trouble? 65
Sharpen Your Survival Instinct 67
Eight Deadly Business Killers 69
The One Costly Error Case 75
Why a Dollar Earned May Not Be Enough 77
Six Tips on Profit Planning 78
Complete Your Own Management Action Plan 81
Any Business Can Be a MoneyMaker 82

Chapter 5: Attacking Problems One by One

The Tourniquet Treatment 86
The Cash Transfusion 88
Fill Your Empty Shelves 94
The Care and Feeding of Creditors 99
Getting 120% Out of 100% of Your Employees 102
Keep Your Customers Smiling 105
To Sum it Up 106
Problem Solving Planning Guide 106

Chapter 6: Cut Your Debts Down to Size

    How to Turn Poverty Into Power............................110
    The Foolproof Formula That Tells You What to Offer..........111
    Negotiate Your Best Deal...................................113
    Taking the Motion Out of Emotion 115
    Sell Future Dollars 117
    The Enemy Within 119
    Effective Ways to Get Their Signature 120
    Five Ways to Handle Even the Toughest Creditor.............122
    Winning Over That One Important Creditor 123
    Your Ten Point Negotiating Checklist.......................126

Chapter 7: Bailing Out Your Problem Loans

    A "No-Nonsense" Look at Your "Nonsense Loan" 130
    Create Your Own Master Plan 133
    Shrinking Your Over-Financed Loan 134
    Turn Choking Payments Into Easily Swallowed Installments 137
    Put Yourself in Your Lender's Shoes 140
    Three Lenders Who Always Play Rough 143
    More Strategies That Can Turn a "No" Into a "Yes"..........144
    Turn Lenders Into Partners................................145
    Winning Ways to Get Even More Money 147
    Know What's Inside That Pin-Stripe Suit...................149
    Why Quick Action Is a Must................................150

Chapter 8: Strong Medicine for Your Sick Business

    A Quick Trip to Solvency 152
    The Case of the Belligerent Bank..........................155
    But Will They Settle for Two Cents on the Dollar?.........158
    Cancelling Costly Contracts 162
    Shrinking Assets Can Bring Powerful Profits 165
    How the Bankruptcy Court Can Help You Get Credit..........166
    The One Essential Ingredient 168
    Can Chapter 11 Help You?..................................169

Chapter 9: Business As Usual: Starting Over Free and Clear

    Why Starting Over May Be Your Best Bet 172
    The Master Strategy 175
    Picking Up the Pieces for Pennies 180
    Finding Cash to Make it Happen 180
    Business as Usual at the Same Old Stand 182
    Harvard, Yale and Jail 184

Chapter 10: Two's Company

    Should You Hear Wedding Bells? 190
    Spot Your Hidden Charms 193
    The New Math: 2 + 2 = 5 198
    How to Structure the Deal to Work for You 200
    What Are You Really Worth? 203
    Thirteen Ways to Get Your Best Deal 204
    Two Blunders to Avoid 206

Chapter 11: Putting It All Together

    A Case of Indigestion 210
    Why Fight City Hall? 213
    The Case of the Corporate Eunuch 216
    A Case of Contaminated Chow Mein 219
    Prescription for a Dying Drugstore 221
    A Final Act 224

Bibliography 229

Index 231

Introduction

Getting into business is relatively easy. Staying in business is another matter. During the turbulent 1980's, hundreds of thousands of businesses will fail and close their doors.

What an alarming statistic! Eighty percent of those who test their entrepreneurial wings eventually crash and return to punching somebody else's timeclock after their investment, hopes, hard work and aspirations vanish under a sea of liabilities.

I see it every day. Walk into any Bankruptcy Court tomorrow and you'll witness businessmen publicly confess defeat in the rough and tumble business game.

It's no crime to fail, but too many people quit while there remains a good chance they could pull their companies out of a nosedive, sail clear of financial obstacles and build the successful business of their dreams.

I wrote this book to show you those proven ways to rescue your financially troubled business. I'll show you specific strategies and techniques that can work for any kind of enterprise, regardless of its problems. You will learn step-by-step methods that can keep you out of the Bankruptcy Court and on the road to prosperity.

This book is long overdue. Go into any bookstore and you'll find the shelves loaded with books selling "success." How to get into business or how to make even more money are recurring themes. Certainly these books have their value; however, it's time we paid more attention to beleaguered business people wallowing in financial despair.

These people aren't looking for their first million. They don't want inspirational pep talks about building castles in the air or how to magically go from rags to riches. They face the more mundane problems of the real business world, and they need concrete plans to fend off creditors, stop checks from bouncing, and survive in the twilight world of no cash, no credit, dwindling assets and skyrocketing debts. Their survival depends on the "no-nonsense" information this book provides.

I've spent 20 years as an insolvency specialist, learning that most small business owners have no trouble dealing with stability or prosperity. But adversity is another matter. When adversity strikes, too many people throw up their hands in despair, releasing the very controls that could produce workable solutions to keep their business in the air.

While most lawyers adorn their walls with diplomas and pictures of dignitaries shaking their hand, my wall is papered with crisp $10 bills. Whenever I agree to represent clients in financial trouble, I make them promise to send me a crisp $10 bill if they are still in business 5 years later.

To remind myself that the strategies in this book do work, all I have to do is swivel my chair and glance at the ever-growing collage of $10 bills.

Every bill represents a unique story. There's Ken's $10. He was in deep trouble with his appliance business and was almost ready to file for bankruptcy and go back to work as a telephone repairman. But he wasn't a quitter. I showed him how to eliminate over $300,000 in debt, turn his profit picture around, and build a growing chain of stores grossing over $4,000,000 a year.

The $10 bill next to Ken's came from two young partners who owned a failing health club. They followed my advice, sidestepping failure to go on and manage a club that provides them each a $50,000 income.

Imagine! Hundreds of bills representing hundreds of success stories. Though each involved unique people like you, each illustrates the message that almost any business can erase its problems, start fresh and go on to succeed.

Since the majority of business failures are small businesses, I direct this book to them. The options available to the small business owner are substantially different from those geared to the large, publicly-held corporation. So are the priorities.

As a small business owner, you as an individual become the #1 priority. You want to protect your investment and your dream of "going it alone." Your survival in the business arena is what matters. Perhaps that survival will be in the form of a fresh start with a new business, or even an imaginative merger with a competitor. So I write this book with you—the individual small business owner—in mind.

Before we start, there are a few things you must know. First, shed your mistaken belief that insolvency is a matter to be handled only by lawyers! Nothing could be further from the truth. In this book you will see in action strategies that many lawyers know nothing about. And these winning tactics depend equally on the management skill you must provide. I therefore ask you to set aside your opinions and misconceptions of what can be done for you until you finish the book. Read carefully. You may find that blueprint you never dreamed possible.

As you claw your way back to success, you will face numerous day-to-day problems. I'll guide you over these operational bumps with proven solutions. Credit is a problem, so I'll give you five surefire ways to obtain it. Cash flow is at a standstill and in these pages you'll discover six quick steps to increase it. Employees? Of course they're demoralized. But I'll show you three incentives to get them working harder than ever. Yes, you know the thorny problems. This book will help you find the answers.

When insolvency strikes, everything becomes a blur as problems keep piling up. We'll attack those problems in a logical and concise step-by-step manner so each problem and every solution is in clear focus. From initial start-up to ultimate prosperity, big problems or small, you'll know just what to do and how to do it.

And I give it to you in easy-to-understand everyday language, avoiding textbook theory or technical jargon. When you put this book down, you'll have new insights and the information that any business person can relate to and effectively use.

Strategy is only one dimension. Your thought-process, willingness and desire to see the business through its crisis is the other. And this book can put you in the right frame of mind so you can go from despair to the courage and stamina you'll certainly need to succeed. You'll take on a new perspective. Looking out for #1 and doing what's best for you will become your war cry as you fight hungry creditors, belligerent employees and ruthless competitors.

Success won't come with a wave of a magic wand. Every real-life story in this book shows how a loser became a winner, but the people involved didn't do it without plenty of hard work, sleepless nights, and a commitment to their own financial victory.

Professional confidentiality required me to change the names and nature of the businesses in the cases. However, every one is true. As I have learned from their successes, so will you.

So read on as your first step in putting your business back on the road to success.

—Arnold S. Goldstein—

Starting Smart

1

Every weekend, my friend Paul packs his bags and heads for the gambling casinos in Atlantic City. Knowing he's fed up with his high level executive position at an electronics firm, I asked him why he didn't save his money and go into a business of his own instead of throwing it into hungry slot machines. "The slot machines give me a 45 percent chance of winning," replied Paul. "If I go into my own business, my odds of success would be only 20 percent."

He's right about the statistics, but that doesn't mean you should close up shop and head for Las Vegas. Far from it. Though you must go into business with success as your goal, you must allow for the very real possibility of failure.

This chapter will start you thinking about failure, not as something, like an automobile accident, that only happens to others, but as a possibility for which you must prepare. I'll show you how to start your business so you can best prepare for the possibility of failure. Even if you are already in business, you may find valuable ways to restructure your business to give you a "soft landing" if you have to bail out.

Playing "What If?"

Who ever heard of planning for failure? Open any business book and you'll see rosy pictures of fat cats in plush penthouse suites, sipping cognac and "wheeling and dealing" their way to a fortune. Fueling your fantasies by reading and thinking success can be fun, and positive thinking does build empires, but full-time dreamers only see one side of the equation, never the "downside" risk. They ignore the possibility of failure, until it's too late. Most dreamers don't start smart by taking at the outset precautionary steps to protect themselves against a less than prosperous future.

Realists, on the other hand, don't fall victim to the "Rose-Colored Glasses Syndrome." Instead, they do everything possible to reduce their risks. Realists understand and prepare for possible defeat.

Consider the dreamer who walks into my office with boundless enthusiasm over her plan to buy a dress shop. She'll spend hours figuring out how to spend the millions she'll make, but she won't spend even a minute asking, "What if I fail? What can I do *now* to reduce or eliminate my risk? How can I best protect myself? How can I start smart?"

I have Sarah in mind. After working as a sales clerk in a leading department store, Sarah finally accumulated $30,000 to buy her "dream" business which was currently grossing $500,000 a year. She was prepared to pay a $30,000 deposit and sign a note for $120,000 to meet the purchase price of $150,000. The deal was basically sound. Sarah enthusiastically told me how she would re-merchandise the store, undertake extensive newspaper advertising, and go discount. With her strategy, she figured to double sales and profits within a year. She had it down to a science, which, coupled with her unbridled enthusiasm, convinced me she could succeed. I listened to her ideas, added some of my own, and spent two hours talking "success."

When it came time to play "What if?," I turned to Sarah, saying, "What do you see as your potential loss if the business *doesn't* succeed?" Sarah laughed, "Don't you have confidence in me? How can you even *think* I'll fail? This business will succeed and I won't waste my time thinking about failure!"

I pulled out the *National Bankruptcy Reporter*, which lists businesses that have filed for bankruptcy during the prior week. Running my finger down the columns, I counted 28 women's apparel shops that may have started with plenty of hope but ended with plenty of liabilities. But

Sarah wouldn't listen. Two years later, her store appeared on the very same list. She was so stunned by the bankruptcy, I didn't have the heart to say, "Sarah . . . remember the 'What if?' "

How about you? Have you asked yourself "What if?" To what extent have you strategically set yourself up for the contingency of failure? Even if you are already in business, it may not be too late to put on your "bulletproof vest."

Recently, our firm supervised the liquidation of a large stereo shop. I had handled routine legal matters for the client, Robert, for years and had pointed out several areas of vulnerability. I advised him to incorporate, reduce his obligations on guaranties, and to remove certain assets from under his name. Like Sarah, he was a dreamer. He would only laugh and say "What for? I've been in business nine years, and business has never been better!" Unfortunately, about a year ago a large discount stereo chain moved in next to him. The competition murdered him. Had he taken the suggested steps to protect himself, he could have avoided bankruptcy and certainly would not have lost over $280,000 in personal assets.

It's never to late to ask "What if?" Even if you have already started your venture, you may be able to take timely corrective action to protect yourself.

Hope for the Best—Prepare for the Worst

You can never completely eliminate risk. Entrepreneurship is always risky. However, "Starting Smart" can minimize risk because it will —

1. Keep your personal investment to a minimum, protecting what you do invest.
2. Protect valuable assets from hungry creditors.
3. Free you from personal liabilities on business debts.
4. Put you in the best defensive posture, so you, not your creditors, have the upper hand if the business goes bad.

"Starting Smart" enhances your chances of success by giving you the upper hand and the ability to keep your personal resources intact so you can bounce back if you do crash.

Why a Corporation Is a Must

"Starting Smart" means choosing the correct form of business organization, and no chapter on risk-reducing strategies would be complete without mentioning that greatest of risk-reducers—the corporation.

If you do go into business as a sole proprietor or with others in a partnership, you are saying to your business creditors, "If my business doesn't pay your bill, you can come after my personal assets to satisfy your bill." It's easy but extremely dangerous to do business without the protection of a corporation.

About 30 percent of all businesses operate without the protection of a corporate umbrella, but if you assemble all the non-incorporated business people, you'll be looking at a long line of dreamers. They'll never fail, so why do they need the hassle of incorporating? Dream on!

Fresh out of law school, I quit dreaming after one of my first cases, which involved a pharmacist who owned three drugstores. His former attorney had said, "Why incorporate and go through the hassles of extra paperwork and tax returns?"

Though the pharmacist didn't fail for the first ten years, one day trouble struck. His locations became ghettos; giant chains moved in and his stores fell under the hammer of Louie the Liquidator. When it was all over, the auction of the three pharmacies brought $45,000. Unfortunately, there was also $200,000 in creditors' claims.

The creditors whooped for joy! My client had a fully paid $150,000 ranch house. With a few carefully timed attachments, the creditors ended up with the house, and my client moved to his new third floor walkup apartment to ponder the most expensive legal advice he ever had—"Why incorporate?"

Look at incorporation as just another form of insurance. You may pay $300–600 to initially incorporate and you may have to pay your accountant another $200 a year to file corporate tax returns. But those modest premiums isolate and protect all the personal assets you have worked so hard over the years to accumulate. You can't find better insurance!

Even if you're now operating without the protection of a corporation, it may not be too late to gain its mighty protection. I recently observed a skillful play of a non-incorporated owner of a hardware store who was in trouble with over $50,000 in bills. His attorney incorporated the business and sold all the assets to the corporation. The owner would make payments on old bills that were directed to him personally, while the corporation would incur new bills under its own name.

A year later, the hardware store went bankrupt with $50,000 in outstanding bills. The bills, however, were now *corporate* obligations, because the owner had retired all the old bills incurred before incorporation.

If you are not incorporated, run, don't walk to your lawyer. Everything you own may depend on it.

Make Uncle Sam Share Your Losses

The IRS is never shy about sharing your profits or gains, so why not make them a partner when you lose money? You can do just that if you take advantage of the little-known Section 1244 of the Internal Revenue Code.

Your attorney can draft a provision in your corporate by-laws that the shares of stock that you buy fall under Section 1244 of the IRS Code. Section 1244 provides that once you purchase your shares, you can deduct any loss on your investment as an ordinary loss. If you are in the 50% tax bracket, and you have invested and lost $20,000, you can deduct the entire $20,000 against taxable income. This could save you $10,000 in taxes!

Without this provision in your corporate books, you can treat the loss only as a capital loss, and this saves you money only if you have a corresponding capital gain in the same year. There are absolutely no disadvantages to a Section 1244 stock issue.

Small Investments Mean Small Losses

How much are you willing to invest in your own business? Chances are you'll quote a figure that's triple the actual dollars you really need.

Time and time again you've heard of people scraping together their last dollar or mortgaging their house to the hilt to come up with a hefty down payment. Of course, if the business fails, they end up losing that hefty down payment.

Every dollar you invest is a dollar you might lose. "Starting Smart" means investing as little of your own money as possible.

Not long ago, two brothers, Mark and Walter P., decided to buy a run-down restaurant in Boston's North End. Believing the business to have "turnaround" potential, the brothers agreed to pay $200,000 financed by a $100,000 bank loan and $100,000 of their own capital.

Fortunately, the brothers wanted to "Start Smart," and they knew that creative financing could substantially reduce their investment and their risk.

First they talked the seller into financing $120,000 on a one-year "interest only" note. This knocked out the need for bank financing, and since the seller agreed to accept the note on a "non-recourse" basis, the brothers would not be personally liable for it. If the business failed, the seller could take it back but the brothers would be off the hook. However, if the business succeeded, the brothers could then pay this loan off from profits or bank financing.

Next, the seller agreed that the buyers could assume $30,000 in outstanding accounts payable owed by the seller. This would reduce the cash investment by an equal $30,000. At this point we had $150,000 of financing in place without the brothers committing a dime of their own.

Next they visited a food wholesaler. Since the wholesaler could foresee sizable sales and profits from the account, he agreed to loan the business $15,000 toward the sales price. The business broker was squeezed for a $10,000 loan from his $20,000 commission, and finally, the cigarette vending company, anxious to retain the location, agreed to finance $5,000 against future commissions.

There it was. $180,000 in financing from other sources. The

brothers no longer had to invest and gamble $100,000. Now their investment was a reasonably safe $20,000.

Unfortunately, the restaurant didn't make it. There were too many factors against it. In the first year, it lost $60,000, in the second, $40,000. Finally, the brothers threw it into bankruptcy.

They did lose their $20,000, but that was far better than losing $100,000. "Starting Smart" for them meant cutting their potential losses by cutting their initial investment.

There are countless ways to reduce initial investment, hundreds of which appear in my book *Own Your Own/The "No Cash Down" Business Guide*.

Some business theoreticians may argue with my approach and warn you of the risk of undercapitalization. They'll remind you that the more debt a business has, the greater the chances for failure.

Bull! Businesses fail due to lack of profitability and cash flow. If your business begins to show signs of success, you can always judiciously add further working capital, always balancing the investment against the risk.

By the same token, an excessive initial investment in an unproven venture doesn't give you the favorable odds you want. It's easy to add cash, but it's difficult to get your cash out once it's invested.

How to Invest Safely

No matter how little you do invest, once you have put together your creative financing package, the next step is to protect even that modest investment so you can recoup it should the business fail.

Assume you find a business that requires a $50,000 down payment. You pay the $50,000 into your newly formed corporation in return for all the shares of stock. On that basis, your entire investment is characterized as "equity" or "capital contribution."

Two years go by and your business becomes insolvent with $100,000 in debts. At auction, the assets bring $50,000. The creditors get the $50,000 at the rate of 50 cents on the dollar, and you as the stockholder receive nothing. Your plight becomes obvious; you not only lost your business, you lost $50,000 besides.

However, you can protect your investment by lending your corporation most of the money and using much smaller amounts to buy the shares.

In the above example, you could have loaned $40,000 to a close friend or relative, who in turn could have loaned the $40,000 to your corporation in return for a mortgage on the business assets as security. Your relative would be obligated to repay your loan only as the corporation pays its debts to him. With your remaining $10,000, you could buy the outstanding shares of the corporation and still be its sole stockholder.

If the business turns sour, your mortgage-holding relative would be entitled to the first $40,000 of auction proceeds (or whatever the corporation owes him at that point) *before* other creditors receive a cent. Once your relative is repaid, he could repay his loan to you. The bottom line is that you will have recouped $40,000 of your $50,000 investment by whittling that investment down to $10,000.

Since bankruptcy courts may nullify a loan made by a stockholder and give "arms-length" creditors priority, I recommend using an intermediary to make the loan to the corporation rather than making a direct loan yourself. A relative's loan is safe as long as he can prove he actually loaned the money.

This is perfectly legal. Should the idea of putting your own economic interests ahead of your creditors shock your conscience, that's morality, not business. You follow your own conscience. However, "Starting Smart" will at least give you a choice.

Review this strategy with your lawyer and accountant, so they can execute the necessary paperwork.

Assets You Never Have to Lose

Turn to the bankruptcy auction pages and scan some of the ads. Look closely at the assets going under the hammer. Many such valuable assets could have been saved had the owners used common sense and placed title to certain assets in the name of someone other than the operating corporation, which could in turn lease the asset.

Real estate offers a common example. Recently, one of the choicest parcels of land on Cape Cod was auctioned off with the other assets of a defunct restaurant. The restaurant itself had liabilities of $200,000 against equipment worth no more than $30,000.

However, the owner had made a serious mistake. When he purchased the real estate, he had the restaurant corporation take title to it. There it sat. A beautiful waterfront building with a value of $250,000 and a low mortgage of $60,000 ready to satisfy creditor claims.

"Starting Smart" in this case would have meant putting the building itself in the owner's personal name, or through a separate real estate trust or another corporation. The real estate could then be leased to the restaurant corporation. Had the owner used this foresight, the real estate and its $190,000 equity would still be his, and the creditors could only grab the $30,000 in equipment. The owner understands that now, but it's too late. It's always too late when you plan only for success!

I have a shrewd client, Cal S., who knew how to "Start Smart" when he went into the high risk printing business. The key to his operation was a sophisticated piece of high-speed printing equipment that cost $60,000.

Cal purchased this item in his own name and leased it to the corporation for a fair monthly rental fee. Five years later, the printing plant folded with debts in excess of $100,000. All Cal had to do was to go in and repossess his machine. The creditors had no claim to it.

Cal has since talked another printing plant into leasing the equipment from him for $15,000 a year. As Cal explains it, "I could have invested the $60,000 in the corporation and had the corporation buy the equipment, but I know the printing business and how risky it is, so I did it the right way. I kept my $60,000 and used it to buy the equipment myself. I had the best of both worlds. I owned the assets the corporation used, and the creditors, not me, took the risk."

Look over your own situation. If your corporation owns real estate, or a piece of high cost equipment, or perhaps even a valuable intangible asset such as a patent or trademark, "Starting Smart" may mean personal, not corporate, ownership of these assets.

Create Your Own Mini-Holding Company

If one corporation is good, more can be better. If you're in multiple businesses, "Starting Smart" means putting each business into its own corporation. With your businesses operating as separate and distinct corporations, the failure of any one will have no legal impact on the others. If all your businesses are owned by one corporation, then the creditors of any one business can go after the assets of the others.

Since the law of probability holds that you will eventually take on a loser if you expand, why jeopardize all your success with one failure?

Roger W. owned three prosperous gift shops under one corporation with annual pre-tax profit over $100,000. When Roger negotiated a location at a new mall, his corporation set up his fourth store. After spending $120,000 in start-up costs, Roger discovered the entire shopping mall and his new store were doomed because a new interchange made access to it by customers almost impossible. A year later, the store showed a $100,000 loss with more losses on the horizon.

What could Roger do? He had a $38,000 a year lease he couldn't give away, and he faced creditors clamoring for $150,000 in overdue bills.

Roger closed the mall location, but his creditors sued the corporation for $150,000, and the landlord demanded his $38,000 a year rent for the now vacant store.

It overwhelmed Roger's corporation. Several months later, he filed for protection under Chapter 11.

Had Roger "Started Smart," he would have expanded through a "mini"-holding company. First, a different corporation would own each gift shop. Each gift shop corporation, in turn, would have been owned by a parent corporation of which Roger would be the stockholder.

When the mall location failed, he could have simply liquidated it, given the creditors the proceeds and walked away from any remaining liabilities. Roger wished he could have "mailed the landlord the keys and forgotten the $38,000 a year lease." Since the creditors of the mall corporation could look only to that one store, the success of the original three stores would have been intact.

Such "mini"-holding companies offer excellent tax advantages. The holding company can file one consolidated tax return for all the subsidiary corporations, so losses from any one shop could offset the profits of another.

Segregate your businesses, and you segregate what you have to lose. Besides, it's fun being president of your own personal conglomerate.

Side-Stepping Dangerous Guarantees

Creditors have an annoying habit of always pushing personal guarantees under your nose. Who can blame them? They know that if they extend credit to your corporation, they severely limit their options in the event it goes bust. That's why they want your personal signature on the dotted line.

Your objective, however, is to confine your debts to the corporation. You don't want personal exposure if you can avoid it. Therefore, you have to know how to sidestep dangerous personal guarantees whenever possible.

Here's how you can limit your personal liability to the absolute minimum.

1. Never guarantee a debt unless you're certain the business can pay it off. Our firm was called upon recently to file personal bankruptcy for an owner of a bakery who succumbed to the demands of a wholesaler that he guarantee the payment of a $12,000 delivery. What a foolish move, considering the owner knew the bakery was already in dire straits and could never pay.
2. Banks and other institutional lenders never lend to small business without guarantees from the owners, so you can't avoid them if you want to get your hands on bank financing. But you can do it the right way. First, make certain the bank secures their note with a mortgage on the business assets. In the event the business fails, the bank is the first to get paid, decreasing your exposure on the note. Second, make certain the liquidation value of the assets is comparable to the balance owed the bank on the note. You don't want business assets yielding the bank only

$30,000 if the note shows a balance of $50,000. They'll chase you for the remaining $20,000.
3. Just because one would-be creditor demands a guarantee doesn't mean they all will. A guarantee is a bargaining point when you seek out a new supplier. Shop around until you find suppliers who will extend credit to your corporation rather than you.
4. Make it firm policy never to guarantee an *existing* corporate debt. Why should you? You have nothing to gain. Let your account go into arrears and credit managers will plead, promise, threaten and cajole to get you to risk your personal assets to back up your now questionable account. Ignore their demands for a personal guarantee. Later in this book you will see just how weak your creditors' bargaining position is, so don't strengthen it.
5. A guarantee is just one way to convince a creditor to extend credit to your corporation, but there are plenty of risk-saving alternatives. For example, you can offer a mortgage on the business assets. Whatever the collateral, confine your creditors' recourse to the corporation. Let the corporation exhaust its resources before you even consider a guarantee.
6. If you must supply your guarantee, negotiate it on a partial basis. Perhaps you have a key supplier to whom your business already owes $10,000. He refuses to extend further credit without a guarantee. If so, offer your guarantee to cover only the fresh credit. That way you won't be personally liable for the existing $10,000. Or limit the dollar amount on your guarantee. One client negotiating a lease in a shopping center was hit with the landlord's demand that he personally guarantee the lease. Rather than promise a blanket guarantee the client negotiated a guarantee limited to $5,000. He was smart. The business did fail and the store still stands empty. Back rents now amount to $87,000, but my client doesn't have to worry. He paid his $5,000.
7. Understand your creditor's position. Without your guarantee, he may decline shipment of a $20,000 order. But he may willingly gamble on a $10,000 order. Be prepared to cut orders to coincide with your company's credit rating.

8. If you have partners, make sure they also sign any guarantee. They enjoy the benefits of the business, so why not the risk? I can tell you one sad story of a 25% owner of a restaurant who guaranteed $86,000 in bills without "bothering" his other three partners. You guessed it. When the restaurant failed, his partners walked away, leaving him to satisfy the debt.
9. If your business shows signs of trouble, give priority to creditors holding your guarantee. Your objective is to pay them before you collapse so they (and ultimately you) will incur no loss.

When I was in law school, I had a cantankerous but wise professor. He always defined a guarantor as an "idiot with a fountain pen." Twenty years and 2,000 cases later, I must confess that more times than not his definition fits. Negotiate, bluff, threaten, and intimidate if you must. Just don't sign on the dotted line unless you have no other choice.

How Deep Are Your Pockets?

Smart players realize that no amount of care or caution can prevent personal liability and lawsuits from following them home once they've closed down a defunct business. They "Start Smart" by starting poor—and staying poor so "would-be" creditors can't find any personal assets to take once the lawsuits begin.

Such "judgment-proofing" is designed to deploy your assets so they always lie beyond the grasp of creditors. You may be a multi-millionaire, but if none of your assets is in your name, you enjoy the financial vulnerability of a pauper.

I had a client, Peter C., who owned a small chain of health and beauty aid stores. His business was in rough shape with on-going losses and debts well in excess of assets. I did everything I could to keep the business afloat, but after two years of fighting, Peter gave up.

Catastrophe struck! First, the IRS put a lien on his home for $60,000, because he was personally liable as an officer of the corporation for unpaid withholding taxes. Two days later, a creditor holding a $15,000 guarantee attached his personal savings account. Still another creditor sued him personally on bad checks, and eventually attached Peter's summer cottage in Maine for $9,000. In the final tally, Peter lost almost every asset he ever owned. Since I was just a legal "pup" at the time, I had yet to learn the lesson: you can't get blood from a stone, so make certain your client is that stone.

Today I insist that my clients "judgment-proof" themselves before they climb aboard. On paper, they look so poor, creditors are more likely to send sympathy cards then subpoenas. The quickest way to defuse a rambunctious lawyer is to convince him he's spinning his wheels chasing a worthless judgment.

If I knew then what I know now, Peter would probably still have his assets. He could have:

1. Deeded his home and cottage into a real estate trust that he could control as trustee. As trust property, it would be free from creditor attack. He could have put them into his wife's name, but that might have backfired. His spouse may have had liabilities of her own. Then again, she might have run off with the 23-year-old muscle-flexing tennis pro at the country club.
2. Taken advantage of the homestead laws provided by some states. (Homestead laws protect a certain percentage of a homeowner's interest in real estate from creditor claims.) By filing a homestead exemption, he could have protected the equity in his real estate from creditors' claims.
3. Transferred stock and bonds to either a trust or perhaps a corporation set up for that purpose.
4. Transferred cash in savings accounts to either a trust account or a closely held corporation, in either case out of his name.

These are only the more common techniques used to accomplish the goal of staying rich while you appear poor. The techniques best suited for you must be left for your counsel, because they depend on a careful assessment of many technical factors.

Timing is crucial. Don't expect to incur substantial debts and try to protect your property two days before the sheriff comes calling. Your creditor can successfully claim you fraudulently transferred it and demand its reconveyance.

However, if you "judgment-proof" yourself *before* you incur the debt or well before the creditors file claim, chances are the courts will conclude the transfer was without fraudulent intent.

Nothing obligates you to be a debtor with "deep-pockets." You can legally, safely and morally shield your assets. "Starting Smart" means having nothing to lose.

Your "Starting Smart" Self-Exam

It's time to test yourself. Take a few moments to review your situation, then ask yourself these questions:

1. Did you look at both sides of the coin, preparing for success *or* failure?
2. Have you taken every known step to keep your investment as low as possible?
3. Have you protected your investment by lending it to your business as a "secured loan"?
4. Do you operate your business through a corporation?
5. Did you purchase your shares pursuant to Section 1244 of the IRS Code?
6. Have you made certain your corporation does not own the real estate occupied by the business?
7. Are your guaranteed bank loans adequately secured by a mortgage on business assets?
8. Are your personally guaranteed debts able to be paid first by the corporation?
9. Have you protected your personal assets by judgment-proofing yourself?
10. Have you carefully reviewed your situation with your attorney and accountant?

If you answered "No" to any of these questions, you have work to do. It won't take long to adequately prepare for failure. Then you can spend all your waking moments planning and working for success.

Taking Charge

2

Business problems bring out the best and worst in people.

Ralph R. needed a stiff drink to face them.

Joan G. procrastinated for months before she could muster the courage to fight them.

Michael S.? You'll find him in San Diego. His style was to run away from them.

Ken T. looked at them as an opportunity to take charge—and rebuild the business to even greater heights. You can almost say he enjoyed them.

Your successful turnaround depends more on your attitude and desire to win than on your financial statements or the laws hidden in dusty law books. Your attitude is the essential ingredient for what your business will or will not become.

In this chapter, I'll turn the spotlight on you. I will help you objectively examine your own thoughts, ideas and attitudes.

Whether you *can* handle the turnaround must be answered. Should you even *try*? That too demands an answer.

You Come First

For years, my law library was stocked only with bankruptcy books. Then I got smart. I cleared away a whole shelf and packed it with no-nonsense psychology books a lay person could understand. Why not?

I've been practicing psychology for years and wouldn't be surprised if the AMA were to pick me up for practicing medicine without a license. But it's unavoidable. Ask any bankruptcy attorney. He will tell you the same thing—you have to know your client!

Unfortunately, too many attorneys, accountants and turnaround specialists don't understand this. They immediately focus on the business instead of the owner, and that's the wrong approach. It must follow the reverse course.

- Your *objectives* determine whether the business *should* be saved.
- Your *desire* determines *if* the business will be saved.
- Your *capabilities* and attitude determine *how* the business can be saved.

Last week I sent Michael's salvageable toy store to auction. It was the only solution. He had a great job offer from an electronics firm in California. He didn't want the business or the aggravation and hard work needed to put it together again. Saving the business just wasn't consistent with his objectives.

Ralph posed another problem. He was on the fence. He wanted his business to stay alive. But did he have sufficient desire to kick his drinking habit, roll up his sleeves and get down to business? We had to assess his commitment. Did he want survival badly enough to achieve it? Fortunately, he did. Today his garden supply firm is financially healthy. So is Ralph. He hasn't touched the bottle since he made up his mind that he had sufficient desire.

Joan wanted her restaurant to live. And she had the desire and commitment to see it through the hard times. However, Joan had another problem. She couldn't handle creditor pressure. That was her Achilles heel. So it became a question of *how* to best accomplish the turnaround. A short vacation while her assistant manager grabbed the helm provided the answer. Joan returned to a solvent business.

Think about it. Examine your own objectives, desires and capabilities. You'll draft your blueprint from what you find.

Define Your Objectives

Success means different things to different people. Surprisingly, many small business owners have not carefully defined it clearly for themselves.

When they do define what they *really* want to accomplish, they often find that their underlying objectives are entirely different from what they initially perceived them to be.

I always start a conference with a new client by asking a rhetorical question. "If you could wave a magic wand," I ask, "what would you like me to do for your business?" An obvious question? The answers are surprising and unpredictable.

Answer quickly and you'll tell me you want to save your business. Of course you do. That's why you're reading this book. But you may be wrong. You have other motives. There's always an underlying reason for wanting the business to survive. Sometimes that objective can best be achieved by *not* saving the business and finding alternate solutions.

Michael S. answered my question. He initially told me he wanted to save his business and have it give him a healthy weekly income. Listen to Mike carefully! He wanted *protection of income*. It's a valid reason. But two weeks later Mike got the offer from the California electronics firm at double the salary he could draw from his struggling toy store. Continuity of the business suddenly didn't seem worthwhile. Since *income* was his objective, he realized he no longer needed his business to achieve it.

The Claflin brothers answered my "magic wand" question less than honestly. "Don't bother us with riddles. Just save our business." Dissatisfied with their reply, I pressed the issue. "Why?" "Because we're stuck on a damn $90,000 note to the bank, and if the business goes down the drain, we'll personally owe the bank the money." Now we were getting somewhere. All the business meant to the Claflins was buying time until they retired the bank note. Keep the business alive we did, just long enough to apply every last dollar of cash flow to the note, finally reducing it to the point where the brothers could pay it off from the auction proceeds. The Claflins real goal? *Avoiding personal liability on business debts.*

Then there was Ann K. "Save it" she sobbed, "I don't want to lose the $50,000 I invested." The message came through loud and clear. Whenever Ann thought of her business failing, all she could see was her $50,000 vanishing with it. We found a competitor who grabbed the opportunity to take over the retail accounts of Ann's distributorship. Ann? She was paid $75,000 not to go back into the same type of business and compete with them. It was easy.

I didn't really have to save Ann's business to *recoup her investment.* Ann's creditors suffered a $120,000 loss, but she more than satisfied her objectives.

Greg thought he was over the hill at 52 and desperately wanted to save the bottling plant he had owned for 25 years. The business was his security blanket, supporting him and his family and putting his kids through college. It was the only business he knew. We could have saved his business, but he came out even better by selling out to a conglomerate who signed him to a 5-year employment contract at nearly double what he had earned as his own boss. It didn't take much conversation with Greg to see what his business meant to him. One word says it— *Security!*

Some owners desperately want to dump their business, but you'd never know it unless you were to dig just a bit deeper. I recall one interesting case in which we didn't have to save a business. Our job was to save an *ego.* Paul was never the type to admit defeat. How could he toss in the towel and still hold his head high at the Rotary Club, Kiwanis, and Knights of Columbus? How could he be the leading spokesman of free enterprise as President of the Chamber of Commerce when his appliance store was about to sink into bankruptcy with $200,000 in debt? How could Paul show his face at the country club or hob nob with his successful cronies on the golf course? Disgrace, failure, outcast: the words haunted him. The business itself meant nothing to Paul, as he finally confessed. "The damn thing is an anchor. It's driving my crazy. I can't even take a week's pay out of it." Paul's appliance store never did fail. But Mort's Appliances did. Who's Mort? A guy Paul found standing in line at the unemployment office. Within two hours, aided by a "takeover incentive" of $1,000, Mort was the new owner. Mort was in. Paul was out. A month later, the appliance store sank, but it didn't bother Paul. He spread the word in his social circles, saying, "I spent eight years building a healthy, thriving company and in one short month this jerk Mort ruins it. Some people just don't belong in business."

Once you understand your objectives, you can find solutions. Sometimes those solutions point to saving the business. Then again, the objectives may be achieved without the business being rescued. It's only a matter of knowing what you really want.

Fight or Flight?

Have you had any flashing thoughts lately of grabbing the first plane to Mexico and starting anew driving a cab while you lick your wounds and forget your woes? If so, you're 100 percent normal. Every embattled owner has such thoughts from time to time. It's nothing more than the old "flight" syndrome. However, most owners choose to stick it out and fight.

The fight or flight syndrome can defeat an accurate appraisal of your own objectives and cloud your willingness and desire to continue on. Decisions are not made rationally. They're the end product of emotion. Oftentimes you have to drain the emotions before you find those rational answers.

Admittedly, creditors climbing on your back, employees jumping ship, competitors sharpshooting your best accounts and customers complaining about low inventories aren't anyone's definition of fun. Quitting can appear to be an attractive, mind-saving alternative. Defensive management can take its toll. Operating under sustained pressure for a prolonged time can turn even the most resolute optimist into a quitter. Desire to continue goes out the window. The business is sure to follow. Carl R. can tell you. "My shoe stores were causing me nothing but sleepless nights. It got to the point where I didn't want to go near them. All I had to look forward to was another day of banging my head against the wall. Your emotional battery is drained. It's easy to say 'get me out.'" Lucky for Carl, he was able to grapple successfully with his feelings before all remaining will to continue escaped. Today Carl's Shoes has several stores with more on the way.

How did Carl change course and re-charge his emotional batteries so he could come out swinging? Follow his advice:

1. Step back from your problems. Usually a short vacation from the situation can clear your head and allow you to look at matters with a new perspective. Carl explains "I remember one particularly horrible day when sixteen checks bounced and I didn't even have the money for payroll. By 5 o'clock that afternoon, I was ready to mail the creditors the keys. Grabbing the few remaining dollars from the till, I took off for a long week-end in New York. It was just enough to screw my head on straight. Monday morning I still had the same problems, but at least my head was clear and I could see some solutions."

Every day clients storm into our office, throw the keys on the desk and demand that we liquidate their business. "I've had it. I quit." But we never take them up on it. "Tomorrow will be soon enough" we say, buying time. Tomorrow always comes, but the clients often don't.

The problem is that troubled owners make the decision under the worst of all possible circumstances and for all the wrong reasons. It's almost impossible to expect someone to sit back and objectively decide what may be the most critical decision of his or her career when that same person is up to his or her neck in alligators and is shell-shocked from fighting everything and everyone.

The army calls it "combat fatigue." Some rest and recreation is their solution. It can also be yours. Get away from the business for awhile. Stop thinking about the problems. Your business will be there when you get back. You'll come back with a clearer head, and you probably won't return with the same desire to throw in the towel as when you left.

2. Salve for your battered ego? The best ointment is reality. Owners look upon their problems as a personal defeat. Self-failure. It may be managerial mishap that caused the problems. Then again it may be external factors that even the best management couldn't counteract. What difference does it make?

If the business failure was caused by factors beyond your control, why should it shake your own self-confidence? Reverse the picture. Managerial blunders aren't likely to be repeated. The mistakes of the past should be looked upon not as defeat, but as a learning experience. It's all part of your managerial growing pains. Who doesn't make mistakes?

I enjoy reminding clients that Ford had 400 MBA's conduct a three-year study before they gave the Edsel the green light. Talk about disaster! Yet, I've never seen a pencil without an eraser.

An inspirational pep talk? Perhaps. However, it's necessary. There's nothing as tragic as an owner wallowing in his own self-doubt shutting the door on his entrepreneurial spirit. I don't have to reach for my psychology books to handle it. I've lived it.

Years ago, my own entrepreneurial spirits were running high. A partner and I decided to build a drug chain and make it the best in the state. From one store, we mushroomed to twelve. We were riding high with success. Then total annihilation. What happened? We made a fatal mistake. We expanded faster than our internal controls. Failure? Well our creditors didn't call it a stunning success. And I had my own self-doubts. My own entrepreneurial spirits weren't gone, but they certainly ebbed. What brought it back to full life? A candid self-assessment. I pulled out a sheet of paper and divided it down the center. "O.K. Goldstein," I said, "on the left side list the things you did right. In the other column list what you screwed up. No cheating!" It wasn't a bad scorecard after all. It's easy to see only your failures. And it's important too. It's equally important, however, to see your strengths. You begin to look at yourself in a different light. I've had other business ventures since. I never make the same mistakes—only new ones. We all do. It's part of the business game.

How about your scorecard? Don't remind yourself of only the mistakes. Look around. What did you do right? Look hard. It can do wonders for your self-confidence.

3. You don't see the light at the end of the tunnel? That's the third reason why so many owners lose desire to continue. They see the problems. They don't see the solutions.

Inability to see business-saving remedies shouldn't be reason to lose the desire to try.

Carl had that problem. Outlining the solutions was critical for turning his "non-desire" into a frenzy of positive activity. When Carl retained us, he had his long shopping list of problems. Losses by the carload, inventory depleted, an overdraft in his checking account, and an expired lease. It looked insurmountable. Carl didn't ask if he should save his business. He had made up his mind. It couldn't be saved. But Carl was wrong. A week later, we had a possible solution. A shoe manufacturer would stock his store and turn it into a factory outlet. The light at the end of the tunnel was beginning to shine, and the "possible solution" turned into a $3,000,000 victory. That's what Carl's Factory Outlet shoe stores rang up in sales last year.

Whenever I sit across from a client who says, "Get me out. The business can't be saved," I refer him to Carl. He can convince anyone that there's no such thing as a hopeless business.

Keep an open mind. As you turn the pages, you'll find others who have shared your problems. And you will find solutions just as they have. The solutions only evaporate when you're not willing to look for them.

The desire to continue must be the result of a rational thought process. You want to survive and are willing to find solutions to make it happen. Oftentimes it's equally logical to let the business go and admit continuity of the business is not in your own self-interest.

- I dumped my interest in our budding drugstore chain. I wasn't afraid to nurture it back to health. It just didn't offer me the challenge or income of my law practice.
- A client decided to sink her troubled boutique because she had a chance to go back to her first love, teaching high school history. Good for her!
- Another owner believed continuing his plumbing business would require him to endanger his already weak heart. Who can argue with wanting to live?

Many owners made the decision based entirely on what they saw as the long term prospects for the business. Even in the most favorable light, some businesses won't pay off well enough to make the fight worthwhile. This is particularly true with small "me-too" businesses that don't have clear money-making potential. The owner may work 60–70 hours a week for several years and be able to squeeze out only a $250 weekly paycheck. Why work your butt off for peanuts?

Personal problems can intervene. Divorce and business failure often go hand in hand. Believe it or not, approximately half of our clients having business problems are going through marital difficulty simultaneously. Do marital problems interfere with the profitable management of a business or do the tensions and stress (and the inevitable lack of money) play a role in destroying the marriage? I'll leave that one for the marriage counselors. Owners suffering problems both at home and at work can only try to separate the two and assess each relationship on its own merits. Easier said than done, of course!

Just the other day, a new client consulted me about liquidating his insolvent luggage shop. After glancing at his financial statements, I asked, "Do you really want to liquidate the business? Assuming we can make peace with the creditors, I could save it." Jon was quiet for a moment and then said, "I thought about it, but the business doesn't really mean much to me. I can make better money doing something else." I had my answer. Jon wasn't merely reacting to a financial crisis, he just didn't give a damn about the business. He's happier at his old job installing fences.

Some people want their business to survive, others don't. There's no right or wrong answer. You have to decide for yourself. Nobody can or should make the decision for you. And it will always be the right decision—provided you have the right reasons.

Will the Real You, Please Stand Up

The highest wall between a business problem and its solutions can be the owner's attitude. To scale that wall, you must understand the limitations you bring to your own situation. Attitude and capability determine *how* the troubled business can be saved.

Meet a cast of characters who illustrate how troubled owners react to their own situation.

The Ostrich

What a challenge! He refuses to believe his business is on the fast track to failure. Excelling in the fine art of "non-awareness," he continues to bury his head in the sand until Louie the Liquidator shows up to padlock the door.

Ostriches come in two sub-species. The first is oblivious to financial danger signals. Liabilities continue to mount, losses climb and assets dwindle. Only sunglasses can overcome the glare of his red-ink-stained financial statements.

Marty provides a perfect example. He invested $30,000 to buy his shoe store. Five years later, the business was dead, but he didn't know enough to bury it. For two years, he worked without a salary. Creditors bombarded him with lawsuits. Marty's game was over, but he continued playing extra innings. His concern in life—a new lease! Marty, the ostrich, pulled his head out of the hole only when we showed him his business had over $100,000 in losses. The ostrich was the last to know.

The other breed of ostrich knows he's in trouble, but tries to fool himself and everyone else into thinking he's not. "Ignore it, it will go away!" is his cry. Hiding in his hole, he cannot muster the courage to admit the problem exists or take the decisive action to solve it. Who can have confidence in the ostrich when it only lays more eggs?

The ostrich requires a special diet: A large dose of reality. It's not easy to get him to swallow it, but unless he recognizes and accepts his situation for what it is, he can't turn anything around.

The Confirmed Optimist

He's a close cousin of the ostrich. While the ostrich doesn't know (or pretends not to know) that he's in trouble, the confirmed optimist realizes he's in trouble but clings to the dream that things will get better by themselves. Just wait until tomorrow. It's always tomorrow. The big sale will come through, he'll discover a new invention, the ruthless competitor down the block will vanish. He never faces the moment of truth, for he keeps pushing that moment into the future.

The optimist requires the same care and feeding as the ostrich. Unfortunately, the optimist, unlike the ostrich, runs the other way when he sees the feedbag filled with the facts.

The Nervous Nellie

The Nervous Nellie can't handle the stress that insolvency inevitably brings. With emotions in high gear, Nellie loses perspective and panics.

Karen was a Nervous Nellie who totally fell apart when her ad agency hit hard times. She was a walking basket case. An overdue bill from the telephone company could send her to the funny farm. The ad agency could have been saved, but Karen wasn't the one to save it. The process would have ruined her emotionally. Fortunately, Karen's husband knew the business and wasn't a Nervous Ned. He stepped in, hired some key people and whipped the company back into shape. Several months later, Karen returned and took command of the business. Her batteries were re-charged. She could handle normal operations, but not prolonged adversity.

I don't scorn the Nervous Nellie. Everyone has his own stress threshold. But what good is a grandiose turnaround scheme if management is in a sanitarium!

Nervous Nellies pop up even when they don't have anything to be nervous about. Lots of owners in this category think their business is headed down the drain when they are encountering only normal business problems or growing pains.

Recently, a Nervous Nellie consulted me about bankruptcy for his company. His problem? Profits for the year were only $27,000 rather than the $50,000 of the year before. Imagine his despair if he had really been in trouble!

The Absolute Moralist

This is perhaps the most difficult managerial type. He wants to save his business and pay all his creditors at the same time. Tell him it's not in the realm of fiscal reality and he'll quote the Ten Commandments and the Boy Scout Oath. Inevitably, reality must set in. But by then, the absolute moralist has not only lost his business, but the creditors get even less than they would have if the moralist had swallowed a dose of logic instead of a morality pill.

The Pirate

He's the opposite of the absolute moralist. His objective is to pay nothing to "no one" at "no time" in "no way." He'd rather rape, pillage and plunder the business for his own gain.

At least the pirate brings to his situation a clear idea of where he's going and how to get there. Unfortunately, he forgets that other people have rights too. Faced with a troubled business, the pirate may decide to take a few short cuts to come out ahead. Unlike the Nervous Nellie, he doesn't need hand-holding. Arm wrestling, perhaps, to make certain he plays by the rules and adopts a turnaround plan that makes sense not only to him but to creditors as well.

The Perennial Pessimist

He, of course, is the extreme opposite of the optimist. His trademark is "gloom and doom." Nothing has gone right or ever will go right. The way he sees it, his sled only goes in one direction—downhill. The pessimist isn't only pessimistic about his chances for recovery. He started the business expecting only the worst and even if the business can be saved, which of course he doubts, the aftermath will be worse still.

The pessimist is not hard to handle, if for no other reason than we have so little to do with him. He lacks everything needed for success. Enthusiasm, interest, imagination, hope and desire are to him only words in the dictionary.

Sometimes the pessimist is only temporarily afflicted. He may have originally been an optimist who only switched gears when his business started to crumble. Reality and a decisive game plan oftentimes arrests the disease. If treatment is successful, he may even return to his former condition as an optimist.

The Dreamer

The dreamer is an interesting fellow. Sometimes it's difficult to find him, unless you look in the clouds.

The dreamer knows he has business problems, but that's all beneath him. How can he be bothered with such mundane matters as losing a few hundred thousand dollars of someone else's money? He's too busy inventing a better mousetrap.

Ideas, concepts and grandiose schemes are his daily diet, as he sits in a dark room contemplating. What's going on in the next room? Well that's not for the dreamer to worry about.

Every organization should have a dreamer, as long as they also have a "doer" who can handle such earthly matters as balancing a checkbook. I usually send the dreamer back to contemplate while I find a "no-nonsense" type to keep the business alive.

The "Buck Passer"

We can speak openly about this character, because it's a safe bet he's not even reading this chapter. He never asks the tough questions about himself. He doesn't have to. Nothing is his fault; he was just victimized by everyone else's misdeeds.

The big problem with the "buck passer" is that he can't look honestly at his own involvement in creating the fiscal fiasco. He's Mr. Right. It's always the other guy.

This bird needs a large dose of humility. I enjoy parading before him a shopping list that points out his own undoing. Sometimes reality sets in. Other times the buck passer storms out. I'm never disappointed. Chances are he'd only blame me if his business ends up down the drain.

Are these people paranoid or sick? Far from it. They're just ordinary people like you reacting in their own special way to the moment of truth. Recognize yourself in the crowd?

How you react to your situation, and the attitude you bring to it is one important factor in selecting the remedy for your troubled business.

All my successful cases have shared that common denominator. The turnaround plan matched the client. The client could handle it and shared the view that it was the best plan for both him and his business. He was comfortable with it. Failures were usually a mismatch. We may have analyzed the business correctly, but we didn't read the client properly. As a bankruptcy specialist puts it, "Designing the 'right' turnaround plan is like buying clothes. You need a suit that fits."

If each of my cast of characters faced the indentical business problem, I'd design the plan that matched the client. The business is the fixed component. Its owner is the variable. It's very much a "people" game.

Assess Your Management Mentality

Excuses, excuses. Everyone has an excuse.

The first group of storytellers complain how bad their business is. I can hear their stories now.

"You can't make a buck with nursing homes—they're over-regulated."

"Variety stores? Dead as yesterday's news, the big boys grab all the business."

"Book stores are all in tough shape. Between chain store discounting and publisher cutbacks on margins, you can't even make a living."

Name the business. It doesn't matter what it is. When it goes "bad," it's the business. I never realized there were so many "lousy" businesses before I began my insolvency practice. At least, that's what these storytellers would have me believe.

Ever meet a masochist? You'll find them in our second group of storytellers. Everything's their fault. They can do nothing right. Sometimes I wonder whether they sleep on a bed of nails as the daily grand finale of their unceasing quest for self-flagellation.

I don't listen to either group. There's no such thing as a bad business or bad management. There's only management that's mismatched to the business. The owner simply failed to measure his own management mentality. He brought to the business a certain capability, however, the business demanded a competency that he didn't or couldn't provide.

Most owners don't see it that way. They refuse to assess the managerial relationship between themselves and their business, unaware that the problems were caused by the managerial mismatch. Devoid of this reality, they don't focus on creating the proper match as part of the turnaround strategy.

With the large corporation, management becomes the sacrificial lamb when the mismatch occurs. In the small enterprise, the owner is the fixed and unmovable object. The business inevitably has to undergo change if the managerial supply/demand are to run in parallel.

Some examples?

Remember Marty the ostrich? He didn't invent the word "inept," but he gave it added meaning. What was his management mentality? Sub-zero! One look at his shoe store and you'd see it. Everything was wrong. Out-of-stocks on best sellers, overloaded on the dead, overdue bills all over the place and three over-paid employees playing poker in the stockroom. But Marty was happy. He loved to sell shoes. Occasionally he even sold a pair.

Now back to our "magic wand trick" again. Marty knew what he wanted. A profitable and solvent shoe store. Could I make it solvent? It would hardly be a challenge. Could Marty make it profitable? Mission impossible. So why fight to make the business healthy when Marty didn't have the managerial ability to keep it off the sick list?

There were only two possible solutions:

1. Hire someone who could manage, or
2. Put Marty in a business that he could handle.

We chose the latter strategy. Marty's still in business. You'll find him selling shoes as owner of a leased shoe department in a giant discount store. He buys all his inventory from one manufacturer who handles merchandising and inventory control. The discount store takes care of all the paperwork. All Marty has to do is sell shoes. That's what he does best.

Bill T. had a measurable level of managerial talent. But it couldn't quite measure up to what his fast-growing candy business demanded. Bill started with a small candy manufacturing business in the basement of his home with sales to local gift shops. The following year, a retail store of his own. Two year later, he had two more stores. Now Bill was really moving. Within a few years, he had eight stores of his own and a franchise network of fifteen stores featuring his candy. Bill could see the business growing, but he couldn't see that it was also out of control. Bill was a terrific candy maker and promoter. But he was in over his head with his empire. In reality, he had the same choices as Marty. Either bring on the people who could provide the necessary management skill or cut back the operation. We decided the fast-growth potential of the business justified a partner with top managerial ability. Bill still owns 60 percent of the business, but what a business it is! This year it will gross over $15,000,000.

Then there are cases where management is actually stifled. The owner has a super abundance of managerial talent and energy but only needs a way to break out and use it. That was Al's story. He was a bright pharmacist who took over his father's corner drugstore. The challenge wasn't there, and Al's interest quickly dried up. I could see it. The business was rapidly going downhill, but Al was too busy flapping his entrepreneurial wings scouting other business opportunities. Finally, Al's interest was sparked. He'd become a specialist in providing pharmaceuticals to nursing homes. Day and night he worked to build his nursing home accounts. The corner drug store? Not only is it still there, its sales are astonishing. You'd never know by looking at it that its annual sales exceed $8,000,000.

Usually the solution is to reduce the over-expanded operation to parallel the owner's managerial ability. Typically, the strong managerial personality will find his own expansion route or rationally abandon the business in favor of one that will challenge him. Then it becomes a recurring theme. At what point will he expand beyond his managerial capability?

Many latent achievers find themselves in a business that doesn't allow for the development of their managerial potential. Al was the exception, but hardly a rarity. He found his avenue of opportunity. Many don't. Rehabilitate their troubled company and they'll return to a solvent, albeit mismatched, business. Sometimes you do them a favor by pulling them out from under their security blanket.

Dennis lost his security blanket. He did, however, find opportunity. He was another victim of "stepping into father's shoes." Bright? You bet, complete with degrees from Cornell and Syracuse. I met Dennis at a social affair. He was on his third high-ball as he spread his tale of woe. It was his dry cleaning plant. The same old problems. Too many creditors and too little cash. Dennis turned the business problems over to me, but the business wasn't the problem. It didn't take long to realize that Dennis had his mind on computer programming. I'd "talk" creditors, and Dennis would tell me about computer technology. During three legal conferences, we spent a grand total of fifteen minutes on solving his business problems and three hours on computers. The right solution for Dennis was not a viable cleaning plant. We sold the business, paid the creditors, and gave Dennis the few extra dollars to start a software programming firm. He's struggling, but he'll make it. The smiling entrepreneur always makes it. Management needs more than competence. It also requires enthusiasm.

Owners seldom evaluate either their managerial abilities or enthusiasm. They shoot for the short term solution—saving the business, and ignore the long term remedy—defining the business they can profitably manage.

Lack of self-objectivity is one reason for the problem. It's difficult to determine your own level of managerial performance. Most owners shield themselves from the question—if they think of it at all—by focusing instead on external reasons for business decline or on the immediate problems. Striking out at the "effect" is the substitute for examining the cause.

The successful turnaround considers reshaping the business to meet the capacity of management. The end product of the carefully conceived strategy is a business that usually bears little resemblance to the business that was in trouble. If the business does retain form, it is inevitably bolstered by additions to management.

Assess your own managerial mentality. It can help you define *what* your business should become, if you are to manage it profitably.

1. Consider the size of the business. Your problems may be over-expansion beyond what you and your management can effectively handle. It's a common problem. I estimate that 70 percent of all troubled companies suffering from acute growing pains have managerial indigestion. While undercapitalization may compound the problem, the key culprit is still the lack of management depth.

Faced with this problem, you are forced to either retrench the business to the capabilities of management or quickly add to the management staff.

2. The Peter Principle must be considered. We all have our managerial limitations. The entrepreneur who can effectively manage the $500,000 firm may not be the one to oversee the $3,000,000 firm. This is an equally common occurrence.

The owner who is in "over his head" may be able to add management staff, but he has to resolve a more important issue—can he effectively lead them?

3. Your business may be too diversified for your managerial capabilities. Expansion can take several directions. Many firms diversify into areas alien to the original enterprise. The owner whose entire background is in retailing now finds himself in manufacturing as well. A food retailer expands into drugs. Mini-conglomerates can make for major disasters.

With many of our diversified clients, we uncover precisely that problem—owners playing in new business arenas that are completely unfamiliar. One trip to their operations and it becomes clear. The original "core" business is alive and well, but the diversified areas are in shambles. Surgery to the business becomes a must.

4. Ask yourself an honest question. Are you happy with the type of business you're in? Let's spend a few moments on this one.

One of the chief reasons for business failure is not managerial incompetence, but rather lack of managerial interest. Many owners don't perform because they can't develop the enthusiasm for the business. Dennis' lack of enthusiasm for his cleaning plant is a prime example.

And it's a considerably larger problem than the case of the motivated owner who simply expands too far or too fast. It's larger in the sense that more owners fall victim to lack of motivation and also that the solutions understandably require more than surgery to the firm or a booster to its management. The only solution for the non-motivated owner is to divest himself of the business and select a new career path.

That advice may apear to go contrary to the thrust of this book. Actually, it's what the book is all about. Saving your business requires management. Management requires motivation and enthusiasm.

How prevalent is the problem? Probably 30 percent of our clients eventually decide they're in the wrong business. A case that starts out as a "turnaround" is transformed into a sale or liquidation. The owner? There's only one direction for the owner, a new business or career path that can motivate him to flap his entrepreneurial wings at full speed.

It goes beyond the question of desire to stay in business. Many mismatched owners have the desire to continue on with the business, but it's their lack of managerial enthusiasm that affects the business. Commonly, these same owners inherited a business, or fell into it not by deliberate choice but by chance. In other instances, the owner had a misconception of what the business would really be like. Reality can be somewhat different than expectation.

These same owners may resist striking out on a new career path since the business represents their security blanket. Maintaining the status quo is always the route of least resistance.

Playing part-time psychologist for the misguided owner can be a challenge. Everyone knows he's unhappy in his business and so does he. Lead him back to the salvaged business and he continues on with a life of misery, managerial neglect and an eventual return trip to our office. Success comes only when you get him to see it that way.

This may be the best time to carefully answer your own question—is the business right for you? Don't let the problems scare you. They can disappear. Pretend the business is healthy. Would it still be the business that can best satisfy and motivate you? You may not be a bad manager after all—once you find your *right* business. Then you can "take charge" and mean it!

The Moment of Truth

I used to think of myself as a legal specialist to the sick business. I was wrong. My goal was seldom the rescue of the business, but rather the rescue of the owner who happened to be caught up in a troubled firm. There is a difference. You have to know yourself, then you can think about the business. You are the locomotive, the business is the caboose. That's the message in this chapter.

It's *your* moment of truth. Why not take a few moments and answer those all-important questions about *yourself*. Try this self-test.

1. What are your specific reasons for keeping the business alive?
2. Can your objectives be satisfied through means other than continuity of the business?
3. Do you honestly have the desire to see the business through its troubled times and put it back on the road to success?
4. To what extent, if any, has your managerial performance contributed to the problems of the business?
5. Do you have the managerial capability to handle the business if it were returned to solvency?
6. What changes in your business are necessary before you can be confident of your ability to manage it successfully?
7. Are you in the right business, or would you be happier in a different business?

Find some interesting answers?

Putting Together Your Winning Team

3

When a Fortune-500 conglomerate begins to flounder, it runs to Booz-Hamilton or Arthur D. Little Co. for managerial wisdom.

When Kaplans' Dresses began its plunge, the Kaplan boys had only to venture to Shmulka Bernstein's Delicatessen, an age-old meeting place for the 7th Avenue garment trade. Side orders of free advice come with every hot pastrami sandwich. "Raise prices—you're giving your damn dresses away," shouts Sam Spiegelman, a coat manufacturer who occupies his regular booth. From across the room drifts the sage wisdom of another caterer to American's fashionplates, "How the hell do you expect to compete when you're 20 percent too high?" Even the counterman has the answer. "Why don't you get out of dresses and into bathing suits? That's where the real money is." You can count on more than a great sandwich at Shmulka Bernstein's. It's the "brain trust" for the entire garment industry.

Misery loves company. But company can be a valuable commodity when your business hits the skids, particularly if it's the right company and you know how to exploit it to help put your business together again.

The successful turnaround is never a one-man show, but rather a team effort. You may not know all the answers yourself, so you must surround yourself with players who do.

When Kaplans' sales plunged faster than its dresses' daring necklines, the Kaplan boys had no answers and weren't likely to find any amidst the salamis and pickles at Shmulka Bernstein's. But they did learn one thing—the survival of their business depended on people who *could* come up with answers.

Ted Kaplan isn't ashamed to admit, "We were walking around in circles. The stockroom was bulging with unsold inventory, and our desks were buried by an ever-growing mountain of unpaid bills. Competitors were stealing our best accounts. What a disaster! But we finally woke up and made the wisest investment of our lives, a ten cent phone call to our attorney."

The Kaplans' attorney called in a top insolvency lawyer, who "quarterbacked" a strong game plan: a Chapter 11 reorganization to put the creditors on hold and buy time to re-group. Two days later, they pulled a sharp accountant on board to put the Kaplans' finances in ship-shape order. He began to control costs and measure cash flow with a critical eye, all according to a budget that made sense.

Next they hired a consultant with an outstanding record for boosting sales, who sold their excess inventory to several discount outlets to generate cash. Then he recommended a top dress designer and an aggressive advertising agency. The new line of merchandise sparkled, and the promotion sizzled. Before they knew it, Kaplans' showroom was bustling with buyers from Macy's, Filene's, Bloomingdale's and Nieman-Marcus. They couldn't manufacture enough dresses to fill all the orders.

And it wasn't just the outsiders who rescued the Kaplans. Harry from shipping worked nights and weekends to increase distribution. Annie from bookkeeping siphoned payment out of the slowest paying accounts and made the credit department a cash producer. Everyone pitched in. The Kaplans didn't have a team, they had an army. No wonder they won the war to save their business.

Today the Kaplan boys still enjoy pastrami sandwiches at Shmulka Bernstein's, but now they're dishing out the side orders—how to turn a nearly defunct dress manufacturer into a healthy $14,000,000 a year money-maker.

Ask Ted Kaplan if they used magic, and he'll laugh. "Of course not. We may be slick, but we got a little too close to our own business and couldn't see the problems, much less find the solutions. It took some hard-nosed professionals to force us to face the facts. Nothing like a winning team to stimulate you to take charge."

What Your Team Will Do for You

George Steinbrenner has his Yankees. Ronald Reagan has his Cabinet. Team effort wins results. Your business probably isn't failing because it's unsound or your management bad. You're just too deeply involved, emotionally and financially, to "go it alone." To survive, you must learn how to locate and use the "know-how" of others.

You'll be the team's captain as it:
1. Pinpoints business problems and finds the right solutions.
2. Chooses and implements the correct legal and fiscal strategies to give you back a healthy company.
3. Helps you establish the leadership so crucial to the "turnaround" process.

How do you scout the best players?

Finding the Right Attorney

Forget your Uncle Joe the lawyer. He may not have charged you when he drafted your will, but what does he know about business insolvency, bankruptcy, and turnarounds?

Your team can't win without competent counsel. Too many beleaguered owners make the mistake of thinking that all attorneys possess equal competence in all areas of law. What fiction! There's no such thing as a totally competent or incompetent attorney. They're all both competent *and* incompetent, depending on the area of law you're talking about. You need an attorney experienced in "saving" troubled companies, a gunslinger who carves another notch on his belt each time he rescues a distressed business from the brink of disaster. A rare breed? You bet. Fewer than one percent of all practicing attorneys can legitimately claim specialization in this area.

Any attorney can handle a bankruptcy, because it's so easy to dump a company into a Chapter 7 or liquidating bankruptcy. No experience needed. Just complete a few forms and sink the business. However, just because a law firm handles many straight bankruptcy cases, that doesn't qualify them to orchestrate a turnaround.

Businesses are liquidated every day, not because they should be, but because the attorney representing the business doesn't know the alternatives. If your attorney can't offer saving remedies, keep looking. To obtain the services of an attorney experienced and qualified to handle your turnaround, you have to knock on the right doors.

Look for someone who:
1. Has experience with your type of business. Knowledge of your industry isn't a must, but it can be a big advantage.
2. Has solid experience with insolvency cases.
3. Can promise the time, effort and commitment a turnaround demands.

His technical knowledge as an insolvency specialist can help the turnaround sail smoothly.

The insolvency specialist inhabits the insolvency system. He has done battle with creditors' counsel before and knows what to expect. Creditors' and debtors' lawyers interact on hundreds of cases, developing a working relationship among themselves while still protecting the interests of their respective clients. As one bankruptcy specialist insists, "It's a lot easier negotiating a plan of arrangement with counsel for the creditors' committee when you're on a first name basis with the guy." It even extends to the Courts. A bankruptcy judge is inclined to trust the words of an attorney who routinely appears before him. The judge prefers competency and a "track record." An attorney "unknown" in the Court has a distinct disadvantage if for no other reason than the Court has no basis to determine either the clarity of his judgment or his veracity.

Expect a seasoned insolvency attorney to have a network of resources that can help your business survive. He knows the banks that lend to troubled companies. He has dealt with accountants who can help put a business together again. Consultants? He'll have a long roster of specialists who can solve any business problem. He's played the game with them before.

Place compatibility high on your list of priorities when selecting counsel. In other areas of law, the personal chemistry between attorney and client isn't as critical, but the insolvency case involves a prolonged working relationship. My average case lasts three to six months and some have lingered as long as two years. During the turnaround process, you'll involve your counsel with everything from legal problems to the effects of the struggle on your psyche as you ride an emotional rollercoaster.

An attorney doing his job will be doing more than tackling creditors or running the company through the courts. He may be the catalyst to coordinate the turnaround team. He'll be involved in the total process of the turnaround effort, and he'll handle the battered ego of management and bring needed objectivity to the situation. If he doesn't orchestrate the turnaround, he certainly will provide the tempo.

Ask yourself these questions before you select counsel: Will you enjoy working with him? Can he give you the support you need? Do you agree on the objectives and strategies to reach those objectives? Can he provide the needed time and involvement?

Shop around. Interview several attorneys before you decide, matching the attorney not only to your problem but to yourself as well.

Here's how to find insolvency specialists who can help you.

1. Ask your family or business attorney to refer you to a specialist. You may feel awkward asking one attorney to refer you to another, however, he won't resent it if he recognizes his own limitations.
2. Check with the Clerk of the Bankruptcy Court for the names of attorneys who routinely handle insolvency cases.
3. The State Bar Association may provide a referral service. Make certain you accurately define your problem because many attorneys deal only with liquidating or consumer bankruptcies, totally different fields. Find a business turnaround specialist.
4. This may surprise you, but your creditors may be able to help. Credit Associations within your industry have dealt with other distressed businesses and frequently know someone who's

capable.

The largest firm doesn't necessarily give the best service. As a small business person, you'll invariably end up with a junior associate in a large firm, so a smaller firm or even a sole practitioner might be your best bet.

Legal representation is a necessary evil: The lawyer is necessary, his fee is evil. Let's take some of the mystery out of it.

1. Don't hestitate to seek legal help because you don't have cash available. If your business flounders, you'll never accumulate the cash to retain an attorney.

2. A competent insolvency specialist will be smart enough to figure out ways to obtain his fees from the business. I've yet to see a small businessman walk into my office with a large retainer. An insolvency lawyer doesn't expect it. If you had the money, you probably wouldn't need him.

3. Both you and your counsel should realistically decide what your business can afford to pay—and when. Your attorney will want his fees as the case progresses, but you will be fighting to keep a cash-poor business afloat. It's as unreasonable for you to expect him to bill you at the end of the case as it is for him to demand a retainer the business cannot afford.

4. Don't demand a fixed fee quotation. It's impossible to predict how many hours he will spend when unexpected problems always develop. Do ask for an approximation, though your final bill will depend on the hours involved, the hourly rate, the size of your firm and the results accomplished.

5. Your remedy will to some extent depend on what your company can afford to pay. For example, an attorney cannot profitably handle a Chapter 11 reorganization for even the smallest firm for less than $10–15,000. This may lie beyond the reach of a corner "Mom and Pop" operation. However, other solutions will fit your pocketbook.

6. When you retain an attorney, you're not really incurring an expense because your creditors, the true owners of the insolvent

company, eventually pay the bill. The creditors allow you to use some cash from *their* business so you can invest in hiring the team to put the business back together.

Wanted: An Accountant Who Can Keep Score

Seat-of-the-pants management causes business problems that only thinking-cap management can solve. You must play the game dictated by the "numbers," analyzing every component of your operations to find not only the key to solvency, but to profitability as well.

My first official act in many cases? Firing a client's existing accountant. No apologies. If the accountant wasn't doing his job, I conclude he can't change overnight into an effective member of the turnaround team.

I see it all the time. Roger E. had no idea how close his furniture store stood to the edge of a cliff. More importantly, he didn't know why he was in trouble because his accountant didn't warn him in time. Only the IRS had some numbers, and they, too, didn't have the full picture. Too many accountants consider preparing year-end tax returns the sum and substance of their jobs.

Your accountant, even during normal operations, must provide the fiscal maps and charts for the business. It's his job to tell you when you're veering off course, and what corrective steps you might take. Without skillful navigation, any business becomes a rudderless ship.

Rigaletto's Restaurant floundered in a typhoon of debts, incurring losses for four straight years. It took Tony Rigaletto two full years to seek outside help. When I stepped in, I found the financial statements inaccurate and out-of-date. I'm always upset when an accountant allows a business to sink so deep without waving the red flag, so I asked Tony, "What did your accountant have to say about your financial mess?" "Nothing," he replied, "he only drops in once a year to have me sign my tax returns and help himself to my famous linguini."

It's a recurring theme. Businessmen everywhere can't tell you whether they're making or losing money. Books and records either don't exist or lay in a shambles. In over 70 percent of my cases, I'm lucky if I can obtain an accurate list of creditors. There may be thousands of accountants, but few know how to keep score.

I don't intend a blanket indictment of the accounting profession. Many are on the ball and yell loud and clear when trouble begins. These accountants work harder than ever to achieve a managerial turnaround and drag their confused, sometimes reluctant client to outside legal help. Others have tried to deal with "ostrich" owners but failed to force them to face their problems. Still others defend their lack of navigational skill by stating, "The client didn't want my help, he paid me only enough to do his taxes, nothing else."

Fortunately, lack of financial data doesn't defeat the turnaround, it only delays it.

If the solvent, ongoing enterprise requires strong fiscal control and management, the troubled company demands even tougher guidance. Stick everything under the microscope. No turnaround can begin until the numbers to support the plan are on the table.

To dig out those numbers, you need the right kind of accountant, one who lives in a world of cash flow statements, cost analysis, break even projections, forecasting, and budgets. He dives in and comes up with all the answers the turnaround team needs to make thinking-cap decisions.

An effective turnaround team lives on numbers, more numbers and still more:

- "Where are we making and losing money?"
- "Are we making or losing money based on last week's sales?"
- "What will our cash position be over the next three months?"
- "How much must we slash expenses to stop losses?"

No business regains a profitable fiscal course without a navigator at the helm.

The perfect navigator can skillfully analyze operations. He's a rare breed, a blend of cost accountant, comptroller and visionary. And the ideal candidate understands the business and can coordinate the numbers with operational practicality.

Comptrollership comes closest to your needs. Comptrollers have the experience and orientation to guide the solvent business and can readily adapt to the needs of the insolvent one.

In recent years, a new professional designation, C.M.A. (Certified Management Accountant), has been awarded to accountants with expertise in managerial accounting (as opposed to auditing, taxation and statement compilation, which is the "bread and butter" of the C.P.A.). A good C.M.A. can navigate your turnaround.

Titles are not important. In many of my successful smaller cases, we relied on bookkeepers, whom we carefully guided by specifying the "numbers" we wanted.

The bankruptcy courts now appoint experienced accountants as trustees to oversee the reorganization of troubled companies under the protection of Chapter 11. Since most of these accountants have a private practice, they could be excellent additions to any team. Not only do they possess the financial acumen you need, but they've handled many other financially distressed businesses. And since the accountant's findings are important to the courts and creditors, it's wise to secure an accountant the court knows and trusts. Your attorney can locate an accountant with turnaround background, or the bankruptcy court can supply a list of court-appointed trustees with managerial accounting backgrounds.

Large firms usually have sufficient "in-house" personnel to do the job. For smaller firms, the addition of an outsider may be unnecessary, because navigation is not necessarily a full time job. For firms with sales of less than $1,000,000, we usually obtain the answers with fewer than 50 hours of accounting time. The accountant will "moonlight" two or three nights a week, until we have all the financial information we need. Then we can make decisions. Subsequently, the accountant should monitor the numbers to see if the decisions were sound. It's only a matter of keeping score. You can't play the game without a scorekeeper.

Consultants Who Mean Business

Your team begins to take shape. On the left sits your attorney who will run interference against the creditors. On your right stands the accountant who will give you numbers you may never have seen before. But wait. Your team may not be complete. You may also need a consultant to "sharpshoot" your operational problems.

The word "consultant" scares people. They envision some guy showing up in a three piece suit, scanning the business for a few hours, then returning in a few weeks with a pristine report complete with charts and tables that might as well be written in Greek. Sometimes that happens. But quite often consultants can give a business a fresh perspective on its own problems, together with proven solutions. And sometimes the best consultants are people who don't even call themselves that, but are, nevertheless, the "experts" from afar who may know more about your business than you do. I call them the "chicken soup" consultants.

I met my first "chicken soup" consultant years ago at the Seaview Restaurant, a fully packed chicken and steak house at a local ocean resort. Its owner, Barry T., had purchased the business several years earlier and seemed to be doing everything right except showing a profit. In fact, his losses had prompted Barry to invite me for dinner. He wanted me to battle his creditors. I was very curious about how such a popular restaurant managed to operate in the red. Barry didn't have the foggiest idea, his accountant didn't have any answers, and I knew nothing about the restaurant business. Our collective knowledge fit in a salt shaker.

However, what we lacked in knowledge, we overcame with determination, turning the place upside down looking for answers. We audited invoices, analyzed customer counts, studied expenses and scrutinized income. My calculator blew its battery. No success! The customers (and the losses) kept pouring in. We needed a "pro."

Our "pro" didn't sport a three piece suit but, as the owner of one of the most successful restaurants in Boston, he had loads of restaurant "savvy." There I sat with all my graphs, numbers, projections and theories—everything but the answer. In walked the "pro" with a simple answer. "Fellas," he said, "you want profits?" "Of course," we chimed. "Then stick your noses in the trash cans out back. They're full of wasted food. We call that 'shrinkage,' and it can swallow a restaurant's profits quicker than a whale. In my own operation, I pay as much attention to the garbage cans as to what's on the customer's plate."

Within two days, Barry took a PhD in "shrinkage" and began recycling chicken into chicken salad and chicken soup and left-over vegetables from the salad bar into cole slaw. Food destined for the garbage pail became profitable menu additions. Cost-of-goods dropped 28 percent. Profits zoomed to $18,000 in one season. The restaurant was saved, all thanks to the "chicken soup" consultant. I seldom handle a case without one on the team.

Note these three lessons:
1. Your accountant and attorney are experts in their own fields, but they don't know yours. Don't expect easy answers to business problems from your attorney. And beyond financial guidance, your accountant won't add much more.
2. Most businesses incur losses (and financial trouble) through operational inadequacies. Owners often know their business well but are still totally lacking in one or more key areas.
3. The best and perhaps the only way to detect and solve operational problems is to call in someone who knows the business. Grass roots problems demand grass roots solutions.

It's all common sense. Since small business owners are usually loners, they are the last to turn to others for answers to business problems, even when they desperately need them.

The larger firm enjoys management depth. Purchasing, sales, merchandising, finance, are all manned by experts. And still they stumble. The small business owner has to do everything; he's a generalist wearing twelve hats. Some of those hats just won't fit.

Hundreds of my own cases were successful not because of legal one-upmanship or the numbers, and not even because the owner had sufficient stamina and enthusiasm to fight for survival. The "chicken soup" consultant deserved the credit.

It can work for you, as it has worked for others. Consider:

Economy Drug. From outward appearances it flourished. So why did it lose money? We called in a successful pharmacy owner, who immediately found the answer. Faulty buying proved to be the

Achilles Heel. The consultant recommended an out-of-state supplier who would sell for 10 percent less. That advice was worth $20,000 annually. Profits appeared for the first time.

Buy-Lo Foods. It was falling victim to its own poor merchandising. We found a retired executive from a large supermarket chain, who within a week had the shelves loaded with the right merchandise at the right price. Sales doubled.

Milani Italian Foods. It derived 20 percent of its sales from pizza and beer for the high school crowd. The owner couldn't see the problem, but an owner of another successful Italian restaurant could. She recommended up-grading the restaurant to a "fine dining" image by dressing up the interior, dropping the pizza and beer and concentrating on higher priced cuisine. Sales increased dramatically and the business began to make money as "big spenders" replaced stingy kids.

Gardner Motors couldn't sell its quota of new cars. The auto manufacturer wouldn't help, so we called in a high-powered dealer handling a non-competitive line. He showed my client a number of effective tricks to really move cars, including advertising on television with a tame tiger. Today, Gardner Motors ranks higher in sales than any dealership in the region.

The small business is only the sum total of the talent, experience and capability of the owner, who doesn't have support personnel and in many cases lacks sufficient prior experience or formal business training. So you're alone, fending for yourself and making countless decisions that affect your bottom line. When you guess wrong (it invariably is a guess) on a few major decisions in a row, or make a sufficient number of minor goofs, your profits turn to losses. And it's all compounded by your inability to detach yourself from your business long enough to be objective and to stick your head out the front door.

Very few troubled firms follow this advice and bring in a consultant who knows the business and can spot and remedy operational problems. The turnaround proceeds with many of the same day-to-day errors that created the losses in the first place. And what happens without the consultant on the team who can provide the firm with an objective appraisal of its own managerial performance? Barry thought he really knew the restaurant business. He even knew "shrinkage" had to be controlled. It's common sense. What he did not know, however, was that his shrinkage was excessive by restaurant standards. And he did not know effective ways to solve it. The owner of Buy-Lo Foods thought he was a merchandiser. Yet it took another supermarket operator to merchandise the business the right way.

It's smart business. Others within your industry can put you on the "fast-track" to renewed profitability. You have only to ask for their help.

Your outside consultants will be easy to find. Here's what to look for:

1. They will be from within your industry. You need someone with experience in your field. Business consultants who are not experienced in your field can only apply general management theory. That's not what you're after. You need practical answers.
2. You probably have an inkling about your own operational weaknesses. The ideal candidate should provide complementary strength in those areas. Business people have reputations. You know who is strong in merchandising, promotion, inventory control, or buying. Every industry has its "heavy hitters" who can strengthen your operation.
3. Your "consultant" should be from within your industry, but not a local competitor. You can find knowledgeable people who don't compete with you. If I needed a restaurant consultant, I'd approach a restaurant owner located well beyond my client's trading area.

Ask your consultant what, specifically, he thinks he can do for you and how long it will take before he begins. You're asking him to take time away from his own business. In most cases, the consultant can significantly improve operations by spending the equivalent of a week or two. In some cases, the consultant quickly locates and hires an employee who can handle a troublesome phase of management on a continual basis. That's what happened at the Buy-Lo Supermarket. The consultant himself performed the initial re-merchandising of the store, then he recommended that we bring on board a young man who had once worked for him as an assistant manager. The consultant trained the new employee for a week, until he was satisfied the new man could maintain the new merchandising strength. Buy-Lo's owner could handle other phases of operation, but he just wasn't a strong enough merchandiser.

Your consultant may never have acted in this capacity before, because he works full time in his own business. On the other hand, I also like to use retired businessmen. They can afford more time and have often been around long enough to have experienced difficulties similar to yours. Business people are generally flattered to be asked, because you're recognizing their business accomplishments. Give them a free hand to review the entire operation. I seldom define the problem, because if you confine the consultant to your interpretation of the problem, you lose the opportunity to detect problems you've never even noticed.

Still, certain guidelines are important. I always ask the consultant to submit an outline of major operational problems. Once he defines these, I can rank them by priority and decide the time, manpower and money it will take to effectively handle them. Be honest with your consultant. Disclose your financial affairs. Let him know that he should concentrate on problems that can swiftly improve your cash position. It's essential, of course, but you can plan for long term profits later.

You may need more than a report or identification of problems. Implementation is vital. The owner and consultant have to decide whether the changes can be implemented without outside help. Who will do the work is as important as defining the work that must be performed.

That's where we dropped the ball on the Beacon Secretarial School case. Beacon ran into problems with shrinking enrollments and high expenses. We called in a sharp operator who headed a similar school in California. Within a week, he handed us a blueprint on how to recruit students, cut overhead, and even attract money from the government. For a $5,000 fee, the consultant gave us $100,000 worth of advice. But it was worthless. The owner of the school stuffed the twenty-page blueprint in his desk drawer, and that's where it sits.

Recommendations are only as good as their follow up. They are valuable only when:

1. You identify who will implement the guidelines.
2. A timetable is established for their implementation.
3. You follow up to see that it's done.

I have found many business people willing to offer several hours—or even days as a free "consultant." Some simply enjoy helping a fellow businessman, others do it for ego gratification and still others conclude they'll inevitably pick up some good ideas from your operation that they in turn can use in their own. Yet I recommend that you avoid free consultation from this type of source. You're not looking for favors. Establish a business relationship so you can demand both time and results.

Many owners are the biggest roadblock to effective use of the consultant. They resent an "outsider" interfering in their operation, and assent to the consultant only because an attorney or accountant insists. More commonly, the owner welcomes the consultant but never agrees with any recommended changes, creating inevitable conflict within the turnaround team. There's no easy answer, but if the recommendations sound logical, try them. You have little to lose and a lot to gain.

I have used more than one consultant for the same business, each focusing on a specific area of operation. This seldom makes sense, however, for the very small business.

Still, no business is too small for outside help. The smaller the business, the more help it may need. When Zisson's Bakery began to lose customers, I called on Harry Winston, Boston's "Bakery King." He showed up in his apron, sampled a few cookies and within two minutes spewed answers, including, "You're using too much salt." In another three hours he recommended a new layout, advertising campaign, and price lists. He even gave us the recipe for a few ethnic delicacies guaranteed to attract any "sweet tooth" within ten miles. Annual sales climbed from $80,000 to $170,000. Harry was delighted to help a fellow baker, boasting, "Why not? I'm still the King! Nothing wrong with kissing a few toads if I can turn them into princes." The Harry Winstons of your field mean business.

Free Help—Yours for the Asking

Others can give your business valuable free assistance.

The SBA sponsors SCORE, a network of retired business executives which brings years of experience to any type business. You don't have to borrow an SBA loan to qualify for their help, either. I have found SCORE to be an excellent source of help, particularly if you can find a consultant from within their ranks who can match his or her talent to your specific needs. Contact your nearest SBA office for the addresses of SCORE representatives in your area.

Another valuable source of free advice may be the MBA student of today who'll be working as a $100 per hour consultant tomorrow. Many graduate business schools have "outreach" programs in which students work with businesses that can use their fledgling guidance. The student gains valuable "hands on" experience, and the business obtains the benefit of modern knowledge.

I rank MBA students in an "outreach" program similarly to SCORE, plenty of good solid "general" advice, but too little of the "nuts and bolts" applicable to your field.

Fremont Catering Services was saved by two inexperienced but aggressive MBA students who knew nothing about my client's business. The students had a picnic with this business that grossed $2,000,000 but couldn't earn a dime. They:

- Negotiated with suppliers for better prices. Prices fell 12 percent!
- Collected overdue payments from canteen owners. A "no-nonsense" collection effort produced over $60,000 in working capital and established a system for keeping the cash flowing.
- Raised some prices and lowered others. Fremont listed for the first time products that added to or subtracted from profits.
- Reduced excess inventory and increased stocks of frequently "out-of-stock" items.

Today Fremont earns $150,000 annually. Our MBA students? They're billing $100 an hour. Fremont was smart. Smart enough to call them in *before* they graduated!

The consultant is the essential, but commonly missing, member of the turnaround team. Solving creditor problems is never enough. Your business requires strategies to return it to profitability. Your attorney and accountant can't do it alone, and chances are you can't do it by yourself, either. That's when it's time to consult additional talent.

Ask Your Key Employees to Help

Lurking within your firm are employees who can assist the turnaround team. And in some cases, their involvement is as important as the owner's.

The turnaround requires a clear delegation of responsibility. Operational changes will come fast and furiously. You'll need all the help you can get to maintain daily operations while you implement changes and shoulder the extraordinary burdens the turnaround will impose.

You can't be a one-man band. You'll need to maximize internal support. The work will proceed more smoothly and many employees will show you talent you never knew existed.

Who to use for what defies simplistic guidelines. The size of the company, the severity of pressing problems, and staff availability all contribute to the perfect blueprint. No two are identical. Can the owner better handle operational matters, or could a key employee perform just as well? Your principal function will be to oversee operations and work closely with the turnaround team. This gives you less time for routine matters, so your employees must pick up the slack.

I always try to meet the key employees of a troubled business, because they provide valuable insight into business problems. Sometimes they offer objective and sensible advice because they watch the company deteriorate day by day. I try to measure both their degree of interest and what added responsibilities they can assume. Forget complex organizational charts. Instead, assign work to people who can best handle it. You can't do everything yourself, and you should be smart enough to know when your employees can do things even better.

Creditor pressure? Delegate public relations to an articulate employee. A "tough skinned" employee who knows the ropes can run interference and field the bombastic, time consuming creditor threats with considerably more aplomb than the typical owner. I always look for that "tough skinned" employee. And I always make him or her part of the turnaround team, so we can keep close watch on the creditor battlefield.

Operational changes? A key person may be the perfect candidate to make them. At Dyson Shoes, the owner ran out of steam and was hours away from a nervous breakdown. On his payroll, however, was an assistant manager who had good strong ideas for the ailing $800,000 footwear house. Even better, he possessed the energy and ability to convert those ideas into reality. The owner supervised but the up-and-coming assistant took over as captain of the turnaround team and worked with us not only to save the business but eventually to expand it into a four-store chain.

You shouldn't place all your employees on the turnaround team, only the one or two who can assume major responsibility.

The turnaround process can be an important tool for detecting and curing deficiencies in your staff. When your people can't provide required support, change the people before you alter the game plan. If Dyson Shoes hadn't had the aggressive assistant manager to spearhead the turnaround, finding the person who could would have been my first priority. The owner couldn't do it, but the job had to be done. It becomes a matter of plugging the hole in the team.

In many cases, we replaced key employees suitable for the solvent enterprise, but who couldn't respond to the needs of the company in trouble.

Capable employees require motivation during the turnaround process. Effective use of their talent bolsters morale. They feel involved, because they *are* involved. Key employees can see what's happening and play a decisive role in making it happen. Adding two or three top employees to the turnaround team can create an enthusiasm that filters down to other employees.

When Graphic Printing over-expanded, we designed a turnaround team which included not only the owner but the sales manager and production manager as well. They had great ideas for expanding sales and production. Why didn't they come up with the ideas before? The owner never asked for their opinions and seemed disinclined to accept them. But as members of the turnaround team, they had an open forum. The sales manager wanted to go after institutional accounts. The production manager wanted to dump some inefficient typesetting equipment and lease a new computerized printer. The team analyzed their ideas and gave them the green light. The sales manager became a ball of fire. So did his twelve salesmen. The production personnel also came to life. Positive things were happening. They could see it and were part of it.

Consider your top employees for your starting line-up. They'll be around after the other teammates are gone.

Partners for Your Winning Team

Partnerships sometimes provide the answer. Why not? Conglomerates sell the idea of corporate marriage on the basis of managerial strength. It can make even more sense for the small firm.

An owner can delegate, but he can't totally abdicate. In several recent cases, the owners had neither the inclination nor the talent to whip their companies into shape. Nor could they find or adequately supervise employees who could.

Ask Ralph K. of Ralph's Stereo Centers. Ralph had it all, $3,200,000 in sales and a prize winning bankruptcy. It had to happen, but Ralph didn't know how to cope with it, and he had no employee with sufficient talent to help. I knew the legal solutions, and the accountant ran the numbers. Two consultants even demonstrated how the business could be turned into a success. But who within the organization could put it all together? Not Ralph. He was too busy drowning his sorrows on the golf course. Ralph never became part of the turnaround team, so to win the game we had to resort to a "designated hitter." That was Arthur who was busy building a Radio Shack store into the pride of the Tandy chain. He acquired a 50 percent interest in Ralph's to be paid out of future profits. Ralph still plays golf. He can afford to with his share of the $200,000 profits the business earned last year.

The starting line-up isn't always the best team. But without management, there's no team at all.

In the previous chapter, I asked you to assess your own managerial mentality. There we focused on your ability to lead your company once it cleared its financial hurdles.

The turnaround process will demand even more managerial strength than the custodial operation. Many owners can't muster that strength. That's when a partnership arrangement can make sense.

Leadership for the turnaround team can come from only one source—the owner. He can delegate substantial responsibility to the employee, but invariably the turnaround can never be more successful than what the owner himself can provide. As with all business matters, management has to come from the top.

Oftentimes that leadership has to be found outside the organization, and hiring one or two key employees may not be sufficient to achieve the leadership demanded.

Many owners recognize their own inadequacies to provide the team with the leadership and sell to or merge with larger firms. In some cases, managerial support is only one of the reasons. The owner may not be looking only for management. Financing or personal profit from the sale can be an incentive for looking to the larger firm. But it's usually a mistake.

The troubled firm can seldom be sold for what the business is—or can be—worth. The timing is off. The owner is dealing from a position of weakness, not strength. Larger firms can only take advantage of your vulnerability to strike the best bargain for themselves.

That's why I recommend looking in another direction. You need management for the turnaround. Your best management sources *can* come from firms even smaller than yours. It may even be an aggressive employee from a competing firm. Those are the bushes to beat. If you can't find the talent within your own organization, you may within someone else's firm. You can usually bring them on board by giving them a small percentage of your company. And if they are successful with the turnaround, you'll end up with not only an ownership interest in your firm, but that ownership interest could be worth considerably more than if you had sold out under a depressed condition.

But think positively. Perhaps you can be the leader who can give the team what it needs:

- **Direction:** to provide blueprints for returning the business to profitability.
- **Coordination:** to insure that all members of the team are doing their job and are moving ahead, as a team.
- **Decisiveness:** to tackle the problems one by one, as they develop.
- **Enthusiasm:** so the team and everyone within your organization knows you expect to win and have what it takes to win.

You need your team and the team needs its leadership. The right players and the right leader can work wonders with any company.

Beverly W. of Hilltop Fashions travelled that road. She now understands the value of a strong team and the need to coach enthusiastically. "Do it all alone? I'd rather remove my own tonsils," she laughs. Why shouldn't she laugh? Hilltop grossed $2,000,000 last year and showed a bottom line profit of over $300,000. Beverly looked clever. She also had a clever team.

Check Your Starting Line-Up

1. Do you have an attorney who knows how to handle your turnaround?
2. Can your accountant keep score and give you all the numbers to guide you?
3. Has your operation been reviewed by consultants who can pinpoint what went wrong, with solutions to make it right?
4. Do you have employees who can work with you to develop ideas and help you perform surgery?
5. Are you the leader who can put it all together and make it happen?

Profits: The Name of the Game

4

The business of business is making money. And you can't save your business without making money.

Face the Facts

Fact 1: Profits provide the only scorecard for rating your business.

Fact 2: Unprofitable businesses always fail.

Fact 3: No easy formula or foolproof system will turn a loser into a winner. Every business demands its own unique game plan for profitability.

Fact 4: Only you can design your business' winning approach to profitablity.

Fact 5: You can make money with any business, provided you remove your blinders, roll up your sleeves and use bold and imaginative tactics.

Fact 6: Ninety percent of all businesses fail because the owners refuse to face the first five facts.

Jerry Caughlin didn't want to face the facts. His small department store incurred whopping losses for five consecutive years. The business was in dismal shape with liabilities triple the asset value. Wanting to save his business, Jerry asked for legal hocus-pocus to try to make his creditors disappear. I could only turn to Jerry and say, "Sorry, I can't help you."

"What do you mean you can't help me," he stammered.

"Just what I said," I replied. "I can't save your business. All I can do is negotiate a settlement with your creditors. Assuming I'm successful and I give you back a solvent company, what happens then? How have you changed your business? How will your business begin to make money, and what will happen if it doesn't?" I shot plenty of questions, but Jerry had run out of answers.

Then I offered Jerry a deal. Handing him a long yellow legal pad, I said, "Come back in two weeks. Show me, and more importantly, yourself, that you can construct a plan to make your company profitable, and I'll help you."

Jerry burned the midnight oil and two weeks later returned my legal pad covered with calculations and ideas. He identified the reasons for his losses, invented a new merchandising and pricing campaign geared for the discount market, added several cost cutting ideas, and even proposed hot new promotional concepts. Drafting the blueprints for profits, Jerry was finally beginning to do his job. It worked. We reduced his company's debt by $2,000,000 through a Chapter 11, giving Jerry the time to test his game plan. Jerry finally realized if he couldn't turn his business into a profit producer, it would eventually fail. He made sure it didn't happen.

The successful turnaround starts with a plan to produce profits and ends when profitability is achieved.

It's common sense. Yet many owners make the same mistake as Jerry Caughlin. They think the turnaround only involves returning the business to solvency. You can maintain solvency, however, only with profitability.

Let's put you through Jerry's exercise. Pull out your yellow pad. You have work to do.

Five Early Warning Signals

In many cases, the clue that the business is losing money doesn't come from the profit and loss statement. The owner may not have studied his statements, understood what they said or had any confidence in their accuracy. Nevertheless, he or she has the "gut feeling" the business is turning bad. Gradually, operational problems appear, and with time, the problems become so acute they can no longer be ignored. Experienced managers recognize these operational problems in the early stages. Less experienced owners usually allow the signals to keep flashing until it's almost too late to salvage the business.

Look for these signals:

1. Decreasing Working Capital

The established, stable business operates with cash reserves within a customary range. Unexplainable decreases in working capital may signal a company losing money.

The start-up or cyclical business can't rely on working capital balances as an early detection signal, and all cash balances have peaks and valleys.

Analyze the trend of your own working capital. Do you notice a declining balance?

2. Shrinking Inventory

Decreasing inventory levels may disguise losses. Goods move off the shelves faster than you can replenish them.

Many businesses fail to detect this early warning signal through failure to conduct annual inventories. At year's end, the owner estimates the inventory and conveniently places it at the same level as the prior year.

Decreases in inventory can go unnoticed because they happen so gradually. Even experienced owners may not observe a decrease from $70,000 to $60,000. But that decrease represents a $10,000 loss.

Conversely, inventory may be building up and may even explain decreasing cash balances. Regine Liquors was a prime example. The business always operated with $10–15,000 in the checkbook. Suddenly, the business became cash poor. The owner panicked, believing he was falling victim to an early warning signal of losses. But he was wrong. It was his new manager. Over-buying was his weakness. Working capital was drained to pay for the rapid build up in inventory. It's a common mistake. Working assets can change form. Yesterday's cash may be today's inventory and tomorrow's receivables.

3. Declining Accounts Receivable

It's part of the equation. A decline in receivables, without a corresponding increase in cash or inventory, signals a drop in current assets. Conversely, a build up of receivables can strangle cash or deplete inventories. Watch your receivables.

4. Increasing Liabilities

If working assets (cash, receivables and inventory) aren't increasing, escalating liabilities can certainly indicate a business losing money.

Owners of the established business watch liability levels closely. They have set up regular payment schedules and can easily detect when bills remain unpaid longer than usual. Less experienced owners may routinely postpone bills another month. Six months later, payments have fallen 60–90 days behind, and a few collection letters from angry creditors appear. It's another gradual process that can escape the unwary eye.

Owners oftentimes have no idea what they owe. I always ask new clients to list their accounts payable. An owner may say $50,000 off the top of her head, but I'll insist on a updated list of every single account. For the first time in years, she'll actually gather up the bills and run them through the adding machine. The result commonly totals double what the owner estimated.

Prepare a monthly payable list. Then you can easily spot creeping liabilities.

5. Loan Defaults

Loan defaults usually offer the final early warning signal. Owners are reluctant to default on loans. First, they exhaust cash and credit. Then they deplete inventory before throwing their loans into default. Once loans go into default, the business is floundering in the terminal stages of insolvency. Surprisingly, many owners may be seriously in default on important loan obligations and still be unaware that their business is in trouble.

Watching for early warning signals can provide timely clues that your business is losing money. However, they're only symptoms. You'll have to dig deep to find the causes.

Take a Quick Trip Through Your Financial Statements

How do you really know whether you're making or losing money? Your financial statements should provide the information needed to assess your profitability or the extent of your losses. They may not tell you *why*, but at least they tell you how much. On the other hand, your financial statements might tell you very little. In fact, many contain a wealth of erroneous information. Small losses may actually be whoppers. Losses may, in reality, be profits. A small business with non-certified statements must allow a considerable margin for error. That error factor can be lifesaving or fatal.

Here are just a few examples of how financial facts get buried.

Skimming income? Jeff T. showed me the P & L for his retail kitchenware business. Losses of $20,000 for three straight years stared at us in black and white. But business had been good. How could it have happened? Jeff finally confessed. In addition to the $20,000 a year he took as salary on the books, he skimmed another $25,000 a year directly into his pockets without disclosing the fact on his financial statements. Why did he do it? He didn't want to pay taxes on the extra income. I won't moralize about it, but small business owners do it all the time. In Jeff's case, a business that appeared to be losing $20,000 a year was really making $5,000.

Inventory? Kevin T. told his accountant he maintained a constant $60,000 year-end inventory. That optimistic guess destroyed the accuracy of his business' financial picture. In actuality, inventory was falling $10,000 a year and had declined to $30,000. The business showed a nominal annual loss of $5,000. After Kevin's accountant factored in the inventory reductions, losses expanded to $15,000 annually.

Worthless receivables? John K. displayed $180,000 in uncollectible receivables on his books. Had he written off the receivables as an expense as he should have done, his fledgling computer firm wouldn't have shown a $40,000 profit but an average annual loss of over $30,000.

64 How to Save Your Business

Any turnaround demands hard, accurate financial data on which to base decisions. Know the score!

1. Disregard prior financial statements. Chances are they will not be accurate enough for your purposes.
2. Have your accountant prepare new statements designed to show accurate operational profits or losses for each of the prior three years.
3. Make the statements as accurate as possible. Disclose non-reported income. Conduct a physical inventory. Isolate and disregard non-operational or extraordinary items that can distort the picture.
4. Analyze the statements carefully. You'll spot important trends in sales, expenses and profitability that can provide valuable clues to the reasons for losses and help determine corrective action.
5. Consider this guide:

Sales:

a) Analyze trends for the past three years. Your business should show an increase in sales of at least 10 percent annually just to stay even with inflation.

b) Decreasing sales? Look at your inventory levels. Decreasing inventory explains why most businesses lose sales. If inventory isn't the answer, the sales lag is probably due to either improper merchandising, lack of promotion or added competition.

c) Analyze sales from a departmental or product line approach. Define where you are growing and where you are falling behind. Oftentimes a business will have excellent gains in most departments only to suffer from sluggish sales in others. You must spot your profit centers.

Gross Profit:

Calculate it as a percentile of sales. Decreasing percentages can be attributable to:

a) Improper buying? You may be paying more for goods this year than you did in prior years. It can be a common reason for declining profits for the troubled company. They begin to operate defensively. Cash poor, they can't bargain for the best prices, take cash or trade discounts, or buy on the best terms. Cost of goods rises and profits shrink.

b) Pricing is your next step. Many businesses are slow to pass price increases on to their customers. This will shrink gross profits. Discounting to increase sales may account for a drop in gross profits, as a percentage of sales, but be justified when dollar profits increase. But it doesn't always happen. You have to consider gross profits in both dollar and percentage terms to obtain the true picture.

c) Merchandise mix? A change in merchandising or product mix can alter gross profits as low profit items generate a larger percentage of sales.

d) Shrinkage? It may be internal pilferage or shoplifting. Don't ignore it. Approximately 20 percent of my clients have unprofitable businesses because of internal pilferage. You can spot it if you watch your gross profit percentages.

Expenses:

Expense items must be evaluated on a line-by-line basis. Study the trend for each expense. How has each expense changed as a percentage of sales? Even a small increase in expenses can erode profits unless there is a corresponding increase in sales. And you have to find those creeping costs, implement sound cost-cutting techniques, and control them with a fine-tuned budget.

You need financial statements that can provide the details. Study the trends within your business. Compare your statements to comparable businesses within your industry, and you will spot those problem areas.

Why Is Your Business in Trouble?

Owners always have an answer. Oftentimes, it's the wrong answer. Everyone cites a sluggish economy, inflationary costs and increased competitive pressures, but these represent *external* reasons for decline. They can be culprits, but they seldom provide the total reason. Here's why:

1. Ninety percent of all businesses fail, not due to external reasons beyond the control of the management, but through managerial inexperience or error. Dun and Bradstreet confirms these statistics.
2. External factors deflect the blame away from one's own managerial inadequacies and create the illusion that the company has fallen victim to circumstances for which owners cannot be held accountable.
3. External factors can create problems for a company and can even strike at the core of the business. However, even in these instances, managers have foreseen the oncoming problem and taken timely and decisive steps to side-step its consequences. It still comes back to management.
4. Most businesses suffer numerous problems. Seldom can only one identifiable reason explain failure. One problem may be more visible than others, but others are bound to exist.

"I'm losing money because the economy is tight and customers aren't spending." And, "Competition is destroying me." I hear this every day.

Recently, I conducted a seminar on "Business Turnarounds" at a local college. I gave each of the 70 participants a sheet of paper and said, "Tell me why your company is in trouble and what you intend to do to make it profitable."

Here are the results:

    43 — blamed the economy

    16 — held competitors responsible

    3 — said they had no idea why their businesses were in trouble

    4 — complained about undercapitalization

    2 — cited one big business error (i.e.—casualty loss and a product defect)

2 — admitted problems with their own management

Out of 70 owners, 59 blamed their woes on just two factors, the economy and competition. Only 12 offered strategies to overcome their problems.

I don't shun these external factors, which can devastate a business. Add to external pressures a marginal operation, and you have a doomed business unless you can effectively:

Sharpen Your Survival Instinct

Businesses that succumb to economic and competitive pressure usually exhibit an operational inflexibility and don't react appropriately to change. When the marketplace changes, they suddenly find themselves out of step, at a loss for solutions.

Your right solution, of course, depends on your unique characteristics.

Survivors come in all sizes and shapes, but they have all removed their blinders and have found imaginative solutions:

Ralston Jewelry knew it was vulnerable to a downturned economy, because its products are historically among the first to feel the crunch of a recessionary market. Owner Syd Ralston explained his strategy. "Our jewelry sales dropped 40 percent. People just weren't spending on luxury items. We cut expenses as far as we could, but it wasn't enough to compensate for the sales drop. We had to increase our sales base by bringing in additional lines. We divided the store down the center and set up a complete leather goods section. The new lines have stabilized sales at a profitable level so we can ride out the economy." *Should you expand your sales base?*

Capeside Motel was smart. A decrease in tourism produced a 40 percent vacancy rate during their peak summer season. Without full occupancy, the motel wouldn't earn enough to cover its annual mortgage payments. But owner Kathy White was a survivor. While nearby motels shuttered their windows, she developed a new promotional campaign, "Rent a room for a week during the summer and get a week's free stay during the off season." She stole the idea from an interval ownership firm selling vacation retreats by the week. With a few ads in the Boston papers, Kathy stimulated an over-flowing crowd. As she tells it, "What does it cost me to give a free room during the off season?" When sales are down, you can either sink under the wave or ride the crest. *Have you tried shrewd promotion?*

Joe A. owned a small supermarket in a downtown area. His Huntington Market did well until a giant discount store moved in beside him. Though I suggested relocating to a spot where he could easily survive, Joe decided to stay and fight it out. He shifted his merchandise strategy to concentrate on gourmet items. Imported groceries and delicacies from around the world covered every corner of his store. Sales skyrocketed. Joe enjoys explaining his increased profits while he puffs on his fat cigar. *"You have to hit the ball where competitors ain't playing."*

Ever hear of "The Pizza Boys"? It was Rico Petucci's clever business-saving idea. He owned one of the hundreds of small, nondescript pizza shops in Boston and was doing fine until Pizza Hut and Papa Gino's hit town. Others figured their pizza-making days were numbered. Not Rico. Committed to survival, he bought a few used Volkswagen busses and advertised home deliveries. "Pick up the phone and call P-I-Z-Z-A B-O-Y-S. Within 30 minutes you'll have your pizza just the way you want it, hot and ready to eat." Rico now has 12 cars on the road, and he's rolling in more than one kind of dough. His newest brainstorm? Pizza Boy's franchises! Rico didn't look at competitors as the end. For him it was a beginning. He calls it *service with a smile.*

Unique stories? Not really. Look around you. Thriving businesses have owners who think positively. The economy? They know there's still plenty of money being spent, so they muster the imagination to capture their fair share. Competition? They know what all survivors know. There's always a way to beat them, no matter how small you may be.

Eight Deadly Business Killers

How many possible reasons are there for business failure? According to one business professor, you may fall victim to any of 4071 potential reasons. What staggers the mind is not the sheer numbers but the reality that 93 percent of the reasons relate to operational decisions.

I have my own list of reasons. And I don't have to boggle your mind with 4071 pitfalls. Eight will do. Having handled over 2000 troubled companies, I have distilled what I call the "Eight Deadly Killers." They strike at the financial heart of most of my clients.

Here's my checklist:

1. Excessive Owner Salaries: Over 30 percent of my cases result from owners who haven't realistically assessed what the business can afford to pay them. They drain the business of needed capital, then wonder why it shows a loss. Inexperienced owners often make this mistake, leaving a job paying $250-300 a week and suddenly finding themselves with access to a business with a $5,000 weekly cash flow. It can be tempting.

Sal K. fell victim to his champagne taste. His record shop had a healthy $300,000 gross, but we had only to scan the expense column to find the answers for the $18,000 loss. He'd augmented a $30,000 salary with another $20,000 off the books. It didn't stop there. His wife drew a hefty $15,000 salary but seldom worked. Fringe benefits? They had it all—life and health insurance, a leased Porsche and winter jaunts to the Caribbean. His total take from his young struggling record shop exceeded $80,000. The new business venture can least afford a hefty owner's salary, because it needs the money to build the business.

You can easily correct this problem by putting yourself on a realistic weekly salary and stopping any expense account nonsense. Unfortunately, it didn't work for Sal. We cut his salary from $30,000 to $18,000 and made certain he kept his hands out of the till. He didn't like the cut in pay or driving his old beat-up VW, so he continued to steal from his own business. The record shop failed and Sal went back to his prior job as a department store stock boy.

2. Excessive Overhead Costs: I spot it in at least 40 percent of my cases. Right down the line, expenses are too high. Sales may be adequate, but the business is slowly choking to death on operating expenses.

Several years ago, I delivered an article to a magazine publisher who had an impressive operation perched in the penthouse of one of Boston's plush office buildings. A swanky receptionist oversaw an equally swanky reception area. The place reeked of success. Unfortunately, its financial statements told another story. I developed a friendship with the publisher, and after several visits, he began to confide in me. His business was losing over $100,000 a year.

Guess where you'll find that publisher today. He now occupies a 12,000 square foot supermarket basement. We made him work day and night with his yellow legal pad, answering tough questions. Why did a magazine publisher need an expensive office suite? Who was he trying to impress? Did his subscribers care what his operation looked like? Objective answers produced annual savings:

$ 96,000 on rent

57,000 in reduced payroll

18,000 on expensive office furniture leases

12,000 in fringe benefits

$183,000 annually

When it's a matter of survival, radical surgery on unnecessary overhead costs can help achieve a healthy bottom line. Survivors cut, cut and cut again, letting nothing escape their scalpels. Lean and mean can win fattened profits.

3. Poor Merchandising: Sales cannot reach profitable levels with insufficient merchandise or poor merchandising strategy.

When inventory turnover is excessive, you may be ordering insufficient quantities of merchandise to support strong sales. Conversely, you may have plenty of goods, but not the right selection or price.

For several reasons, merchandising problems are difficult to correct. Insufficient inventory requires capital or credit that may not be readily available to the failing business. Excess of undesirable inventory presents less of a problem, because all you have to do is dispose of it and re-align your inventory.

Merchandising problems help explain losses in one-third of retailing cases.

Betterman's Fashions had inadequate merchandise levels. The high traffic mall location was excellent, but Sally B. couldn't pump sales over $150,000 a year. Even after she cut expenses drastically, her business couldn't succeed without at least $250,000 in sales. After interviewing several of Sally's customers who left the shop empty handed, I learned that they were disappointed in the lack of variety in styles and sizes of clothes at Betterman's. Sally was trying to do business from an empty wagon. Adding $30,000 in fresh merchandise did the trick.

Be careful when analyzing the thinly merchandised business, because the inadequacy may stem from other problems. In some instances, the owner starts the business poorly capitalized, which is reflected in weak opening stock. The business never gets off the ground, because inventory can never rise to an effective operational level. In such a case, the turnaround goes slowly because it must conquer a tarnished image with customers. In some cases, the owner had necessary capital to properly merchandise the business but played too conservatively. Conrad Clothes had money and credit to merchandise the store properly, but their idea of effective merchandising never coincided with the customers'. We had to convince Conrad to buy $25,000 in new lines.

At the other end of the spectrum lies death by strangulation. Finneran Health and Beauty Aids almost fell victim to it. Finneran's sprang for every sales pitch it heard. Revlon would offer a $1,000 deal with an extra 5 percent margin. They bought. An hour later, Max Factor's salesman would be pushing a super colossal special that was too good to pass up. Again they bought. When Finneran's came running for help, I glanced at the financial statements but couldn't believe my eyes. Sales were only $240,000, but inventory sat at $160,000. Inventory almost coincided with debts. A one-time only 30 percent sale slashed excess inventory to $90,000, and the business began its comeback.

4. Bad Location: Even strong internal management can seldom produce a profit for the retail business that suffers from an unsuitable location, particularly when the business demands high traffic.

At least 30–40 percent of my retail clients could point to site location as a cause of inadequate sales and profitability.

Every retail industry publishes comparative statistics, including ideal sales per square foot. When sales fall below industry averages, you can bet it's due to bad location if not improper merchandising.

Harvey B. had opened a new pharmacy two years earlier in a small town south of Atlanta. By industry standards of $120/square foot, his 2400 square foot store should have been giving him sales of $290,000. With sales at only $120,000, something was clearly wrong. We inspected his store and found it to be well merchandised. That wasn't the answer. When I paused to look out his back door, I saw a cow pasture. To the right stood the tombstones of a nearby cemetery, to the left an auto salvage yard. I could see everything but prospective customers.

The solution? We settled with the creditors for 20 cents on the dollar and found a downtown location with 2000 square feet of attractive space. In one weekend, Harvey relocated his business and sales shot up to $7,000 a week.

Owners commonly have trouble assessing the viability of their location and try to counteract poor customer traffic with increased promotional or merchandising efforts which rarely work. Calculate your sales on a square footage basis and compare it to averages. If you come up short, move to a location that can produce profitable sales.

5. Improper Pricing: This ranks high on the list of profit destroyers for manufacturing firms, although it can be equally bothersome to wholesalers and retailers.

As many as one-third of all manufacturing firms fail due to improper pricing, whereby management prices the product entirely on the basis of existing market conditions or competition rather than on production costs.

Retailers and wholesalers can readily detect improper pricing by analyzing gross profits on their P & L statement, but it's not so easy for a manufacturer who must rely on cost accounting to calculate unit costs. If each unit loses money, the whole enterprise will lose money.

Pricing is far from an exact science. You may price low to increase sales, but watch gross profits drop. Price too high, and sales suffer.

Dakota Brick lost its balance on the pricing tightrope. It priced its decorative brick at 40 cents each. It seemed reasonable. Competitors were selling the same item for 45–50 cents, so why not come in lower and snare a hefty percentage of the market? Three years and $470,000 in losses later, Dakota faced the awful truth. It cost 44 cents to produce each brick! Remember the businessman who, when asked how he could afford to sell every item at 20 percent below his cost, quipped, "Easy, I make it up in volume." Dakota Brick didn't laugh when I told them that joke.

Even the corner variety store can improperly price. Whenever I see a financial statement that shows shrinking gross profits, I always turn first to pricing.

Camden Variety panicked when a supermarket moved in around the corner. Camden knocked 10 percent off all their merchandise in a futile attempt to stay competitive, but it was ludicrous for a corner "Mom and Pop" store to try beating a discount chain on its own terms. To compensate for the reduced prices, sales would have to jump by almost 40 percent. But sales hardly changed. Customers still popped in at the same rate for their quart of milk and loaf of bread. The few cents savings didn't mean a thing to the customers. But ask the owners of Camden Variety what impact those few cents had on profitability, and they'll show you a P & L statement for 1979 showing a $14,000 profit, followed by a 1980 statement showing a $17,000 loss. All it took was a few pennies here, a few nickels there.

I can't give you a magical pricing formula for your business. But I can give you some strong advice. Know your cost and review your pricing. Unsound pricing practices destroy businesses.

6. Absentee Ownership: Businesses under absentee ownership suffer the highest mortality rate of all. The reasons are simple. Not only is the absentee owner unable to keep daily track of the business and continually motivate his workers, he easily falls victim to employee theft, fraud and neglect.

Whenever we represent a business under absentee ownership, I don't look for one big problem to hit me in the face. Instead, I look for several subtle ones, not dollars, but nickels and dimes. Small losses can add up to an avalanche.

I have files full of horror stories.

Fenway Fruit and Produce had four stores, with three under absentee ownership. To become profitable, they trimmed to their original location and slashed $120,000 in employee theft.

Capital Auto Parts had to hire a private investigator to discover an employee going home every night with a lunchpail full of parts. The employee had built his own sports car.

Whitehall TV's eight-store chain couldn't account for $200,000 in missing inventory. Nobody had the answer, not even the people running the branch stores. A security firm found the answer. Two managers conspired to falsify records.

A business needs a boss on the premises who has an interest in what goes on. Without direct supervision, unprofitable events are bound to happen.

In most of our cases involving absentee ownership, we either consolidated the assets into surviving stores the owner could supervise, or we sold the branch locations.

7. Over-Expansion: Building too much too fast can destroy profitability quickly.

Flushed with initial success, too many owners grow helter-skelter without an adequate supply of capital or personnel. The business grows too fast for tight managerial controls to detect losses. Newer acquisitions or areas of expansion may have a profit potential but might not reach that point before they bleed the parent company dry.

Lally Family Restaurants made that error. They owned three profitable restaurants and in one year expanded to three more. It was too much for the fledgling chain. Start-up costs, first year losses and construction over-runs siphoned off the financial reserves of the chain. Survival came only through a long and expensive Chapter 11 reorganization and liquidation of two of their newer restaurants.

The over-expanded business must cut back on the size of the operation until it retrieves profitability.

One turnaround specialist thinks that 70 percent of the firms growing faster than 20 percent annually will eventually outgrow their financial and logistical capabilities. Of those that stumble during the growth period, fewer than one-half will survive. Sometimes a business can become too big for its own good.

8. Inadequate Financial Controls: Authors have written entire books on this subject. To an extent, it encapsulates all the managerial blunders that can kill a business. Most managerial errors originate in a discrepancy between a plan and financial reality, but management frequently ignores the controls needed to measure the impact of a decision after implementing it.

While most business experts point to insufficient financial control as the major or sole cause of problems, I disagree. The troubled business rarely surfaces with one definable, easily solved problem. I see financial ineptitude as just another symptom of poor management. If an owner isn't savvy enough to demand and use accurate financial information to stay on top of business, it's likely managerial ineptitude will filter into every phase of an operation.

In most cases, problems exist everywhere. Weak buying habits, sloppy pricing, high costs, non-existent inventory controls and ineffective merchandising hurt the enterprise. Such problems don't come in neatly tied packages with clear labels. Some stand out while others hide. When you uncover one area of loss, you find two more. Fix those two, and you still have to contend with the first. It all comes down to basic controls. The owner simply doesn't know enough about his business to make the right decisions. He gets lost flying by the seat of his pants.

Scan the list. You too may be victimized by one or more of these exceptionally common reasons for error.

The One Costly Error Case

It happens. A business can do everything right and still find itself in financial trouble.

Miracle Muffler almost blew their entire manufacturing operation when they started making a new muffler line. The mufflers worked beautifully unless you happened to exceed 60 m.p.h. Before discovering the defective alloy, 80,000 were shipped. Bombarded by law suits, Miracle descended like a lead blimp. At last count, claims exceeded $2,000,000. Through a Chapter 11, the business narrowly escaped disaster. One technical error after years of sound, profitable management almost plunged the company into insolvency.

I just completed a case for a food wholesaler who suddenly found himself on the financial ropes. It was a strange story. One of his drivers hit a pedestrian who obtained a $250,000 judgment against the company. Two months earlier, the wholesaler's insurance underwriter had been placed in receivership, leaving my client to satisfy the claim from the cash register. Bad management? Economy? Nope, just plain bad luck.

The "one costly error" cases do crop up. With these firms, it's not a matter of finding profits. They've had years of profitable operation. Then suddenly, lightning strikes.

If the reason for losses is apparent with this type firm, solutions may not be. Strategy depends on the nature of the loss.

Miracle Muffler could knock out claims through a Chapter 11. But what about re-building customer confidence and good will?

In many cases, the culprit is not a casualty loss, product defect or a technological blunder. It's marketing vulnerability. The firm is dependent on one customer, and when that one customer vanishes, the entire business erodes. I see it often. A bus firm loses a municipal school bus contract and income plummets by 90 percent; a printer loses an account who gives it the lion's share of his business, or a sub-contractor who leans on a general contractor for business suddenly finds itself standing alone.

When the one costly loss doesn't impair sales, the remedy can usually be found through elimination of the debt the loss created. When the error, however, takes its toll on sales, survival becomes a challenge. Of all my cases, the ones that have the highest mortality rate are those that are tied to one customer and suddenly find that sales base is gone.

Some succeed by paring down the size of their operation a̲_ _ _ _ _ _
out in new directions in search of new customers or markets. Most fail
to survive due to either an inability to quickly and effectively reduce
overhead and debt or failure to find alternate sources of income.

The "one costly error" case does drive home an important point.
Insolvency doesn't have to creep up on you. It can take you by surprise.

Why a Dollar Earned May Not Be Enough

Even a profitable business may become insolvent. Do you generate
profits only to find yourself sinking deeper in debt? You may be
operating your company with a negative cash flow.

One financial specialist estimates that 80 percent of all businesses
fail due to cash flow problems. Although most cash flow cases involved
companies with operational losses, cash flow problems can also afflict
the profitable enterprise. Cash flow problems *can* destroy your business
faster than operational losses.

Bancroft Bakery started its business with a five year $100,000 bank
loan. The bakery generated operational profits of $10,000 a year but was
obligated to pay $20,000 annually toward the principal on the bank note.
Principal payments on notes are not considered an expense on the
P & L statement, so the $10,000 did not jump out at me. Still, the
business operated with an annual $10,000 negative cash flow. How did
Bancroft cover that $10,000 annual cash drain? Working capital eroded,
inventories fell, and other debts went unpaid. Eventually, the business
collapsed like a deck of cards.

Problem loans explain many cash flow problems. (See Chapter 8).
Other reasons include rapid build-up of inventory or slow receivable
collections.

Inadequate profitability is an underlying cause of every cash flow
problem. Owners venture into business deals with optimism about
what the company can produce in profits. Unfortunately, profit
projections are usually over-estimated. When the business fails to
produce the projected profits, the company pays its fixed obligations by
drawing on working assets. Eventually, the business fails, unless the

owner restructures the debt to coincide with profitability or increases profitability. The latter goal is, of course, the preferable route. It's also the more difficult one.

In a substantial number of cases, the business cannot be expected to produce more profits. The business may have reached its full level of profitability and still be without sufficient cash to handle committed expenditures.

Recently, we handled a retail pharmacy that produced a $24,000 profit on sales of $400,000. A 6 percent net profit is above national statistics for drugstores. The same business was choking on note payments that demanded $35,000 annually. It was unrealistic to look for the cure through a build-up of profits. The solution had to be a modification of the note payments to coincide with profitability.

The bankruptcy courts are loaded with profitable companies who were in the same predicament. Sure, they made money. But they didn't earn enough, or perhaps earn it fast enough to cover the checks that had to be written.

Searching for profitability is only one objective. You have to measure that profitability to see whether it can conform to your cash flow needs.

I demand cash flow statements to give me the answer. Whether the business can be made sufficiently profitable to cover the required expenditures becomes the key question. When planned profits come up short, we attack the disbursement side of the ledger.

Earning a few dollars may put you on the right side of the financial ledger, but it may take many more dollars to keep you there.

Six Tips on Profit Planning

The turnaround requires a specific approach to regain profitability. Many businesses fail, not because they can't find the right blueprint, but due to faulty execution.

Keep these points in mind:

1. Take Quick Action

In my own cases, I demand attention to profitability at the commencement of the case. I don't necessarily expect a final blueprint before we start, but I do count on a commitment to consider profitability as a foundation for success.

As a practical matter, initial efforts in the turnaround case focus on pressing operational problems and fending off creditors. This is the emergency stage. Cash flow and protection of remaining assets take priority. The question of profitability is deferred but never forgotten. It should surface once the firm is beyond the emergency stage and management has daily operational matters under control and can step back and take a hard decisive look at the business and where it's heading. heading.

Long-range planning is oftentimes impossible at the commencement of the turnaround. Management may have little idea as to what the firm will look like once it emerges from the turnaround process.

Nevertheless, where logical initial plans can be formulated, it should be done as quickly as possible. It not only provides immediate financial strength, but of equal importance, it increases the confidence of creditors and employees.

I'll seldom walk into a first meeting with creditors without a plan to find profitability. The ship needs a rudder. It has to at least appear that it's finally on course.

2. Seek Short-Term Profits First

The well designed plan concentrates on business changes that can occur rapidly, producing the most certain, significant and immediate profitability improvements. Long term profitability can always arrive at a later date, but you want to stop losses today.

Tackle the obvious areas first. Set up a priority system based on changes that can dramatically increase profits (or stop losses) and that can be accomplished in short order.

In most of my cases, clients start with a cost cutting program. From there they define product lines or operating divisions that are constant money-losers. But it always follows a concentric pattern of hitting hard and fast the items that do not have to wait for a final plan.

Pay attention to changes that not only increase profits, but of greater initial importance, changes that increase cash flow. You have a cash-hungry business. What changes can you put into motion today to increase cash today and profits tomorrow?

3. Be Realistic

Your plan must work. "Pie-in-the-sky" theories will only distract you from making concrete operational changes.

The realistic plan offers detail, has hard numbers to back it up and shows how the changes will impact on profitability.

Short-term profit strategies can be precise. However, even long term planning demands an end result that matches the problems of the company.

Lack of reality can be the major stumbling block for many firms fighting for profitability. On paper, the idea sounds intriguing, but it lacks operational practicality. The troubled firm cannot afford more mistakes. It has already had its share of managerial blunders. Future plans have to work. That's why I'll always encourage a client to elect a safer course that may generate modest profits, instead of an alternate plan that represents a greater potential but also an increased gamble. Safety is part of reality.

4. Stress Capability

Your plan must fit the financial, personnel and logistical capabilities of your firm. Since you have limited resources to work with, assess them against the resources needed to implement the plan. Many owners have sound business ideas which would represent a perfect solution, *if* the company had the resources to put the plan into play. But they don't. They can only work with what they do have or can obtain. Once the plan goes beyond those capabilities, it becomes nothing more than an idle dream.

Back up your plan with a list showing the resources needed to achieve it. Scan the list. Are there any needed resources you don't have? It can put you back on the right course.

5. Remain Flexible

Very few plans follow a straight line but instead take necessary "zigs" and "zags" along the road.

If initial tactics don't achieve desired results, switch to new strategies. You can look only so far ahead. Therefore, you should consider the path to profitability as a long process. It's seldom based on an initial plan sketched in stone. Proceed step by step, never looking too far ahead. Always measure the impact of the steps you have taken. Then take a few more steps.

In most of my cases, the final road to profits followed a path that was considerably different from the one first conceived. What appeared logical at the beginning was replaced by alternate routes that could be discovered only once the process began. Stay on the lookout for those bends in the road, and don't be afraid to consider them if they make sense.

6. Execute Decisively

Some people dream, others do. Once you've designed a plan, emphasize careful execution. Establish timetables. Define who will be responsible for each component of the plan. Allocate the needed resources. Write it down in black and white so you have a step-by-step guide to follow.

I make every client complete what I call a Management Action Plan (MAP). It can work for you.

Complete Your Own Management Action Plan

The "MAP" provides a detailed planning and control mechanism. It will put you on a clearly marked path and keep you there. Stressing the basic who, what, when, where, how and why, it guides your employees and turnaround team.

Design your own Management Action Plan.

Company _____

Date _____

Problem	Remedy	Result
Specifically define the problem.	Define the planned action. List who is responsible for each phase, costs and timetable for implementation and completion.	Define expected result and whether results were achieved and other corrective strategies required.

Follow-up is essential. Stay on schedule. Compare results to goals and take corrective action when results aren't achieved. Watch your priorities. Solve the problems that devour profits first. You can go after the small problems later.

Does it work? You bet! The MAP is our number one navigational tool. We define the problems and provide the detail for how we'll attack them. On a weekly basis, the turnaround team reviews the plan, adds to it, and begins to "bang a few heads" when things don't get done. But it's all part of progress. It's how the troubled company transforms itself from a sick firm into a healthy enterprise. It comes from "doing." It's our answer to that old adage, "You need a plan that works—then you have to work the plan."

Any Business Can Be a Money-Maker

When I first began consulting financially distressed companies, I thought some businesses were born losers and could never show a profit. Then I met Charlie T.

His life centered on his old movie theatre; a loser when he bought it and still a loser. Empty seats and old re-runs were his trademarks. "Dump it," I counselled. "The damn business is losing over $40,000 annually, and it'll never be profitable. Face it, Charlie, you've got a loser on your hands!"

Charlie didn't see it that way. "True," he admitted, "as a *theatre* it is a loser." But Old Charlie could see beyond what I could see. Three weeks later, he had ripped out the seats, sold his projection equipment and was rapidly turning the defunct theatre into a consignment art gallery.

Today, Charlie's Wintergate Art Galleries exhibits over 800 paintings from local artists. And it's always swamped with customers. Charlie's making plenty of money and couldn't be happier. Last year he netted $147,000.

Charlie never lets me forget my "good" advice and always sends me his tax returns, not to impress me, but to make sure I learned my lesson. I have. Here's a note he sent me this year: "Any business can make money. All you need is an owner who knows how."

Attacking Problems One by One

5

You've heard of the "haves" and "have-nots." Well, I've discovered a new club I call the "have-not-paid-for-what-they-haves." Warning: Initiation fees are high, and to qualify, you must successfully negotiate a problem-solving obstacle course.

The club's Grand Exalted Ruler, Phil T., had a long list of "haves" and an even longer list of "not-paid-fors." Phil owned five restaurants. But he hadn't paid for any of them or for the debts from operating them.

Lucky for Phil, he was the determined type. He knew that he couldn't keep the restaurants unless he could clear the hurdles. Here's how Phil relates his experiences on the obstacle course: "When a business goes sour, you don't have one problem. You must deal with dozens of different problems. Saving your business requires you to define each problem and find solutions."

Phil recounts those problems. "Our employees knew the business was in trouble. Our best people were 'jumping ship' and the 'hangers-on' just didn't seem to give a damn."

Cash? He could never get his hands on enough of it. Each day he'd scramble to take in enough money to cover the checks written several days earlier.

Credit was an even bigger problem. Suppliers lined up ten deep trying to collect what Phil owed. "Do you think they'd deliver any more goods to our 'deadbeat' account?"

He couldn't fool customers either. "Come up short providing the goods or services, and they'll drop you like a hot potato. How many times can you tell a customer you don't have this or that item, before you run out of customers?"

Competitors? "They hovered around us like vultures. One was waiting for our auction so he could pick up our equipment dirt cheap. Two more stole some of our best help. Our landlords were besieged with phone calls to throw us out so our competitors could move in."

"To survive, you need more than a game plan to make the business profitable," says Phil, "and that means more than erasing your debts. You have to clear the operational hurdles to keep the business intact while you fight for renewed profitability and solvency."

Phil's right! Many businesses can devise a way to find profitability and convince their creditors to accept ten or twenty cents on the dollar and go away. But it takes time. And during that time, you'll be operating with a shortage of everything. Cash, credit and inventory, even customers disappear or reach dangerously low levels. And you'll have surpluses too: non-productive employees, creditors trying to drain what little cash you have before you go "belly-up," customer gripes and competitors trying to pick you clean.

The surviving business throws a defensive shield around its operation and scrambles for sufficient assets to run the company while it cuts draining payments and expenses. Those that stumble on the obstacle course allow assets to fall to the point that the business can no longer maintain itself.

Preservation and accumulation of assets to create the financial platform to build from must be the first step in the turnaround process. Smart owners protect the "viable core."

This chapter will guide you through the obstacle course and show you how to clear the hurdles one by one.

The Tourniquet Treatment

The troubled company doesn't need a bandaid but a tourniquet to stop it from bleeding to death. Drastic action and quick moves will pump in the plasma needed to restore health to a sick business.

You must:

1. Increase cash reserves.
2. Obtain needed credit.
3. Obtain inventory and goods.

But what good is a financial transfusion if your business can't stop the money drain? You'll need a tourniquet to:

1. Choke costs.
2. Stop the money flow to creditors.

You're after more than positive cash flow. You want to restore your asset base so you have adequate cash and inventory to continue operations until you can regain profitability.

Businesses that fail to apply the tourniquet invariably end up in what I call "bankruptcy spin." Lack of cash or credit starts the vicious cycle. Inventory shrinks as you deplete it to cover debts, and the cashless business can't replace its inventory. Reduced inventory in turn creates lost sales and customers. Reduced sales generate even less cash to the already anemic business.

Eventually, the company bleeds to death; the business reaches the point where it has empty shelves and no cash or credit.

Winslow Foods lay near death on the operating table. In its prime, the business enjoyed $2,000,000 in annual sales. With several years of operating losses, the working asset base (cash + credit + inventory) evaporated.

- Cash? Winslow suffered a bank overdraft of $12,000.

- Credit? The business had a list of 148 creditors.

- Inventory? Almost none. To sustain a respectable sales level, Winslow needed $80,000 in inventory, but its bare shelves contained less than $15,000 in stock. Without goods to sell, sales plummeted to $400,000 annually, a far cry from its prior sales and even further from the $2,500,000 in sales needed to achieve profitability. Winslow didn't survive. Its owners couldn't raise capital or credit to replenish inventory. Without inventory, the business couldn't become profitable.

Some companies allow themselves to bleed to death, neglecting to apply the tourniquet while they still have assets to employ. Such companies seldom get up from the operating table.

The Cash Transfusion

Cash is life blood for the ailing company. And it's the one commodity it has most trouble getting its hands on.

Fortunately, finding cash for your company merely requires imagination and a hard look at assets you can quickly convert to cash.

Follow this "money-finders" checklist:

1. Reduce Inventory

Your firm may be operating with *excess* inventory. Though low inventories can prove fatal, liquidation of excess inventory can provide a quick cash transfusion.

It's a two-step process: 1) Define the safe inventory level needed to sustain sales and 2) sell the excess.

Your firm may be over-loaded with inventory and resultant debt. Are you operating with too little cash? Many firms over-buy in order to squeeze a few extra discount points from suppliers, concentrating on gross margin rather than turnover and cash flow. If you're in this position, reverse the process. Consider a "cash raising sale." Price slashing coupled with extensive promotion can convert dollars sitting on your shelf into hard money for your checking account.

This strategy works in at least 30 percent of our cases, when owners have loaded shelves and an overdraft in their checking accounts.

Sanborn Drug Co. didn't know what it had in inventory. The financial statements said $45,000, but I was suspicious. One look in its basement and my suspicions were confirmed. What a mess. Cartons of merchandise were piled to the rafters. Old merchandise and new deals all thrown in together. No wonder the business was strangling. We called in an inventory team to sort and count the merchandise. Grand total: $90,000. And that was only the basement area. Another $70,000 was loaded on the shelves.

I grabbed its owner, Al T., and gave him a quick lesson in economics. Reaching for a $3.00 bottle of vitamins collecting dust in one of the boxes, I asked "What do you think this is?" "A bottle of vitamins," he sheepishly replied. "Wrong. It's $3.00 and its $3.00 that could be in your checking account," I countered. Al was beginning to learn an important lesson. Merchandise is money and you have to look at it and treat it as money.

A week later, Sanborn had its promotional flyers in the mail. Cosmetics at 50 percent discount, pens at 40 percent off and 1001 other items at bargain basement prices. The merchandise poured out and the money poured in to the tune of $47,000. Think about it. Al had a cash vault under his feet. He just couldn't see it.

2. Sell Unneeded Assets

A successful transfusion requires liquidity. You may lack excess inventory you can liquidate, but you may have other assets.

Excess equipment can produce cash. Examine everything in your operation. Is any equipment gathering dust? How much can you get for it? Many firms over-invest in tangible assets, buying the newest and best of everything.

Jack Wyatt from Wyatt Import doesn't sit behind an $8,000 marble top desk anymore. Surgery on his business included stripping his business of the desk, designer rugs and lamps, and over $40,00 in other non-functional equipment. Today you'll find Jack sitting behind a $50 desk he picked up at a flea market. But at least he still has a desk to sit behind.

Survival under a turnaround may mean stripping your company of every item of unproductive equipment. Nothing should escape your attention. Ask Jack Wyatt about a "bare bones" company. He lost more than his fancy office furniture. New trucks were replaced by older vehicles. Six new cash registers were traded for used models and $5,000 cash, an unused conveyor belt system found a new home with a buyer who forked over $7,000. From ceiling to floor, if it wasn't nailed down, it was a candidate for sale or less expensive replacement. Your assets either have to be working for you as they're supposed to, or you make them work for you as cash in your checking account.

3. Consider the Sale/Leaseback

The sale/leaseback involves selling functional equipment for immediate cash, then leasing the same equipment back over time. It gives your company the cash to fund today's operations. You can pay the lease costs out of future profitability. It's a perfect solution for the firm that needs the equipment to operate.

We have successfully disposed of trucks, computers, office furniture and even cash registers under a sale/leaseback plan. You can even tap real estate.

Here's how it worked for others:

Apex Plumbing Supply, caught in a cash squeeze, sold four trucks to a leasing company and raised $38,000. Monthly lease costs for the same vehicles? $600. But the $38,000 was critical for Apex to survive today. It provided the cash to handle creditor claims under its Chapter 11 and provided additional working capital for inventory.

Taylor Advertising did it with office furniture. We unloaded over $60,000 in furniture to a firm specializing in leasing office furnishings and they rented the same furniture back for $900 a month.

The outright sale wasn't the answer in these cases. These businesses needed the equipment to operate. They also needed cash. The sale/leaseback gave them the best of both worlds.

The sale/leaseback works for firms which own equipment free of mortagages or liens. Call firms that sell that type of equipment. Many of these firms will buy and lease back such equipment.

4. Turn Receivables into Cash

Make this a high priority. Dead or slow-paying receivables can choke you to death.

Develop a "no-nonsense" policy. Overdue accounts should receive a strong and firm follow up. Only an aggressive attitude can turn old receivables into cash. Don't worry about antagonizing a few customers. Lay it on the line. You need cash, and you need it now!

Tie a "carrot" to the stick. Offer a quick payment discount of 10–15 percent. Most customers would rather pay a reduced amount today to avoid the prospects of a lawsuit for the full obligation later.

The troubled firm often has trouble collecting receivables. Customers may even anticipate your demise and switch to another supplier. Why pay you when they can hold onto your money and perhaps settle with your bankruptcy trustee for a fraction on the dollar? Others conclude that holding out will eventually find you so desperate, you'll settle for much less. If your customers know you're operating defensively, they may try to take advantage of you.

You must use extraordinary efforts to collect. An aggressive collection policy worked for Plymouth Photofinishers. To restore the business to liquidity, they needed a $40,000 cash transfusion. Retailers owed the business over $100,000 in receivables and $80,000 in receivables were over 90 days in arrears. We couldn't waste time. Within two days, we put a man on the road to visit the old accounts. It was the old "carrot and stick" routine. "Pay the bill within seven days and deduct 15 percent. Payments not received will be immediately turned over for suit." The $80,000 in deadbeat receivables produced $42,000 within a week. You need a "no-nonsense" policy to survive.

Extend your cash strategy not only to collections but to your credit policy as well. Slow payers should be avoided, because they'll have an adverse impact on cash flow, which may outweigh the profitability of the account. An "all cash" policy may be unrealistic. But you could be equally foolhardy continuing a policy that tolerates slow payments. Strike a balance between cash flow and profitability before extending any credit.

Consumer credit to retail customers is another matter. Switch charge sales to credit card transactions. Few troubled retail businesses maintain a charge policy once cash becomes a problem. "Plastic" is the alternative. As one retailer accurately says, "If customers can't get credit cards, they're not proven credit risks."

Holbrook Books shrewdly cut out its private charge accounts and now accepts only American Express and MasterCard. As Ted Holbrook tells it, "We had $30,000 in receivables on the books. The money was good, but it still tied up $30,000. Once we switched over to credit cards, our liquidity immediately improved. We didn't lose customers, we gained working capital."

5. Borrowing

Conventional borrowing appears low on my list of money-raising opportunities. Small businesses in difficulty have limited ability to get financing. Even when the business has adequate collateral to secure a loan, most bankers will flunk the business as a loan candidate on the basis of an erratic credit history.

If you are willing to pledge personal assets such as a mortgage on your home, bank or SBA loans may be available. I seldom recommend doing so, because a turnaround is speculative at best. Don't risk your personal assets on it.

However, limited amounts of capital *can* be raised through bank financing. You may re-finance vehicles, factor accounts receivable or assign receivables to the bank for a quick cash transfusion.

6. Employee Loans

I learned a lesson from several of the Fortune-500 companies suffering from financial anemia. Employees have a stake in the survival of their employer, so why not ask them to throw a few dollars into the cash pool? That's precisely what Chrysler did.

Intrigued with the idea, I have since tried it out with a few of my clients operating high-payroll, labor-intensive businesses. My proposition: pool 10 percent of gross wages into a 12 percent interest loan to the company. In some cases we approached only the high earners without cutting into the smaller paychecks of the lower paid employees.

It works! Not only does it raise cash, but it quickly separates loyal employees from those about to abandon ship anyway.

Ask John Irwin about it. His employees single-handedly saved his electronics firm. He cut his staff from $200,000 annually to $140,000. The employees fortunate enough to remain on the payroll were "encouraged" to lend 15 percent of wages to the firm. Within a year, John's checking account was $20,000 ahead. It may seem like a drop in the bucket, but as John insists, "When you're bleeding to death, every drop counts."

7. Digging Into Your Own Pockets

Don't! I know it's tempting, but it's the wrong move. Here's why:

It's risky. I have hundreds of clients who decided to throw "good" money after "bad." In 95 percent of these cases, they might as well have tossed the cash down the drain.

Adding capital usually indicates that you haven't developed the "mean" and "lean" attitude. It's easy to add cash from your pocket. It takes imagination and discipline to raise the same cash internally. Adding your own cash today may defer death, but it seldom eliminates the funeral.

There are better alternatives. The business *can* raise cash internally. The business *should* raise the cash from its own hidden resources. If the business can't, then you should re-evaluate either the business itself or your management ability.

Unfortunately, it happens all the time. The business starts its long glide downward, and its owner keeps plugging holes with money. First personal savings go, then the mortgage on the house. Finally the owner cashes in the life insurance policies until there's nothing left to throw into the business. Check writing is easy, problem solving is tough. Don't take the easy way out, because it will prove harder in the long run.

A cash transfusion from your own pockets should be considered only after you have stabilized the business, resolved creditor problems and have the business on a profitable course. Fresh investment capital makes sense only when you're ready for a fresh start.

8. More Cash-Raising Possibilities

Consider imaginative ideas that have worked for others.

Cabot Sales, a financially distressed sundry goods rack jobber, decided to retrench and stop sales to accounts in a neighboring state where delivery costs made them unprofitable. But he didn't abandon the accounts. He "sold" the accounts to another supplier for $80,000 and a percentage of the first year's profits. *Customers have a value.*

Mansfield Health Club advertised a special one-year membership fee of $300 in advance. It was a bargain compared to the $480 standard charge over 12 months. Over 200 members joined, adding $60,000 to the coffers. *Prepaid fees or charges can boost cash flow.*

Beaconway Drug tapped its tobacco supplier for a $15,000 three-year loan. The selling point? Beaconway Drug owed the supplier

$20,000 and offered the supplier a mortgage on the business to secure the entire $35,000. *Suppliers will lend money if you make it attractive.*

Brody Supermarket sub-let space to a branch bank. The annual rent (paid in advance) raised $12,000. Three weeks later, Brody rented the basement area to a small newspaper publisher for $10,000—prepaid! The roof? It wasn't carrying its weight, so a month later a billboard occupied it. Brody had another $6,000. *Imaginative use of space can generate cash.*

Sonar-Alarm Systems of Indiana didn't have much cash, but it did have a patented alarm system. The company's financial plight required fast thinking to raise fast cash. It licensed the alarm to another firm in Arizona for $15,000 and a percentage of sales. The cash kept Sonar-Alarm alive. Encouraged, they tried the plan elsewhere. Today Sonar-Alarm has 16 licensed dealers and plenty of cash. *Exploit the value of proprietary rights.*

Fill Your Empty Shelves

You can't sell from an empty wagon. When sales depend on adequate inventory, you must have that inventory. Empty shelves result in a silent cash register.

The enterprise that has or can raise cash can easily solve the problem through normal buying.

The solution becomes more complicated for the firm with empty shelves that lacks the cash to fill them. That's when the fight for survival becomes interesting.

I recall a saying of one client who nursed his business back to health, "Any idiot with money can buy goods. It takes a genius to do it without cash or credit."

Try this approach! First, determine your inventory requirements. In most of my cases, we design a "model" inventory, then we compare that to existing stock levels. We can quickly determine what the business needs both in merchandise and dollars. Obtaining merchandise is another matter.

Follow these successful strategies:

1. Exhaust Available Credit

You may have more available credit than you think. Most suppliers may insist on C.O.D. payments, but others will open a credit line for you. First, approach prior suppliers you have fully paid. Even recent suppliers whose bills are not yet overdue may be willing to ship additional goods on credit. Review your supplier list. Calculate available credit. Use it to put merchandise on your shelf today.

Protect your suppliers. You don't want to load up with inventory today just so you can eliminate debt tomorrow through a composition agreement or Chapter 11 reorganization. Rather, you want to save your company. Under Chapter 11, creditors would forfeit all or part of their claims. That shouldn't happen to creditors who provide goods for rehabilitating your firm.

The best way to protect suppliers extending rehabilitation credit is to set up a "trust mortgage." Your attorney can handle the paper work, which will grant suppliers who extend new credit a pro-rata interest in a mortgage on your business assets.

Here's how it worked for Plaza Optical, desperately needing $15,000 in additional inventory to survive. Unfortunately, Plaza owed optical supply firms and other creditors over $50,000 already. Three suppliers agreed to ship the $15,000 in merchandise on an extended payment plan, and we set up a trust mortgage to protect the $15,000. Plaza would eventually pay this debt in full, but we could still employ all other remedies to cut the $50,000 prior debt down to $10,000.

If we had simply loaded the shelves with merchandise from whomever we could have conned into giving us some credit and then announced insolvency in an effort to escape all debt, including that created by new shipments, our creditors could have proved we ordered the goods without the intent to pay for them, which could create both civil and criminal problems. It's difficult to prove intent, but every business owner should have strong business ethics. The correct procedure will not only allow you to sleep nights, but it will give you considerably more credibility when negotiating with creditors in the future.

2. Collateralize Your Credit

The trust mortgage works best when dealing with multiple suppliers. However, if one supplier can satisfy your needs, offer that supplier a mortgage on business assets to secure payment on future credit.

Your business may have substantial assets—and equally substantial debt. However, your assets may not be already pledged. A major supplier may decide that a first mortgage on assets will secure him adequately.

It worked for "Big T" Health and Beauty Aids, whose inventory was worth $20,000. To survive, "Big T" needed a $20,000 inventory transfusion. "Big T" owed general creditors over $100,000, but its business assets were unencumbered. A major wholesaler owed $20,000 understandably would not extend more credit, so we offered to give the wholesaler a mortgage on all business assets to secure additional credit of $20,000. Though the original $20,000 debt would remain unsecured and remain on the general creditors' list, the first mortgage would fully protect the wholesaler for the additional $20,000. If the business failed, the wholesaler would enjoy first claim on $40,000 worth of inventory, fixtures, and equipment. If the business survived, not only would he obtain full repayment on the $20,000 in new credit, but he would have a profitable customer. Banks won't lend to the troubled company, but creditors may agree to stock your shelves if you offer proper protection.

3. Collateralize Past Debt for New Credit

"Big T's" wholesaler dropped the ball, because they could have demanded that we secure by mortgage not only the new credit but the existing debt as well.

Collateralizing past debt to win additional credit provides a powerful negotiating point for the business with adequate collateral.

We didn't have to go that far with "Big T." However, Harvey's Superette did. Harvey's needed an additional $25,000 in stock to survive. Its principal wholesaler, owed $16,000, wasn't impressed by our plan to offer a mortgage to secure the additional $25,000 credit line, even though the business contained sufficient collateral. Therefore, we offered the wholesaler a mortgage to cover not only the $25,000 but the old indebtedness of $16,000 as well. We reminded the wholesaler that if he wouldn't agree to it, another supplier would. The original wholesaler would not only continue to risk his $16,000, he'd undoubtedly lose a customer too. A week later, Harvey's shelves bulged with the inventory needed for survival.

4. Offer "Purchase Money Mortgages"

Even the fully mortgaged business can get additional credit with a "purchase money mortgage."

Here's how it works. Normally a supplier will refuse to extend an insolvent business additional credit, because it'll lose its money if the business fails. When the business has existing mortgages, the supplier knows the mortgage holder has first claim on assets.

But the "purchase money mortgage" creates an exception. If a supplier adds new inventory under a mortgage and notifies existing mortgage holders about the situation, that supplier enjoys *first claim to the goods he shipped*. It's technical, and requires your attorney's help, but it can save a business.

It saved Cape Stereo, which owed $30,000 to a bank holding a mortgage. Inventory had fallen to $25,000. To operate the business profitably, the store required an additional $30,000 of equipment. Suppliers wouldn't touch it. If Cape failed, the bank held first claim on all the assets, including new inventory shipments. In a few days, we located a supplier who agreed to ship $30,000 in new inventory, payable when re-sold by Cape. With a "purchase money mortgage," he would have *first* claim on his own goods. What did he have to lose? Today, Cape Stereo grosses over $1,000,000 annually. Without the purchase money mortgage, it would have simply been added to our national bankruptcy statistics.

5. Consignment Goods

This method can help the heavily mortgaged business, providing the supplier the same protection as a purchase money mortgage. If your company fails, the supplier can reclaim his consigned goods. You pay for merchandise as you sell it. This "no-risk" situation can attract a supplier to an insolvent enterprise.

Lancaster Dresses used consignment merchandise to stay alive. Today, it deals only with consigned goods. Lancaster owed its prior owner $50,000 on a mortgage note and owed trade suppliers another $70,000. Because Lancaster had little to sell, sales had dropped from $300,000 to $100,000. Profitability could only reappear if $40–50,000 in new stock rolled in. Existing suppliers? No way. They were scrambling to collect the $70,000 owed them. When we contacted three dress manufacturers in New York City, we asked them to ship their "overstock" on a consignment basis, with Lancaster to provide weekly accounting and payment on all dresses sold. The manufacturers liked the idea. It helped them move excess inventory. As Lancaster sold the dresses, the suppliers got their money. If Lancaster folded, the manufacturers would get their dresses back, because they held title to them until sold, thus protecting them from claims by other creditors. Lancaster discounted the dresses by 20–30 percent and propelled itself to profitable sales of $4,000,000 annually.

This approach works well for the clothing, shoe, furniture, housewares, appliance and stereo industries and can work in any field that's highly competitive at the manufacturer level.

6. Build New Product Lines

Business survival demands adequate inventory to achieve profitable sales. No matter how hard you try, you may fail to gain credit within your existing product lines. However, you may find credit for merchandise you've never handled before. Not only can it give you added inventory, but it may generate sales as well.

Many of my clients survived because they used their imagination in this way.

Westlawn Drug couldn't obtain a dime's worth of credit for its conventional drugstore lines, so it redesigned its layout and devoted 60 percent of its floor space to giftware, plants, artificial flowers, and imported candy, all provided under credit or consignment.

Remember Cape Stereo. It solved part of its problems when it convinced a supplier to ship stereo equipment under a purchase money mortgage. But it didn't stop there. It also brought in a complete line of movies for video-recorders on a percentage-of-profits arrangement. Movie rentals and sales now generate 30 percent of its sales.

Pier 2 Books ran into trouble when its book inventory shrank. Publishers wouldn't ship, and the business couldn't raise the cash to add to the book inventory. Owner Betty N. hit upon an idea. She added a coffee bar featuring imported coffees, sandwiches and tasty croissants. With an $1,800 investment, she doubled sales for her crumbling shop.

Phoenix Furniture is now called the Phoenix Patio Center. Its credit was dead in the furniture industry. But that didn't spell the end for owner Walter S. Walter hooked up with a new patio manufacturer who wanted an outlet in Arizona. The manufacturer shipped its entire line on consignment. It not only saved the business, it gave it a new beginning.

7. Consolidate What You Have

Does your business run two or more locations? Most multiple unit operations have insufficient inventory in each location, but if they consolidate the inventory into fewer locations, the surviving locations can become viable. One healthy store beats two sick stores.

This was the right strategy for "New Dimensions," which owned three greeting card and gift shops with bare shelves. We closed the two smallest stores and moved the inventory to the best location. The surviving store then operated with a healthy $60,000 inventory instead of an anemic $26,000 stock level.

Remember Winslow Foods? It failed because its owner didn't know how to fill the shelves. When the store was auctioned, two young chaps took over the lease, even though they didn't have the money or credit to stock the store either. They didn't want to. They leased the departments to others who could. A butcher set up a "meat boutique." A produce man ran his own vegetable stall, and a local baker established an outlet for day old items. A food wholesaler leased the grocery department. In two months the store was flying high. The imaginative owners coordinated the advertising and operated the cash registers, collecting $80,000 in rents and 1 percent of sales. As they figure it, "We'll earn about $70,000 net annual profit from the business, and not invest a nickel in inventory." Imagination can be as valuable as cash or credit.

The Care and Feeding of Creditors

Cash, credit and inventory can pump in business-saving plasma, but while you undergo your transfusion, tie the tourniquet tight. You can't afford to allow money needed to sustain and rebuild the business to bleed away.

Creditors head my list of culprits who can drain cash more quickly than you can take it in. It's an interesting paradox. When creditors know you're in trouble, they push as hard as possible for as much as possible before your business collapses. Pay them what they demand and you won't have to wait long to collapse.

Many businesses *do* fail because they allow themselves to be "bled" to death by creditors. Creditor A, who is owed $4,000, agrees to accept $200 per week. Creditor B, owed $700, gets $350 per month. Creditor C, not to be outdone by the others, squeezes $500 per month payments on his $12,000 bill. Creditor D decides to recoup his $6,000 debt by withholding trade discounts on future orders. Before you know it, you're paying out a dollar-fifty for every dollar coming in. In the meantime, you have to replenish inventory C.O.D. and stay on top of your operating expenses. The result? A hemorrhage and sure death.

To compound the problem, the business will pay out $20–30,000 over a several month period before it fully realizes its debts are excessive and need restructuring. Intead of cutting the original $150,000 owed, it ends up performing surgery on $120,000. What did the $30,000 payments accomplish? As one veteran will tell you, "They still call you an S.O.B., they still won't extend credit. Whatever roadblocks they could throw in your way over $150,000, they can and will use at over $120,000. Whatever you pay creditors before you restructure your debt doesn't help a bit. It's money down the drain." Every dollar you pay prior to your compromise or reorganization plan represents a dollar that could have strengthened your business. Remember the drop in the bucket?

Survival means saying "no" to creditors pushing for payment on past debts. Saying "no" can save you thousands of dollars during the time you're slowly realizing you're in trouble and creditors are beginning to fear they'll end up with only a fraction on the dollar.

A "no-nonsense" policy can keep money in your till.

1. Make absolutely *no* payment on past bills owed trade creditors.
2. If a supplier refuses to ship C.O.D. without payment on a prior debt, switch suppliers. Few suppliers enjoy a monopoly. Payments on past bills may equal or even exceed your profits on the new shipment. Once you call their bluff, most suppliers will agree to ship C.O.D. without payment on a past debt.

Attacking Problems One by One 101

3. Don't allow creditors to recoup payment by withholding trade or volume discounts, promotional allowances or other purchasing incentives. You want the same price and allowances as any other cash customer.

4. If you return goods for credit, insist on a credit against *future* purchases. Don't let anyone apply the credit to the prior balance.

5. Refuse to provide collateral, a mortgage on business assets, or a personal guarantee, unless you are receiving a big benefit, such as additional credit, in return.

6. Forget excuses. Your check is *not* in the mail. Your accountant does *not* have your checkbook. Your check writing hand is *not* in a cast. You aren't paying because you're trying to rehabilitate the company. Be honest. Say you need time to decide what to do with your creditors' old bills. You know it, and your creditors know it, so why not be honest and just say it? Creditors will respect you and won't badger you for payment every day until you run out of excuses.

7. Never acknowledge your debt or the fact you're in trouble in writing. Do it verbally but avoid specifics. A written admission of insolvency can give your creditors ammunition to throw you into bankruptcy.

8. Don't be intimidated. That's the key to success. Creditors can be intimidating. They'll threaten bankruptcy (less than 1 percent follow through), they'll threaten lawsuits (your attorney can tie them up in court for months) and they'll threaten to report you to the credit association (by now you probably have no credit anyway). In reality, general creditors can do very little harm. They're toothless dogs who love to bark.

9. Refer all legal correspondence to your attorney. He'll know the best way to handle your creditors' counsel. Also, refer to him any unusual collection practices or harassment. Federal and state laws prohibit certain collection practices. Your attorney can stop that.

10. Post these rules by your telephone. That's what my clients do. On a weekly basis I'll review their checkbook to make certain they're living by the rules, for I know that every check issued to reduce a prior debt is a meaningless drain on cash flow. I admit that you're the one on the firing line. You face hostile creditors every day and it can be tempting to write them a check to get them off your back. Yet survivors know how to say "no."

A final suggestion: If you have trouble turning a deaf ear to creditors, delegate this task to a thick-skinned employee who doesn't have his life savings and heart's blood wrapped up in the business. Appoint a "Vice-President, Accounts Payable."

Getting 120 Percent Out of 100 Percent of Your Employees

Expenses, of course, are another cash drain. Operational stability requires slashing expenses to the bone. Payroll expenses head the list. You must pay less and get more.

Employees represent not only a considerable expense to the troubled firm but a major asset as well. To increase productivity and morale with the staff, it is usually better to trim personnel rather than ask for salary concessions.

Jim Rice, a Boston-based turnaround expert, specializes in personnel management for the troubled small firm. He offers this advice:

1. Be candid with your employees about the financial problems of the firm, what you plan to do, and how you plan to do it. Valued employees leave because they fear the future of the company. They develop insecurities when they don't know where the business stands.

2. Estimate your personnel needs based on a "hard nosed" staffing policy. Then reduce that number by 20 percent. Most owners over-estimate their personnel needs. After you make cuts, you can always re-hire. Many employees can wear more than one hat.

3. Discharge excess employees all at once. Gradual discharges increase insecurity and anxiety. Define who is staying and who

is going, then get it over with. The survivors can then get on with their work without worrying about a next week's "pink slip."
4. Select personnel on the basis of need. Seniority, affirmative action and discrimination problems are never as important as putting together the staff who can help a business survive.
5. Measure productivity. Whenever possible, formulate wage policy tied to measurable productivity: commissions on sales, quotas on production, incentives for collected receivables, and expected output of billable hours.
6. Build a "bandwagon" effect. Your employees must realize that survival for the firm depends on *their* efforts. Make them feel important. If employees fail to expend the needed effort, let them go. Remaining employees will respect you and work even harder to save their jobs.
7. Consider "non-compete" agreements with key personnel. Managerial level or sales employees may stay on with the thought that they'll pick up your business if it fails. Have them sign a "noncompete" agreement, promising not to solicit your customers on behalf of any future employer.
8. Reduce expense accounts and fringe benefits first. Pension plans mean less than "take-home" pay. Cut back the least visible compensation areas.
9. Establish rewards and incentives. If you're asking employees to work harder, perhaps for less pay, you should make sure they'll benefit from the future success of the company. Let them know what they can expect and when. It's best if the rewards reflect the company's return to measurable levels of solvency as profitability.
10. Handling employees properly can be a major hurdle for the troubled firm. Many owners cite it as their number one operational problem.

It was for Williams Tobacco, a mid-sized tobacco and candy wholesaler which was striving for new life under a Chapter 11 reorganization. Its staff of 45 employees was falling apart. Two of its top salesmen left to join a competing wholesale firm. The rest of the staff were out looking for new jobs or taking advantage by not producing. Morale was at an all-time low and so was productivity.

Williams Tobacco took charge and followed the right approach:

a) It reduced its staff from 45 non-producers to a hard core skeleton crew of 28. Weekly payroll costs were slashed by $5,700. The staff reduction was coupled with additional work assignments and dropping unprofitable accounts that needlessly consumed manpower. Mel Williams didn't play games. He evaluated each of his employees to decide who should stay and who should go. He sums it up, "You need a cohesive staff of producers. When you demand 120 percent from your employees, you need the workers who can give you that 120 percent."

b) Communication helped restore confidence. The attorney and accountant for the firm joined in the first meeting. Rumors came to an end as the employees were given the facts. Thereafter, Mel Williams met every week with the employees and gave them an update. The employees knew what was happening to the company and the role they were expected to play in its survival.

c) Standards for performance were imposed. Salesmen had sales quotas. The credit department had its collection objectives. Everyone knew what he had to do.

d) Cutting fringe benefits and expenses came next. Health insurance was dropped and the pension plan discontinued. Employees went along with it, knowing it was a temporary measure.

e) Incentives? Motivation is the key. Williams promised its employees a bonus of one month's pay when the company came out of Chapter 11. Additional bonuses tied to profits were on the horizon for future years.

One reason why Williams survived was because it knew how to squeeze 120 percent out of 100 percent of its employees.

Many businesses fail to survive because they don't intelligently restructure their payroll to fit their new needs. The best employees leave, and the least productive remain. Payroll costs remain excessive and the company receives less, not more from each payroll dollar.

I have seen companies reduce payroll by 45–50 percent and *increase* productivity. You *can* get more with less! Bear that in mind when you write next week's payroll checks. Should you turn your tourniquet another notch tighter?

Keep Your Customers Smiling

It's always hard to keep customers happy while you re-build the firm.

Customers will leave you in droves once they experience drops in inventory or service. And they'll have plenty of encouragement. Your competitors will offer predictions of your immediate demise and encourage your customers to turn to them before that happens.

As I write this book, a large wholesale drug firm sits in Chapter 11 reorganization. Boston has no shortage of drug wholesalers. Offering strong incentives, five competitors have hit the road to convince retail drug accounts to switch. Attractive credit, extra discounts, better service, a complete line of goods, even a paid vacation to Acapulco to those who shift allegiance.

Follow these effective tactics to keep your customers happy:

1. Give top priority to maintaining adequate inventory. There's no substitute for it. Customers may give you a second chance to deliver, but rarely a third.
2. If you can't adequately supply or service all your accounts, pull back and preserve the inventory and service needed to retain your most profitable accounts. Let the marginal or unprofitable accounts go. Don't spread yourself too thin.

    Megansett Poultry lived a day-to-day cash flow existence. It provided poultry products to 300 retail accounts. But with tight cash, it had difficulty handling all its accounts. It took the wise approach by concentrating on the chain accounts representing 80 percent of its volume.
3. Don't play games with prices. Some desperate businesses try to raise prices to bolster cash flow. The few extra cents won't mean

much but this can antagonize customers. Instead, announce incentive discounts for cash or quick payments. Cash flow counts. Increased profits can come later.

4. Look like a survivor. Make your customers believe you're playing for keeps. Like employees, accounts jump ship out of insecurity. Years ago, we had a client whose printing firm was sliding downhill fast. It had about six months to live. Competitors were moving in for the kill: "XYZ Printers won't be around long, so send us your printing!" To counter, we spent $600 on a billboard beside XYZ's plant: "Under Construction—New Facilities for XYZ Printing." Of course it wasn't true, because XYZ had to scrounge up the $600 for the sign. But it worked. We sent pictures of the "construction site" to all XYZ customers. The competitors didn't know how to react. Customers believed the sign. You have to look successful to stay successful, even if you're broke.

To Sum Up

The following pages contain an outline of the most important operational problems with suggestions for analysis and planning. Use it as your checklist.

Problem Solving Planning Guide

Problem	Analysis/Planning Tips
Cash:	
1. Define Capital Needs:	• Working capital should be equal to at least one week's sales for retail businesses and 2–4 weeks' sales for wholesalers and manufacturers.
2. Obtaining Cash:	• Sell excess inventory • Sell excess equipment • Collect overdue receivables • Factor accounts receivable

	• Vehicle financing
	• Employee loans
	• Sale of customer lists
	• Prepaid charges or fees
	• Supplier loans
	• Rents for space
	• Sale/license of proprietary rights
3. Cash Control:	• Restrict credit
	• Control purchasing
	• Reduce operating expenses
	• Stop creditor payments
	• Extend loan payments

Inventory:

1. Define Needed Inventory Level:	• Calculate effective inventory level using an inventory turnover formula
2. Obtaining Inventory:	• Exhaust existing credit lines
	• Collateralize new credit
	• Grant purchase money mortgages
	• Acquire by consignment
	• Expand into new lines
	• Consolidate inventory
	• Exchange slow inventory for fast movers

Personnel:

1. Define Personnel Needs:	• Reduce staff to budgetary and minimum operational needs
	• Evaluate each employee for operational benefits

2. Motivation:
- Conduct initial meeting
- Plan weekly meetings
- Solicit employee ideas
- Implement incentives

3. Increasing Productivity:
- Assign expanded duties
- Define productivity goals
- Measure performance
- Delegate and supervise

Customers:

1. Define Customer Base:
- Analyze each account for profitability
- Determine key accounts

2. Assess Service Needs:
- Analyze your ability to provide goods/services to customer base
- Maintain "in-stock" situation
- Offer incentives to maintain accounts
- Review and resolve customer grievances

Cut Your Debts Down to Size

6

Remember the old saw, "If you can, do; if you can't, teach"? My old friend and client, George P., suggests we change it to: "If you can, pay; if you can't, write a letter." Here's one George recently received:

Dear Creditor:

We owe you $96,000. However, our business is failing. The only way I can save it is to pay you $8,000 as full settlement. That's more than you will get if I go bankrupt.

Please advise.

Sincerely,
XYZ Company

After spending several minutes clutching his heart, George rushed to my office. "Read this damn letter. If that deadbeat at XYZ thinks I'm going to walk away from $88,000 he's crazy. I want my $96,000 and I want it *now*! Go after him."

After reading the letter several times, I had to applaud its author's logic. XYZ had put old George in a "no win" situation, but George, of course, didn't share my appreciation. He just sat there popping nitroglycerin pills and muttering, "That S.O.B. not only has the audacity to offer me 8 cents on the dollar, I had to pay 12 cents postage due on the letter!"

I sent George home and got to work ascertaining our position *vis a vis* XYZ. A few hours later, I confirmed that XYZ was totally mortgaged to the bank, and if the business collapsed, George and other general creditors wouldn't see a dime. XYZ held a strong bargaining position.

I gave George two days to recuperate and then gave him the sorrowful news. After the usual breast-beating and hair-pulling, George agreed to send XYZ a letter accepting the $8,000 offer, thus kissing $88,000 goodbye. The other creditors followed and within a few days, XYZ had reduced over $250,000 in debts to about $17,500.

Can they get away with that? You bet. Every year creditors with billions of dollars of receivables on their books agree to accept pennies on the dollar, knowing that pennies are better than thin air. As one credit manager aptly says, "What they owe is a statistic. What they can afford to pay or what you can actually squeeze out of them is reality. So we settle, not on the basis of 'what ought to be'—but 'what is.'"

Shrewd debtors know this and use it everyday to eliminate burdensome debts that stand between them and a fresh start.

A quick glance at some of my own files will prove just how little creditors will accept.

Creditors of a hardware store agreed to take 12 cents on the dollar—reducing $200,000 in liabilities down to a more manageable $24,000.

A nursing home settled with its creditors for 20 percent, payable over two years. Over $500,000 in claims shrivelled to $100,000.

A pet shop relieved itself of $80,000 in liabilities when creditors, unwilling to take a chance on the auction value of Cocker Spaniels and Guppies, agreed to accept $10,000 instead of the $90,000 owed.

These same debt-reducing techniques can work for your business. In this chapter, I'll show you how to achieve quick out-of-court settlements that can dramatically shrink your debts.

How to Turn Poverty Into Power

Even if you have no money, you still have strength, strength which comes from the very fact that you don't have money. This paradox makes a lot of sense when you consider that your business' poverty provides your creditors with only two options: a) accept whatever you offer them, or b) throw you into bankruptcy and get even less. Isn't that precisely the message XYZ sent George?

Poverty creates for creditors the old "damned if they do, damned if they don't" situation.

The job is to orchestrate your poverty-power to your advantage. Here's how:

1. Calculate your settlement offer.
2. Sell it as if your life depends on it!

The Fool-Proof Formula That Tells You What to Offer

In the next few pages, we'll deal with the hard economic reality of your business. You'll learn how to extract a settlement figure from a jumble of numbers.

Your first step is to figure out just what your creditors can expect if your business goes under the hammer.

Step 1. Call in an expert appraiser or a well-recognized auctioneer to evaluate your tangible assets and give you a written opinion as to what he would expect them to yield at auction. Your attorney can probably estimate with fair accuracy what your accounts receivable would generate in cash. Now you know how much money will be available for creditors if you fail.

Step 2. Calculate the amount that would go to priority creditors. The following stand at the head of the line:

- Auction fees and costs of liquidation
- Debts owed secured creditors (creditors holding a mortgage on business assets)
- Taxes due any taxing authority

Step 3. Subtract the priority claims (Step 2) from the total asset proceeds (Step 1). This shows what general creditors can hope to get as full settlement should you go under.

All you need to do to persuade unsecured creditors to accept your offer is to make that offer slightly larger than the base minimum.

Joe A. used this formula to design a settlement offer his creditors quickly grabbed. As the owner of a small supermarket, Joe had a marginal operation; but it would see him through until he retired. Joe decided it was time to stop "skating on thin ice" and rescue the business from the brink of insolvency. A quick glance at Joe's balance sheet showed a mortgage on the business of $40,000 and unpaid withholding taxes of $15,000. He owed his unsecured creditors $100,000. How much would they settle for? In a bankruptcy proceeding, there would be only $2,500 to carve up. Here's how it looked in crystal clear black and white:

Table I Appraised Liquidation Value at Auction

Assets	Cost Value	Auction Value
Inventory	$100,000	$40,000
Fixtures and Equipment	50,000	25,000
Total Auction Value		$65,000

Table II Payment of Auction Proceeds

Auction Proceeds: $65,000

Priority Payments:

Auction Costs	$ 6,500	
Auction Ads	1,000	
Secured Debt	40,000	
Taxes	15,000	

Total Priority Claim $62,500

Net for General Creditors $2,500

Joe had the ammunition he needed to structure a settlement. Any offer over 2.5 cents on the dollar would clearly benefit the creditors.

No one could argue with our numbers. A respected auctioneer had estimated the liquidation value of the assets, and the priority claims were firmly established by a certified statement from an accountant.

Joe offered 8 cents on the dollar, and the unsecured creditors jumped for it!

Negotiate Your Best Deal

Numbers can be convincing, but creditors bring more to the bargaining table than a calculator. They show up with anger, suspicion, irrationality, doubt, desire for vengeance, and the full array of human emotions. To succeed, you must defuse irrational thoughts with your rational numbers. In other words, never overlook the human side of the settlement equation.

Though you can illustrate the bleak alternatives for the creditors should they not accept your proposal, the reverse is also true. What happens to you if the creditors decide that the satisfaction of throwing you into bankruptcy more than makes up for the few cents they might lose? While you're telling your creditors to accept 4 or 5 cents on the dollar rather than 1 or 2 cents, they'll remind you that unless you cough up 50–60 cents on the dollar, you may end up without a business.

If a compromise can't be struck, the creditors have something to lose, but so do you. As with most negotiations, your success depends on your bluffing ability.

Joe played poker skillfully. Armed with the fact that 5 cents is more than 2 cents, he walked into a meeting with his major creditors. After the usual preliminaries, Joe threw his proposal on the table. "Boys," he said, "if you settle for 5 cents on the dollar, I can have your check next week."

Figuring he'd pay a lot more to save his business, the creditors began to test Joe. They put out their feelers to find out just how badly Joe wanted to keep his business alive so they would know just how far they could push him.

I'll never forget Cecil, the credit manager of the baking firm whom

Joe owed $28,000. Cecil was a master negotiator. After patiently hearing Joe out, Cecil turned to the debtor and spoke in a soft tone, "Joe, you don't want to lose your market. We'll *never* accept 5 percent. Perhaps we'd let you stay in business if you paid us 10 percent now and another 10 percent a year for the next 9 years. At the end of 10 years, we would be fully paid, and you'd still be in operation."

There it was. A creditor staring at 2 percent if he didn't strike a compromise, cajoling Joe to pay 100 percent for the privilege of keeping his company.

But Joe examined his cards thoughtfully. He put down his cigar, extracted a prescription vial from his vest pocket and popped a few saccharin tablets which the creditors assumed were life-sustaining heart medication. Slowly Joe drawled, "The truth is I would rather quit the game and retire to Florida. I'm not getting any younger. With a bad heart and all... The only reason I'm here is out of respect for you boys. I'd hate to see you get screwed if I walked away from my business."

How convincing! Joe pulled a master bluff by forcing his creditors to think about their self-interest.

Two hours later, Joe had his deal: 8 cents on the dollar. Riding down in the elevator, I asked Joe what he really would have paid to keep the store. "Probably 50–60 percent. But they didn't have to know that."

If Joe's story doesn't convince you, Tom's might. His fabric chain owed general creditors a whopping $300,000. In this case, I represented a creditor, a supplier owed $25,000. Ten of the major creditors arrived at my office to negotiate a settlement with Tom, who walked in with his pert wife. Tom sketched a heart-wrenching tale of woe and offered the creditors a deal that would give them 15 percent immediately and 10 percent for each of the next 2 years, for a total of 35 percent.

With a few key questions, I got the information to fill in the blanks of my formula, and I calculated that, considering the excessive bank mortgage, we would receive nothing if the business failed.

So why did Tom start out with a generous 35 percent offer? A little more probing, and I soon had the answer. Tom desperately wanted to stay in business, but he had made a fatal mistake by showing that burning desire. He kept repeating that he would do anything to keep the business going. His wife started to cry whenever a creditor brought up the possibility of locking the doors.

Tom was ultimately willing to deal on our terms. When it was all over, Tom agreed to 25 percent down, financed through a second mortgage on his home, and 15 percent for each of the next 5 years.

Tom benefited by spreading out his debt. But he ended up paying 100 percent.

If I were Tom, I would have thrown the keys on the table and said, "Gentlemen, it's yours. I have a great new job lined up in California. But, since I'm an honest, hard-working guy, I'll listen to any proposal you care to make."

The supplier I represented had been willing to settle for 10 percent as full settlement, so Tom might have countered with 5 percent. A few ill-advised words from Tom, and a few tears from his wife cost Tom $285,000.

Taking the Motion Out of Emotion

Remember my client George, who is still clutching his heart over his lost $88,000? He's always been a victim of his emotions. I've always believed that people like George might do better and live longer if they stuck to soap operas and stayed out of business.

If you're a debtor facing twenty creditors, you have to deal with twenty different people, each with his or her own unique set of emotions. You must be able to detect what each is really thinking and be prepared to deal on a one-by-one basis.

Let's consider the cast of characters you're most likely to find sitting around the creditor's table.

Over on the right-hand side of the table sits The Cynic. He thinks you're a crook who pillaged, plundered and raped the business to bring it to its knees. Many creditors will think the worst of you until you prove differently.

Honesty is the only tactic that will convince The Cynic you really are just a genuine good guy who fell on rough times. Tell him how the business got into trouble. Point out the problems that created the losses, skyrocketing interest rates or product development over-runs. One sure way to silence The Cynic's snarl is to invite the creditors to select their own accountant to go over your books so they can see your honesty for themselves. It's amazing how seldom creditors will follow through on such an offer, but if you resist, they'll go to any length to find what you're hiding. I had a client, a professional engineer who operated a product design firm, attend a creditors' meeting and throw his own payroll check stubs on the table. In the past year, he'd taken only $8,700 out of the business. The creditors were instantly sympathetic.

Next to The Cynic sits The Moralist. His attitude is common. You owe him $1,000; he wants $1,000. Anything less is immoral, unconscionable, and un-American. He listens only to "what ought to be," never "what is." All you can do with this character is slowly present the facts of life in his own language. After all, you're moral, too; but you at least know you can't get blood out of a stone. Often, The Moralist will go along with the other creditors because he's one of your smaller creditors. For him this may be a new experience.

Sitting over there at the end of the table is The Avenger, who doesn't give a damn about the $50,000 you owe him. He can live with that loss, but he wants vengeance for the $500 in bad checks you gave him and is angry over the $2,000 order he shipped before you confessed your "insolvency" to him.

Find out what The Avenger's so mad about and offer to make good on bad checks or pay 100 percent for recent shipments. Never let nickels thwart big dollars.

Next to The Avenger squirms the credit manager who has been chasing you for $12,000 for the last six months. He's not thinking about you but himself. How does he explain a $10–11,000 loss to his boss? Sometimes a reminder of all the dollars you have paid his firm over the years and all the future dollars you'll pay if you remain afloat will help him save face.

Is there a lawyer in the crowd? You've heard of ambulance-chasers. Well, there are also bankruptcy-chasers with their own self-serving thoughts. Such a character may actually relish a nice bankruptcy case because he may end up a trustee, thus getting a far bigger fee than he could ever get from the pittance you're offering his client.

Don't lock horns with The Bankruptcy-Chaser, just leave him to your own lawyer to neutralize.

Finally, there's Charlie, that dear cantankerous old soul, who loves playing The Spoiler. Pay him or he closes you down, a hobby he professes to enjoy. Some creditors enjoy playing tough guy. There's only one solution when you come up against Charlie. Look him in the eye and stand your ground. Remind him you don't really care, but you hope he won't do anything rash that will hurt his colleagues. Then let the other creditors work on him. Peer pressure usually softens him up.

These are but a few of the characters you'll meet. Your ultimate success depends on your ability to identify and sell them individually.

Remember the famous line of Don Corleone in *The Godfather*— "Never get angry. Never make a threat. Reason with people."

Sell Future Dollars

Years ago, I discovered a magic ointment to salve the wounds you are inflicting on your creditors.

The story involved Nathan T., a "street-smart" operator of a large seafood restaurant that leaned on the edge of an ocean of debt, $200,000 in liabilities that the business could never repay. But the restaurant was finally enjoying excellent patronage and was worth saving, if only Nathan could whittle the $200,000 down to $50,000.

I spent several hours on the formula and figured that the creditors might come out with $20,000 under a bankruptcy, so I advised Nathan to start at that figure and, if necessary, let the creditors negotiate him up to $50,000. However, Nathan didn't much need my formula or its numbers, because he knew how to handle people.

The creditors' meeting was held in a drafty, austere law office in downtown Boston with parchment prints of old whaling ships on the wall. Fifteen angry creditors sat fuming for old deadbeat Nathan to show up.

After he arrived ten minutes late, Nathan remained calm as the creditors fired their threats, innuendos and insults around the room. After each salvo he would just sit back and hang his head like a scolded puppy who'd had an accident on the new oriental carpet.

When the creditors finally ran out of steam, Nathan slowly stood up and said, "I've listened to you for the last hour. Now please hear *me* out."

Turning first to Sam, his meat supplier whom he owed $25,000, he began, "Sam, how much business have you done with me since I started the restaurant?" Sam had no ready answer, but Nathan did. "$1,600,000 over the past 12 years," snapped Nathan. "So you want to argue with me now about a lousy $25,000? If I stay in business—you know it's finally booming—how much will I buy from you in the next 10 years?" Again Sam shrugged. "I estimate $2,000,000 before I retire. Before we're through doing business with each other, you will have seen $3,500,000 of my hard-earned money. I wish I had your $25,000, Sam, but I don't. Why can't we simply call it a small discount on past purchases or a sales expense on my next $2,000,000?"

Now Sam played the dejected puppy. Nathan had painted the big picture, showing Sam to be an ungrateful tightwad. One look at his face and you knew Sam would not only tear up the $25,000 obligation, but apologize in the process.

Next Nathan stared at Harry, the recalcitrant produce supplier who 20 minutes earlier had screamed for $40,000. The curtain rose on Act Two. "Yes, Harry, I owe you $40,000, but over the past 8 years I've shelled out $957,000 to you. In the next 10 years I'll fork over another $1,300,000. $2,300,000! Not bad Harry. The $40,000 represents less than 1½ percent of the business we'll do together. Since when is 1½ percent a big discount?"

By this point the other creditors wriggled in their chairs, but that only spurred Nathan on. Around the table he went, confidently spouting the numbers. When all was said and done, $200,000 amounted to a tiny fraction of the business the creditors had enjoyed and would enjoy if Nathan's restaurant continued operating. Maybe Nathan wasn't such a bad guy after all, but whether he was good or bad didn't really matter. The creditors decided to go along with Nathan to insure future sales and profits. No one wanted to lose such a money-making account.

Finally, the largest creditor blurted, "Okay, Nathan, old buddy, what do you propose as an equitable compromise?"

Nathan appeared to mull over the question. "I don't want to insult you by offering you a few measly bucks to share. If you'll send me a cancelled invoice out of my long standing friendship, I'll charter us a cruise to Bermuda. That will properly launch the next ten years of prosperity." After a quick toast to Nathan, the meeting was adjourned and $200,000 in pressing, long overdue bills disappeared like smoke.

Leaving the meeting, Nathan lamented, "That damned cruise will cost me $8–10,000, but under the circumstances, I can handle it." You could hear him chuckle all the way to the bank. I never did send Nathan a bill, because I was afraid he'd send *me* a bill for the lesson he'd taught me.

It can work for you. Add up your past business with creditors, then project even larger figures for the future. Many creditors will quickly come to the conclusion that keeping your business alive may mean even more to them than it does to you.

The Enemy Within

Lurking in your mind is your most dangerous enemy—your conscience. As you read this book, is your conscience yelling, "Hold on, something's wrong. Goldstein's telling me that I should do everything possible (albeit legal) to deprive my creditors of payment in full. That's not right!"

Remember The Moralist who's so wrapped up in "What ought to be," he never sees "What is"? When your conscience starts to scream, listen to your survival instinct. Every penny you hand your creditors is one less penny you can use to turn your business around and continue pouring dollars not only into your pocket but the pockets of your creditors as well.

I'm not trying to referee a possible conflict between your morality and your instinct to survive. Only you can do that. However, 80–90 percent of my clients eventually feel sorrier for themselves than their creditors because they, not their creditors, are fighting for their lives. Every feather they let the creditors pluck from the chicken simply means a balder chicken.

Madeline offers a good example. She went into the record shop business undercapitalized and inexperienced. Within two years, her business was woefully insolvent with $100,000 in bills. Still, Madeline was making a small profit of $5,000 a year.

It didn't take long to figure out that liquidation would bring her creditors about 8 cents on the dollar, so I suggested we offer them 10–15 percent with the hope we would end up with 20 percent.

Madeline wouldn't hear of it. She emphatically said she wanted to keep her business going and pay all creditors in full, no matter how many years it took. I reminded her that if we gave the creditors all of her $5,000 annual profit, it would take 20 years to pay them off. She got mad at me. "The creditors trusted me when they extended the credit, and I *never* default on a debt!" With that, she slammed out of my office. As you might expect, the creditors happily accepted Madeline's 20 year payout proposal.

Five years elapsed before I next heard from Madeline. She came into my office a changed woman. "I'm working my ass off, taking home a pauper's salary so I can pay off my creditors, but they won't give me a dime of credit. They treat me like a leper. Frankly, it's not worth it. Can you go to the creditors and settle for the minimum? If they're going to treat me like this, I'm stupid for putting their interests ahead of my own."

Wouldn't it be wonderful if every business could pay all its bills and give its owners a fat profit? But as Madeline found out, that doesn't always happen. Any business has limited financial capabilities and cannot always satisfy everybody's demands or objectives. Who comes first? That's for you to decide.

Effective Ways to Get Their Signature

Getting creditors to accept a fraction on the dollar requires shrewd tactical planning. First, you have a decision to make. Should you try to compromise the debt with all your creditors or perhaps only the few largest? Scan your list of creditors. If 80 percent of your debt is represented by 6 large ones and the remaining 20 percent is scattered among 30–40 others, focus only on the 6 who really count.

Some business people ignore creditors owed less than $200, because they're not worth the time and effort. A small creditor owed $75 may sabotage your overall proposal since it all means so little to him.

Lawyers call settling with the largest creditors a "composition agreement," whether it's immediate payment of a fraction on the dollar, full payoff over a prolonged time period, or a combination of the two. Using the formula and your negotiating skill should dictate your proposal.

The first key to a composition agreement is equality, whereby every creditor receives the same percentage on the dollar.

The second key is for you to get 80–90 percent of all creditors to accept your proposal.

Those are the legal keys, but strategy will govern how you communicate and sell your composition agreement. And the first step in any strategy is communication. Many lawyers make the mistake of drafting a letter explaining the problems and the proposal, attaching an assent form for the creditor to sign and return. This package goes to all creditors, while the beleaguered business person anxiously sits back and waits for signed assent forms to arrive in the mail.

Unfortunately, the debtor too often finds more rejections or lawsuits in his mailbox than assent forms. Why? Bad communication, bad salesmanship.

Turn your major creditors into the sales force you need to put your proposal over:

1. First, meet with two or three of your largest creditors, selling them individually. If you win converts, they can serve as the "nucleus" of support to convince a larger group of creditors.
2. Next, convene a meeting of your largest creditors, including your 2–3 supporters. Strong allies in the crowd can inject the right positive tone into the meeting and keep negotiations going your way.
3. Once the majority of your largest creditors supports you, request they form a committee and accurately report to all other creditors that your proposal is fair and reasonable and in everyone's best interest.

Don't forget to put yourself in the shoes of your smaller creditors, who know nothing about you except for the fact you owe them a little money.

If your creditors receive a letter from a creditors' committee, confirming the miserable facts and proudly announcing the best possible dividend, who can refuse? Instant credibility and a flurry of acceptances!

Five Ways to Handle Even the Toughest Creditor

Nevertheless, it's never completely smooth sailing. If you need 90 percent of the creditors to accept, but you get only 65 percent, it's time to hit the road and do some hard selling to bring the "hold-outs" into line:

1. Meet with the "hold-outs" individually. Find out specifically why each one's turning you down so you can counter with logic. Letters from you or your creditors' committee may not convince someone, but an "eyeball to eyeball" meeting may.

2. Persevere. It takes time for many creditors to cool down from the maddening thought they're about to lose money. Time can be a great healer, eventually turning blind fury into the clear thinking you need to win votes.

3. Don't let a middle management executive or credit manager block your road. Remember, they work within a bureaucracy and have someone else to answer to. That someone may be just the one to whom your ideas make sense.

4. Employ peer pressure. Use one or two of your influential and friendly creditors to intervene. I find this the most successful method of all. One case I recall involved a tobacco jobber whose largest creditor was owed over $400,000. No matter what we tried, we couldn't convince him to accept a 50 percent settlement over three years. After two months of striking out, we asked two other creditors to try their hand at it. They succeeded. It turned out the creditor thought my client had diverted some of his

merchandise to a friend's basement, which was untrue. Though the creditor would never tell us about it, he confessed his fears to his peers, who laughed him out of his misconception.
5. **Send in your lawyer.** Lawyers have their own brotherly language. If you can't succeed with the creditor, perhaps your attorney will have better luck with your creditor's attorney.

Thorough calculations and skillful negotiating can get your creditors voting to give you a fresh start with a healthy balance sheet.

Remember Nathan? He summed it up even better. "When everyone's in the same sinking boat, the solution is a meeting of the minds, not the banging of heads."

Winning Over That One Important Creditor

Perhaps your debt isn't scattered amongst many suppliers. You may be in a business that deals with one major supplier representing one overwhelming debt, while all your other bills are nothing more than a smattering of nickels and dimes. If that's you, then you have a different strategy to follow.

Give it some thought. How would you get that all-important creditor to wipe out 70–80 or 90 percent of what's rightfully due him?

For starters, you can use the formula to prove how little he will get with your failure. Coupled with that can be all those creditor-convincing negotiating strategies that you've learned in this chapter.

However, when your target is only one creditor, you can use even more imaginative solutions than when dealing with an entire pack. You are no longer bound by a deal that requires constraints of "equality." You can design a settlement that puts you ahead in your "one-on-one" contest.

Holly S. was one of the more imaginative entrepreneurs I've seen in action. Ten years ago, she started an interesting business that turns colorful fabrics into decorative wall coverings. Over the years, she expanded her initial downtown store into two additional high-powered locations in local malls. But expansion took its toll. So did the high interest rates on her bank expansion loan and spotty sales due to dwindling consumer spending.

The business still showed a profit, so it was worth saving. Covering expenses wasn't a problem and Holly was confident she could pay for new merchandise as it arrived. Her one obstacle to survival was a whopping $115,000 owed to a Norwegian fabric firm that served as her principal supplier.

Holly was smart enough to know that since she needed this supplier's business, she had to compromise and yet not alienate.

Holly's formula showed a probable 20 cents on the dollar payment to the supplier if the business collapsed. Moreover, using what Nathan taught me about selling those future dollars, we could play up the $250,000 annual purchases. But unlike Nathan's creditors, the Norwegian supplier drove a hard bargain. His potpourri of money-extracting measures included his cancelling $70,000 of the $115,000 debt, conditional upon Holly:

1. Paying $10,000 of the $35,000 balance immediately, with the balance payable over two years with 22 percent interest.
2. A mortgage on the business assets to secure the $25,000, two-year note.
3. Return of excess inventory worth $20,000.
4. Holly transferring to him 25 percent of the stock in her company, with the proviso that she could buy it back if she ever made good on the debt the creditor cancelled.
5. That the debt cancellation was conditional further upon Holly buying and paying C.O.D. on at least $250,000 a year in new purchases for each of the next five years.

Holly had to go along with these demands. She played her negotiating game but the creditor matched us with his own brand of logic and rational thinking.

Today, Holly is glad she went along with it. Last year she grossed over $6,000,000 in her expanding chain, and of course, she finally did buy back her 25 percent stock interest.

Holly proved Nathan's philosophy to be correct. But she adds an important point. "You're not trying to get your creditor to lose. You just want to win."

Holly's story shows you the many variables that can be factored into a "one creditor settlement." Certainly, many of these same variables and negotiating points may be raised even under an "all creditor" composition, however, it's unlikely that the bargaining will be as extensive or acute as when it's one creditor that stands between you and solvency.

I have found that success in dealing with one creditor depends more on the attitude and management style of that creditor than any hard quantitative or purely mathematical considerations. It's almost a matter of personality.

We have witnessed many cases where a significant creditor casually agreed to cancel even 90–95 percent of his debt with little more than a sincere phone call. Others choose to ignore all the rationality of the situation and push for full payment.

Looking back over my cases and the question of why one creditor is such an easy sell and another remains unyielding, I discovered a common denominator with the successful cases. The answer is the smart debtor involves the creditor in his business problems before he strikes for the compromise.

The Kendricks are a perfect example. As a father and son team, they owned a fuel oil business grossing $600,000 a year. Over the years, they purchased all their oil from one wholesale distributor, who finally ended up being owed $100,000. The Kendricks involved the wholesaler. Every week, they would solicit advice and guidance from the creditor, and gradually the creditor became a virtual consultant to the business.

Several months later, the Kendricks proposed a 20 percent settlement with this same creditor. He knew the problems and subconsciously he must have shared some of the responsibility. Resistance was negligible as we handed him the settlement papers. I doubt we would have the same result if we had taken this creditor by surprise.

Remember, creditors are only people. Your success depends on more than numbers. It requires you to put yourself in his shoes. If you were that creditor, would you accept your proposition? When you say "yes," you have something to sell.

Your Ten Point Negotiating Checklist

You have your negotiating points, and the creditors have theirs. They want as much as possible, as soon as possible, and with your survival instincts finely turned—your goal is just the opposite.

As you do battle, keep this handy checklist at your fingertips. It includes virtually every negotiating point that's bound to arise and the counter-points you can effectively use.

1. How Much Will You Pay?

Start with 10 percent more than what your "fool-proof" formula shows they'll get under a bankruptcy. Increase your offer in increments of 2 percent if you must—but only with their even greater concessions. Don't forget your attitude and other negotiating strategies.

2. How Much Now and How Much Later?

Offer as an immediate payment only what the business can afford to pay without tapping personal resources. Future payments should never exceed more than what your accountant calculates as surplus cash flow.

3. Length of Payments?

Creditors will try to get you to pay off the entire amount, no matter how long it takes. Don't mortgage your future for more than 2–3 years. Convince them that for you it's just not worth it. Therefore, your total payment should never exceed the sum total of cash on hand, and positive cash flow for the next 2–3 years.

4. What About Return Goods?

Merchandise that you can return for credit has a value equivalent to cash. You can use excess or unsaleable inventory as a negotiating point. However, needed merchandise must be bartered the same as a cash payment.

5. Will You Give a Mortgage to Secure the Balance of Your Payments?

A mortgage on business assets is a reasonable demand. Use it as a bargaining tool to get other concessions.

6. What About Interest on the Balance?

If you propose a pay-out over 2–3 years, this point will certainly arise. Interest at the prime rate is reasonable. However, this too is a concession tool. Your best argument is to remind the creditor that if your business does go bankrupt, he may have to wait 2–3 years for his small dividend, and the bankruptcy courts don't pay interest.

7. Will You Personally Guarantee the Payments?
Go back to chapter one. You may find just the maneuver to side-step that request.

8. Guarantee of Future Purchases?
Your creditors may like those prospects of future sales—and condition their settlement on your living up to your rosy projections. That's not unreasonable, but it can be tricky. If you do agree, make certain that a) you get the same price as any other cash customer, b) what you agree to buy can be easily handled, and c) you can cure any default by adding what you didn't buy to the following years' requirements.

9. How About Shares of Stock in Your Company?
This demand is not common. However, some creditors decide that if they can't make out as a creditor—why not become a partner? Be on the lookout for this if you are a larger or "fast-growth" business. My advice is to fight it. If you do have to succumb to survive, then never give more than 25–30 percent of the stock and couple it with a "buy-back" option.

10. Salary Restrictions?
While you're paying off the creditors, they may want to tell you what you can take out of the business. It's not a common demand, because creditors know compliance is difficult to monitor. If you must restrict your salary, demand a salary level you can live with and a cost-of-living escalator.

When you walk out of the creditors' meeting, add up the score. Ask yourself the tough questions. Do you now have a business that really gives you that fresh start? Can you confidently say your business will now survive and prosper? If not, read on. Perhaps your creditors only need a stronger dose of "business saving medicine."

Bailing Out Your Problem Loans

7

There's an epidemic going around. One banker calls it "payment paralysis." Its symptoms? The patient can't pick up a pen and write loan payment checks. Laments the same banker, "I can't understand it. The writing hand works fine when it comes to borrowing money."

Payment paralysis is sweeping the land. Over 600,000 businesses are seriously in default on loans due banks and other secured lenders, a staggering number compared to only five years ago. And economists predict that within the next year or two, one out of every three business loans will be in default with the other two not far behind.

Crippling interest rates and recessionary sales and profits combine to create a cash flow crisis that few businesses can avoid. Bankruptcy attorney Jeff Kosberg sums it up, "Businesses are dropping like flies. It's not just that sales and profits are down. It's their inability to continue to pay old loans that no longer fit into their financial picture–and the inability to re-finance with a workable loan that would."

Are there cures for the problem loan? You bet! In this chapter, you'll find workable solutions for the unworkable loan, whether your adversary is the bank, SBA, supplier, or even a private lender holding a mortgage on your business assets.

I don't promise that your problem loan will disappear overnight. However, even an overwhelming, "business busting" secured debt can be whittled down to a level and payment plan that can make sense both to you and your mortgage creditor once you know how to turn your poverty into more power.

Secured creditors can put up quite a battle, since they hold your mortgage. While general or unsecured creditors yell and scream for payment, banks and other secured creditors can easily turn today's business into tomorrow's auction.

Read the fine print in your loan papers and you'll see their power:

- A bank can apply all your deposited funds against overdue loans the instant you go into default. This "offset" provision can destroy your working capital.
- A secured lender can immediately take possession of your pledged collateral and sell it. No long, drawn out court or legal proceedings are necessary, only a simple foreclosure notice, a padlock and a willing auctioneer.
- If you signed a personal guarantee, which most banks and other lenders obtain from the owners of small businesses, your home and other personal assets will be in jeopardy.

Fortunately, secured creditors don't have all the power. You have some business-saving strategies of your own. Let me show you how you can use them to your own advantage.

Take a "No-Nonsense" Look at Your "Nonsense Loan"

You may be victimized by what I call the "nonsense loan." It's never difficult to spot. It's the loan that never made sense and was destined for default even before the ink was dry on the loan document.

Bankers and SBA officials can be blinded by faulty business ideas and unrealistic predictions about what a business is or can become. Major creditors hungry for a new account can extend ridiculous amounts of credit with the mistaken belief that your mortgage gives them all the protection they need. A seller of a business can get an inflated price, taking back an equally inflated mortgage to finance the purchase on terms the business will never pay.

Lulled by your agreement to pay, these creditors frequently overlook the important questions—can you pay—and what is their position if you can't? Businessmen with their hand out for loans can be like kids at the cookie jar. Lenders can be like the parents who aren't smart enough to put the lid back on. The businessman ends up with the bellyache, but that doesn't get the lender his cookies back.

Fairfax Nursing Homes was a victim of its own nonsense loan. A bank loaned it $400,000 to take over and expand an old convalescent facility. To handle the loan payments, Fairfax would require annual sales of $1,200,000. With every bed occupied, the nursing home couldn't generate more than $800,000. A supposedly smart businessman and a supposedly astute banker never bothered to figure it out. A simple cash flow projection could have saved the bank a $180,000 loss.

The SBA? My files are full of their blunders. An interesting case involved a $120,000 loan to the Edgewater Restaurant. Edgewater installed everything from new ceilings and floors to an eight-foot fireplace to keep the customers warm and cozy. Edgewater was a show place. It had everything a restaurant could hope to have—except a lease. One month after the renovations to the building were completed, the landlord thanked Edgewater's owner (and the SBA) for the improvements to his property and kicked the restaurant out. Total salvage value of Edgewater's assets? $2,400. The restaurant wasn't even in business long enough to make the first loan payment.

The SBA didn't invent the "nonsense" loan, but they are certainly it's best salesman. It's inevitable, as their mission is to make loans that even banks turn down. To hear it from one un-named SBA loan officer, "If we were to call in all our delinquent loans—and collect, we could almost balance the national budget. But strong-arm collection techniques won't turn the delinquencies into dollars." The SBA may deal with faith, hope and charity when they write out the checks. Thankfully, they become more realistic when it comes time to collect.

Suppliers can be self-victimizers. A hardware wholesaler financed the start-up of a client's hardware store by giving him $40,000 in opening inventory on the strength of a business mortgage. Through additional credit over a two year period, the debt skyrocketed to $80,000. The business stagnated and couldn't even afford the interest payments. Foreclose? Hardly a favorable alternative as the assets wouldn't bring even $20,000 at auction.

Business sellers may think they have scored when they sell a business at a ridiculous price and then make the even more foolish mistake of financing it. Ben C. had a big smile on his face when he sold his variety store for $80,000. How could he help but smile, since he knew it was never worth more than $50,000. But the gullible buyer agreed to the $80,000 with only $5,000 down. Ben would finance the $75,000 balance with what turned out to be a near worthless mortgage. Three years later, the business failed, crushed by the excessive loan on a business that could never pay it. Ben didn't smile at the auction, not when the depleted inventory and battered fixtures went for $7,000.

Nonsense loans have the element of predictability. They are unsound to begin with. However, you can be equally victimized by a loan that is reasonable when made, but becomes unworkable as your business declines. Since the logic of a loan is predicated on both sufficient assets to cover the debt and profits to repay it, a decline in either and you *now* have a nonsense loan.

The nonsense loan seldom has a winner and a loser. In reality both the borrower and lender lose. The businessman loses his business. The lender loses a substantial part of the loan balance. How it happened can at best be a learning experience. What can be done about it? Clear thinking so both borrower and lender do end up winning. Your objective is to save your business. That's what "winning" means to you. Winning to the lender means ending up with more than he would receive if your business failed. It's the same concept you effectively used on your general creditors. Only this time, you will fine tune it to catch your secured creditors' ear.

Secured loans aren't chiselled in stone. They are only pieces of paper. Usually it makes sense to tear them up and start all over again so both you and your lender come out that winner.

Intertex did it. Several years earlier, they started a leased telephone equipment company to compete with Ma Bell. It didn't take long before they owed a major Boston bank one million dollars on a long term loan. Then other competitors moved in, cut prices and not only stagnated sales but destroyed profits as well. Interest loans alone ate up over $180,000 in annual cash flow. Then Intertex turned off the spigot. The loan fell four months behind. Then came the predictable default letter demanding immediate payment of the entire loan. Ken B., the feisty president of Intertex, remembers that moment, "I suddenly realized what a crazy game we were playing. We had no hopes of paying the bank and we knew it. They had no hopes of receiving payment and they knew it." Several weeks later, Intertex had a letter from the bank reducing the debt, to $100,000. Over $900,000 in debt vanished!

Magic? Of course not. Charity? Hardly. The essential ingredient was the reality that both Intertex and the bank were being victimized by the same bad loan. The die was cast. The bank could foreclose, but then what? Instead Ken used the master strategy that can release the strangle hold of any nonsense loan.

Create Your Own Master Plan

Over 50 percent of my insolvency cases involve problem loans. Every success story required a master plan that:

1. Slashed the debt down to size.
2. Cut payments to what the business could afford—and still survive.
3. Convinced the lender that the renegotiated loan was far better than foreclosure.

That's precisely how Intertex did it. Their assets had only a $150,000 value. Further, the cash flow of the business could support monthly installments of only $2,000. A $100,000 debt level would make sense from both an asset perspective and equally from a "payback" viewpoint. Anything beyond that amount was only an unworkable statistic.

Now, put yourself in the banker's shoes. They thought about a foreclosure. However, after their appraiser estimated the $150,000 in assets would bring only $60,000 at liquidation, the $100,000 began to look attractive. Secured creditors are in the same position as unsecured creditors when you start to cut their debt down to size. They too know you can't get blood from a stone. The only difference is that secured creditors know they'll have the benefit of their collateral to help recoup what is owed. But those few dollars are seldom more than they'll receive if they allow you to stay alive.

Consider your own situation and how you can turn those objectives into hard numbers that will work for you.

Shrinking Your Over-Financed Loan

When is a business over-financed? Turn to accounting or finance texts and you'll find various ratios and formulas to spotlight excess debt. They make sense—but not for you. These ratios are for the solvent operation. The insolvent enterprise has to play by different rules.

I use a simple formula. A business is over-financed when the debt exceeds what the business is worth. I wouldn't necessarily recommend that excess leverage when starting your business, but that's not your situation either. You're already in over your head. Now you have to work in reverse to see how much debt you have to bail out to avoid drowning. Matching the total debt to the business value is what I call the *survival ratio*.

Here's how the *survival ratio* worked for others.

Beacon Packing Company, a small meat processor, owed its bank $240,000, secured by all corporate assets. General creditors were on the books for another $150,000. Total debt: $390,000.

What was the business worth to the owners? They believed the business couldn't be sold for more than $150,000, free of liabilities.

The solution: we cut the bank's loan from $240,000 to $135,000 and the general creditors, in a considerably worse bargaining position, agreed to accept 10 cents on the dollar, or $15,000.

Allegro's Tuxedos was another story. They owed the SBA over $300,000. Trade creditors were owed only $20,000. The value of the business? $100,000. After months of "red-tape," we cut the SBA down to $100,000 and didn't even bother to compromise the general creditors. The business now had debts that exceeded the business value by only $20,000. But it was close enough to justify the fight for survival.

Amit Builders, according to its owners, wasn't worth more than $75,000. It owed its bank $300,000 on a secured note and trade creditors

$100,000. The total debt exceeded the value of the business by a whopping $325,000! The bank agreed to reduce its loan to $60,000 and the general creditors reluctantly settled for $10,000. They had little choice. Under a bankruptcy, they would have been completely wiped out. Now the numbers came into line. If the business is worth only $75,000, how can you justify debt in excess of that amount?

Intertex was smart enough to see it that way. Its president, Ken, knew the bank would have been happier letting the one million loan ride, hoping the business, someday—somehow would be worth an equivalent amount and be finally able to make a dent in its obligation. But as Ken realized, that someday wasn't today. Today Intertex couldn't be sold for more than $100,000.

But some owners don't see it that way. They'll foolishly struggle on with excessive debt as long as the creditors let them. What they don't realize is that in reality they're not working for themselves. They're the indentured serf to the creditors. They owe so much money that it's unlikely they'll ever see an equity or net worth in their own business.

In calculating what a business is worth, I ask my clients to consider the value of the company to them. At this point, I'm not interested in the book value of the assets or the liquidation value. We take a different approach requiring the distressed owner to decide what he would pay for his very own business.

Now let's assume that your business is worth $100,000 to you. If you have debt in excess of that amount, you have a *negative* equity. You won't begin to build an equity or net worth until you reduce the debt to the business value. Why continue on with the business? You're only wasting valuable time working to reduce creditors' debts and still have nothing to show for it but a weekly paycheck.

It's common sense, but many business owners can't see it. I ask them to think about their home. What if it had a fair market value of $100,000 and mortgages and liens against it of $200,000? Isn't it true that they would have to pay down the encumbrances by $100,000 before they began to build their first dime in equity in their own property? Wouldn't it make appreciably more sense to forfeit the house to the creditors and buy another house where payments would turn into equity? Of course. It's just more difficult to see this logic when you relate it to a business.

I'm not always successful in selling this message. Many owners instead choose to struggle against overwhelming debt that far exceeds the value of their business.

Henry K. is in for an unpleasant surprise. He owns a car wash mortgaged to a bank for over $350,000. The problem is the car wash isn't worth more than $150,000 to Henry or anyone else. My proposition was simple enough. Let's cut the mortgage down to $150,000 and begin to build some net worth. Not Henry. Every month he sends out an interest payment and a few extra dollars for principal. I figured it out. The way Henry is paying the note, the balance won't be reduced to $150,000 until the year 2073. I don't think it'll mean much to Henry then. Henry will continue to be a mere serf for the bank until he removes his blinders.

Excess debt can be rationalized by owners when they believe the business will rapidly increase in value. Perhaps I wouldn't have encouraged Henry to reduce his debt if we were convinced his $150,000 car wash would quickly increase in value to $350,000. Then at least the debt/value would be in parity and the payment checks would be building an equity in the business.

Sam S. was another owner who didn't seem bothered by the $90,000 he owed the banks, despite the fact his small superette wasn't worth much more than $50,000. To hear it from Sam, "I know the business will never be debt free since I can barely make the interest payments. But I'm not interested in building equity. I'm able to take home $22,000 in annual salary, so I look at the business not as an asset to build net worth on, but as a week's pay."

Sam's idea of looking at his business only for present income probably doesn't match your own objectives. You are in business not only for cash today but to build net worth tomorrow. And you can't build net worth until debts are cut down to the value of the business.

The company with excess financing needs surgery to survive. Don't be afraid to pull out the knife.

Turn Choking Payments Into Easily Swallowed Installments

Cutting debt down to size is only part of the battle. It's equally important to restucture the loan to bring payments in line with your cash flow and ability to pay.

The over-financed business usually suffers the double dilemma not only of owing too much but also being unable to meet the payments required by the excess debt. The strategy then is not just to reduce the debt itself—but to re-align the monthly payments besides.

Conversely, there are many loans that are not excessive but still demand payments that strangle cash flow. Rescue requires decisive action to re-write the terms of the loan to coincide with cash availability.

An owner ending up with loan payments that he cannot handle is a way of life in business. It's even more acute in an era of high interest, short term loans. For the troubled business, the problem goes even further. They have to reduce monthly installments to the level where the payments are *less* than available cash flow after payment of operating expenses. The surplus cash flow is vital to replenishing working capital, inventory, and the payments due general creditors on their compromised debt. Cash hungry best describes the insolvent company. Starving secured lenders can leave that needed cash on the table for you.

Consider the example of Classic Clothes:

After three years of operation, Classic was finally going to break even. However, its problems included a secured $120,000 bank loan requiring monthly payments of $2,400. General creditors were owed piled up debts of $140,000. Since the business had a value of $160,000, we decided to let the $120,000 due the bank stand. General creditors, however, compromised their debts down to $20,000. The financial statements took on a rosier complexion, but cash flow was still a problem. After payment of operating expenses (not including bank payments), the business would have a positive monthly cash flow of only $1,500. How could it continue to meet its monthly installments of $2,400 without depleting inventory?

Our plan was to get the bank to accept only monthly interest payments for three years and defer all payments on principal. Since interest payments were only $1,000, Classic would end up with a surplus monthly cash flow of $500. It wasn't much, but it was enough to handle the payments due general creditors on their reduced debt and prevent a drain on the assets of the business.

What can *you* really afford to pay on your loans? Only a carefully prepared cash flow statement prepared by your accountant can give you the answer. It may be considerably less than you think.

It was for Classic Clothes. If they continued to blindly pay $2,400 a month to the bank, they would only dig a deeper hole by $900 a month. To further weaken their position, they wouldn't have the cash to pay creditors on their compromised claims. Without reducing loan payments, the business would never fly. A year or two later, the payments would choke it out of existence. The cash flow statement gave us the hard numbers that spelled "reality" to both Classic and the bank. Eventually, Classic will increase its monthly loan payments, as cash flow improves.

Once you know what you can afford to pay, the next step is to renegotiate the loan to reduce the payments to size.

Try these proven cash flow problem solvers:

1. Extend the loan. Short term loans may be re-written as long term obligations. That approach helped save Ajax Cleaners, which owed its bank $20,000 on a three-year note. Crippling $800 monthly payments turned into easily handled $400 installments once the loan was extended to seven years. This was critical to Ajax. The $400 a month saved on notes satisfied the claims of unsecured creditors whose debts were piling up. Banks prefer 3-5 year notes. But don't let that fool you. Extending the loan to 7-10 years is a possibility even with the toughest bank.

2. Deferring principal payments. This is a frequent solution to reducing stranglehold payments. As long as lenders receive interest, they may be willing to freeze principal payments until your business is back on its feet. Figure out the portion of your monthly payments that represents principal. It may be significant. It was for Broadway Drugs.

Broadway was paying down a $50,000 loan in three years. It hurt. What the business needed was $20,000 in inventory to bring merchandise back to a profitable level. Trade creditors wouldn't extend it a dime in credit, so we turned to the bank note. Monthly payments of $1,600 dropped to $700 once the bank agreed to put the note on an "interest-only" basis. Over two years, Broadway used the $900 saved on the note to replenish inventory. It did the trick. Sales increased from $280,000 to $360,000 and losses of $10,000 turned into profits of $14,000. Now Broadway is paying on the principal, and it can afford to.

3. Suggest a moratorium on all loan payments until profitability and cash flow improve. It's a "tough sell" proposition, but lenders may go along with it if they believe it's the only way to save your business—and their loan. I've used it successfully many times. Kendwich Stationery Supply proves that lenders may consider it in their own best interests to allow your entire loan to "float." Kendwich owed its prior owner $60,000 on a five-year, 15 percent note. Kendwich had another problem. It owed general creditors $100,000. They would compromise the debt to $20,000 if they received payment within one year. The only place the $20,000 could come from was the note payments due the prior owner, who expected to receive $18,000 within the next year. The prior owner realized that if he didn't go along with it, the business might fail and he certainly wouldn't recoup his entire loan. His begrudging acceptance released the business—saving $20,000 for the general creditors.

When the lender is well collateralized, you may meet with less resistance. In a recent case, we talked a bank into deferring all payments on a $30,000 loan. It didn't bother them. They were holding over $180,000 in collateral. The build-up of accrued interest was insignificant against its security.

4. Re-finance short-term business debt with long-term real estate loans. Real estate loans for a firm owning property can be a shrewd alternative to short-term business obligations. That's how Wareham Restaurant worked its way out of steep monthly payments on a $50,000, five-year equipment loan. Borrowing $50,000 on the corporation's real estate allowed it to spread its payments over twenty years, simultaneously reducing interest by three points. Monthly payments declined from $1,450 to $525. Wareham enjoyed an immediate infusion of more than $900 a month to pay other debts and restore the business to profitability.

There are solutions to those payments that can destroy cash flow and your business. It's always a two-step process:

1. Calculate what you can afford to pay.
2. Design a payment plan that doesn't exceed what you can pay.

Put Yourself in Your Lender's Shoes

Restructuring your debt and/or payment plan requires not only a convincing alternative to foreclose but also the ability to sell it. The successful formula is one part arithmetic, one part psychology and two parts bluff. Survivors never leave out an ingredient. Neither do lenders, who have their own strategies and ideas—all designed to keep their loan intact while you continue to slave away paying down the impossible. Here's what you'll be up against. Be prepared!

Lenders can be a fountain of optimism. Caught in a cross-fire between cancelling part of their debt and a foreclosure which will get them even less, lenders use always the third alternative—the chin-raising pep talk to motivate you to "stick with it." Maintain the "status quo." Hope that someday and in some way the business will be better. Catch the hidden message?

Carl did. He owned a "steak house" restaurant beholden to a mortgage-holding bank for $180,000. With other creditors pressing for $90,000, it was all too much for Carl's Steak House. Carl figured the business to be worth about $220,000. He also knew that the same business wouldn't sell for more than $100,000 under the auctioneer's hammer. So Carl's strategy was to restructure the total debt between $100,000 and $220,000. Threatened with a possible liquidation, the general creditors settled for $30,000 payable over three years. That's when we moved to the big leagues. It was time to perform some further surgery on the bank.

Borrowers may suffer from "payment paralysis," but lenders have their own affliction. They hear only what they want to hear. Carl's banker was a chronic case. Carl explained the problem and told the banker the loan soured his incentive to continue and his ability to pay. Cut the loan from $180,000 to $120,000; extend payments for three additional years and accept interest only for the first year were our demands. The message was loud and clear—re-work the loan or foreclose and end up with $80–90,000 after legal and auctioneer's fees.

The banker didn't "hear" a word of it. "Stick with it, keep working and eventually you'll make it. All you need is staying power," was all he had to say. The classic "pep talk." The perfect "put off." It was all a lot of baloney. How could Carl stay with it? It would take years before the debt was reduced to an acceptable level. Payment? By continuing the loan installments, within two months Carl wouldn't have the working capital to buy a carrot. Optimism is easy to sell. It can be fatal to buy. Two days later, we were back. It was time for the "bluff." "Either re-write the damn loan or we're filing for bankruptcy." Suddenly, the banker's hearing improved. Within twenty minutes, we had the commitment to cancel $60,000 in debt and a new payment plan.

Lenders will do anything to avoid a debt reduction. They prefer to extend payments, as long as necessary, to eventually obtain 100 percent of what's owed. That's reasonable—to the lender. Virtually any loan can be repaid if the borrower wants to spend the rest of his life in serfdom.

Lenders know that with patience, the business may someday grow to the point where the loan can and should be repaid in full. Those hopes and visions may have danced across the mind of Carl's banker. Perhaps next year or in five years the business will expand and be healthy. The bank will then be back in the driver's seat.

Consider tactics. The old "stall" game can give the lender the edge. Mr. Banker looked sharp even with his hearing disability. Perhaps he was just pre-occupied with the thought of buying time until he could find a buyer who would pick up the restaurant under foreclosure for $180,000.

The time to strike is when you have poverty on your side. Be decisive and act decisively. There's a *quid pro quo* in your deal. You're offering the lender substantially more than a foreclosure would bring. In return, you expect the lender to meet your needs by reducing the excess debt to an amount you can live with.

Additional collateral? Lenders love collateral; they also know you don't really want to lose your business. It's the reverse bluff. This time, they're telling you they'll perhaps reduce the loan slightly and even extend or defer loan payments—if only they had more collateral. Why not a second mortgage on your home? How about your wealthy father-in-law's guarantee? Of course the lender wants more collateral. Both you and he know he hasn't enough collateral behind his loan now. That's why you have the upper hand. If the lender had adequate collateral, you wouldn't go near him. One wrong look and he'd have you in foreclosure.

Every case has to be decided on its own, but I have learned from experience that it's best to keep the upper hand by refusing additional collateral.

Take a lesson from Jimmy D., the owner of Bay City Landscaping. He owed his bank $120,000 secured by four sputtering trucks and an equally valueless assortment of landscape equipment. The pile of junk at auction might—if the bank had a lucky day—bring $25,000. It was another example of the "nonsense" loan. I asked Jimmy what the business was worth to him. "About $50,000" was the answer. He agreed the trucks and equipment had a value of $25–30,000 and the good will and existing customers added another $20,000. It was clear. Either the bank would cut the loan to $50,000 or let them take the equipment. Jimmy could then buy or even lease new trucks on a seasonal basis and continue with a new corporation.

But grass grew under Jimmy's feet. The bank saw their vulnerability and turned it to an advantage. They listened to my demands to reduce the debt to $50,000 or go to auction for $25,000 but they gave Jimmy another deal. The bank would reduce the debt to $100,000 and even extend the payments, if Jimmy's mother would give the bank a second mortgage on her home (with $80,000 equity) to further collateralize the loan. Jimmy liked it. After all, he was saving $20,000.

New England grass stops growing in September. That's also when Jimmy's payments to the bank stopped. Two months later, the bank collected their entire $100,000 after foreclosing on Bay City's trucks and his mother's house. Nice guys do finish last.

Three Lenders Who Always Play Rough

You can look at your excess loan and your anemic collateral and decide you have the convincing argument to reshape your loan. Sometimes you're right, but in other cases it's self-deception. You can walk straight into a booby trap unless you know precisely your creditors' alternatives. Here are some booby traps to watch for:

The low-interest loan: Money has a value and its interest rate controls that value. Sarah forgot that lesson. Her bakery owed the bank $50,000 on a four-year, 10 percent interest loan. Sarah didn't demand a substantial concession once her business ran into financial trouble—only a one-year deferral of principal payments. Three days later, the bakery was padlocked and on its way to auction. Liquidation proceeds netted the bank only $27,000, but they came out the winner. They could re-loan the $27,000 at current interest rates of 18 percent and come out even better than collecting the entire $50,000 at 10 percent. Before you negotiate with your lender, ask yourself what your low-interest loan would be worth in today's high interest market.

The collateral with an underestimated value: Another potential booby trap. An auctioneer may see one value, but your secured creditor may see a totally different value. Ask Sonny T. of Clarendon Liquors. He owed his liquor wholesaler $90,000, with the debt secured by a mortgage on the inventory. Sonny's objective was to talk his supplier into a settlement of $50,000 based on his estimate that the inventory of $100,000 would bring only 50 cents on the dollar at auction. Fifty cents on the dollar may be what it was worth at public auction but not to the liquor wholesaler. He foreclosed, reclaimed $100,000 in re-saleable inventory that he could sell again for $100,000. Why should he settle for $50,000?

Spence loved foreclosures, particularly when he was doing the foreclosing. He sold his pizza shop six times and foreclosed five, making money every time. His game was to sell the shop for low cash down and accept a high-interest secured note for the $50–60,000 balance. Inevitably, the pizza shop would fail. Do you think Spence would accept $10–15,000 and walk away? Nope. Spence would always end up his own high bidder and buy it back. The next day he'd have another "for sale" ad in the paper. You can't bluff Spence with a foreclosure.

It's simple reality. Spence would do only what any other high-powered, savvy lender would do—maximize the value of the collateral by taking it back for himself rather than see it go for a dime on the dollar auction.

Lenders can put a premium on your collateral and laugh at your auctioneer's report. Make certain you look at it through their glasses.

The SBA guaranteed loan: Don't try to bluff a bank backed with an SBA guarantee. They can take a hard stand. If you default, the most they can lose is 10 percent of what's owed, since the SBA guarantee will cover them for the remaining 90 percent. Show the bank a problem loan and they'll show you a foreclosure.

Negotiations should be at the SBA level. It's the bank's money, but it's ultimately the SBA's risk. And you can be successful in compromising or extending an SBA loan if you have the solid facts to back your request. The SBA knows how to deal with the problem loan. They have plenty of experience.

More Strategies That Can Turn a "No" Into a "Yes"

Borrowers seldom understand why a plan that appears to be in the best interests of the borrower and lender alike is turned down. Lenders have their reasons, and once you discover them, you can frequently find a solution and turn that "no" into a "yes."

A bank secured by inventory of a card and gift shop refused to extend payments on their defaulted $20,000 loan. Their reply? "Double the payments or we foreclose." Their reason? The bank knew that if they foreclosed now, the inventory was sufficient to generate close to $20,000 at auction. A year later, the inventory might be depleted and they'd be in a considerably weaker position. That's a common problem for the troubled company. The natural inclination of the lender is to accelerate payments to reduce the loan before the business fails. It's a position completely contrary to the objectives of the business trying to conserve capital. The solution is to convince the creditor that the collateral will remain at no less than their current level during the payback period. It's a legitimate cause for concern. You should respond by agreeing to a clause in your loan documents granting the right to the lender to foreclose if the inventory (or other collateral) diminishes. Back it up with an offer to submit periodic appraisals to monitor collateral levels. Lenders may cooperate once they're convinced they won't be in a worse position due to their delay.

Lenders have their own problems. There are various fiscal or regulatory reasons why your proposal will—or will not—be accepted. A bank may have incurred extraordinary losses during the year and decide they'd rather defer your problem until next year. Another bank may decide a foreclosure and resultant loss today will look better on this year's financial statement. Banking regulations may dictate how far a lender can go. Find out the real reason for the "no." It's vital in order to turn it into a "yes."

Your personal financial condition may be part of the problem. One bank foreclosed on a loan only one month in default. It wanted to protect itself on the loan by proceeding immediately against the owner under his personal guarantee. Why? The owner was going through a divorce and the bank wanted to attach the owner's home before he lost it to his wife. Convincing a lender that your personal financial condition remains solid can be an important tool.

Turn Lenders Into Partners

Have you considered turning your lenders into partners? The idea can work.

A Boston-based high technology firm escaped the dilemma of finding cash to pay down its $1,500,000 loan by having its secured lender convert the debt into a 35 percent ownership interest. It was a smart deal for everybody.

The lender realized the firm couldn't repay the loan, but why foreclose and end up 20–30 cents on the dollar while killing a business with growth potential?

Defer the loan? It was a possibility, but the lender also realized that the five year loan would have to be extended to over fifteen years, and since the business needed cash for research and development, every payment would impede its growth.

The owners of the firm came out ahead too. They realized that owning 65 percent of a debt-free, fast growth company was better than owning 100 percent of a firm destined for foreclosure.

The concept of converting business-busting debt to ownership equity is more common than you think. It can be the perfect solution if:

1. The firm has growth potential and can attract the eye of the lender from an investment viewpoint.
2. The debt is excessive, forcing the lender either to foreclose or extend the loan beyond what it considers reasonable from a loan viewpoint.

Here are a few more examples of how loan/equity conversions have saved businesses and turned both borrowers and lenders into winners!

Heritage Toys owed its major supplier over $200,000 on a secured-loan basis. Heritage's problem was that it couldn't meet the stiff $5,000 monthy payments on the debt. Foreclose? The supplier would end up with perhaps $100,000. Salvation was in turning at least part of the debt into equity. After a month of negotiation, the supplier agreed to accept a 45 percent stock interest in the firm to cancel $100,000 in debt. The remaining $100,000 balance was extended three further years, cutting the $5,000 payments to an easily handled $1,200. Heritage came out ahead in other ways. With its supplier as a co-owner, the business was able to buy goods at even better prices.

Seymour Textile used the same tactics to its advantage. A private lender held its $60,000 mortgage. A crippling labor strike threw the firm into financial chaos and the note into default. The deal? The lender would cancel $40,000 on its note and invest an even further $20,000 into the business in exchange for 40 percent of its stock. Seymour survived! Ralph Seymour justifies it this way, "Without the debt reduction and the infusion of additional cash, we had about two weeks to live." Now hear it from the lender's side—"If Seymour had collapsed, we wouldn't have received our full $60,000. We're better off with a solid loan of

$20,000 and 40 percent of a company that has growth possibility."

What you will have to give up in stock in exchange for a release for all or part of the note will depend on many variables. The collateral value, growth potential of the company, and negotiating ability are all factored into the situation. Your accountant and attorney can give you the guidelines that will work best for you.

Be realistic. You're asking the lender to forfeit all or part of his debt in return for the hope that his ownership interest will someday be worth more than his note is worth today. A lender with a solidly secured note on a corner "Mom and Pop" retail store won't be excited about swapping the note for stock. Companies—even the small firm with sales of less than $200–300,000—can, however, make that convincing case if they can show the lender that the firm does have growth opportunity. Your bargaining chips increase when that same lender is sitting on a loan he wishes he had never made.

Banks and the SBA may not be in a position to end up in partnership with you, but private lenders, SBIC's, venture capital groups, or suppliers holding your mortgage may be perfect candidates.

Start-up firms understand the concept when they seek initial capital. Oftentimes, the lender will demand a percentage ownership in the firm to make the loan. The combination of debt/equity makes sense to many lenders. It can work equally well for the troubled company saddled with a creditor who may just decide that an ownership interest is the perfect "workout" of a bad loan.

Winning Ways to Get Even More Money

Let me share a secret with you. Lenders may consider it a smart move to lend your troubled company even more money—particularly when you're at the doorstep to bankruptcy. Sometimes you don't even have to ask. They have their checkbook open before you even show up.

A few dollars now may keep your business afloat so it can pay off the bigger dollars later. It doesn't require nerve to ask for more money, only common sense.

Kathy P. had plenty of both. Her gourmet shop owed a local bank $40,000 and was already four months behind in payments. Trade creditors were beating down her doors for $30,000, but Kathy didn't even have enough money to cover next month's rent. Someone with less spunk might have called it quits. Not Kathy. She knew where the money was and how to get it.

I enjoyed the show. Kathy walked into the bank to drain it of even more money. Sitting opposite her was Mr. Pinstripe, complete with cigar and large mahogany desk. Kathy launched into her business-saving monologue, "I need another $6,000 to save *your* loan." "What do you mean *save my loan?*" asked Mr. Pinstripe. "Without another $6,000, I'll have to close my doors. According to the auctioneer, the assets will bring only $15–20,000, so you stand to lose $20–25,000. I want to avoid that. $6,000 will cover my operating expenses until I can get into the big Christmas season, and then business should be o.k." Mr. Pinstripe frowned, "If we have a loss on your business loan, we'll sue you for everything you have under your personal guarantee." "Go ahead," quipped Kathy, "I have a list of my personal assets right here for you. Let's see. A Timex watch, a K-Mart portable radio and oh yes, a nine year old B/W television." Pinstripe caved in, Kathy got her $6,000 two days later, along with an extension on her loan. It was a smart move for Pinstripe. Kathy did repay the $6,000 once the Christmas season was over, and after a few more years of struggle, she finally had fully paid Pinstripe.

In many cases, a properly handled infusion of additional capital can get a distressed business over its financial crisis. It can be a shrewd move when:

1. You can prove the additional capital is necessary to survive.
2. The lender can be satisfied that the additional funds can be repaid at a predictable date.
3. The lender will otherwise face a loss if the business fails.
4. The additional capital is not excessive in relation to the potential risk of loss to the lender.

It works even better with trade creditors, particularly creditors who have lots to lose if your lender calls in your loan. More than one creditor has subsidized a troubled business by making its loan payments in order to keep it operating. A wholesale grocery firm advanced a client struggling to meet its loan payments over $20,000 to keep the business afloat, until it reached its peak selling season. It worked out fine. The business survived and repaid not only the $20,000 but over $80,000 in past bills owed the same creditor. Without the loan, the business would have failed and the creditor would have been lucky to see 20 cents on the dollar.

A pool of creditors loaned a boat repair shop $50,000 to cover its winter notes. Again it was a smart move. During the following two summers, the business repaid the $50,000 and made a sizeable dent in its other bills.

Your creditors have a stake in the survival of your business. In fact, they may have even more at risk. Your financial problems are equally theirs. Sometimes they decide *their* investment can be better protected with a few extra dollars.

Know What's Inside That Pinstripe Suit

Don't be misled into believing that successful loan strategy is only a matter of numbers, or legal and financial alternatives. These may provide the framework for solving the problem loan, but it's still a people game. Personalities and psychology play an important part.

Every successful loan workout not only has a proposal that is logical for both the borrower and lender but also has a borrower and lender who work in good faith to find that logical solution. Failures? Perhaps it is an erroneous perception of what is logical. But I don't think so. Whenever a negotiation with a secured lender fails, the lender invariably ends up with less than what he would have received under the proposal. But that's to be expected. Otherwise, the proposal wasn't logical in the first place. No, it isn't the plan that fails, it is an inability to sell the proposal.

Lenders may wear three piece pinstripe suits, but you have to know what's inside that suit. No two lenders react the same way to a problem loan. Some are exceptionally reasonable and lenient. Others take a hard stand and cling to the "pay or foreclose" theory. And they mean it. Different banks follow different policies. It doesn't stop there. Even within the same bank, one loan officer may spell success while the other represents defeat.

Since we can't dissect the attitudes of all lenders, I can only emphasize the need to know what's inside that pinstripe suit before you call a meeting. It's essential. You're in the same spot as a batter checking out a pitcher. You have to know what they're likely to throw at you.

It doesn't take much. A few phone calls can get you the answer. Bankers have reputations. Others in your position have sat across their mahogany desks with their tales of woe. They can tell you whether Mr. Pinstripe throws "high balls" or "sinkers." It's all part of being prepared.

Why Quick Action Is a Must

Every problem loan has its solutions. The danger that plagues the troubled business is the possibility that the owner either doesn't recognize the loan as a problem or continues with it until the payments strip the business of inventory and working capital. The business is no longer viable, because it no longer has the assets to generate either sales or profits.

As one banker states, "I have seen many businesses struggle to make heavy note payments and then throw in the towel once they've seen they had nothing left but debt. Shelves stand empty, working capital is depleted, valuable accounts have abandoned ship. They have nothing to build or even sustain the operation. The viable 'core' is gone. It's unfortunate. Had the same owner faced the reality that he had a loan he couldn't handle—and taken timely and decisive action to solve it, he would be in business today."

As Mr. Pinstripe will tell you, "Come to me with any reasonable proposition that will save your business—and as much of my loan as possible—and I'll listen. What scares me most is not the business person who knows he's in trouble and wants to battle me over the loan, but the business person who simply scuttles the business that could be saved." Did you hear Mr. Pinstripe? "Talk to me!" That's what they all say, "Talk to me." And they always listen.

Strong Medicine for Your Sick Business

8

October 30, 1981 was a bad day for Al Jaspen, owner of Jaspen Photofinishing. At ten o'clock, his bank notified him that it was foreclosing on his mortgage. Two hours later, an I.R.S. agent showed up and padlocked the front door of the shop. By three in the afternoon, the sheriff handed Al his sixth creditor lawsuit of the week. After all these years of struggling to build a successful business, Al could have been facing a bleak and penniless future. But Al was smart.

By 4:30 that same afternoon, Al told the bank to forget foreclosure, then he called the I.R.S. and told them to come get their padlock. The lawsuits? The next morning they had a new home—a fat plastic trash bag next to the other rubbish cans.

Did Al wave a magic wand to make the creditors disappear? Did he inherit a million dollars from his rich aunt in Toledo? No, Al used even stronger medicine—a petition for reorganization under Chapter 11 of the Bankruptcy Code.

Chapter 11 protects a business from its creditors while management seeks to reorganize its financial affairs and cut a new deal to reduce its debts.

Unlike Chapter 7 of the Bankruptcy Code, which is designed to liquidate a distressed business, Chapter 11 has the opposite mission—it helps keep the business alive by providing a troubled company the opportunity not only to rid itself of burdensome debt, leases and contracts, but also to gain a better chance to obtain new credit, raise fresh working capital and do just about anything necessary to save the business from death.

Chapter 11 is part of the Bankruptcy Code. Just as a Chapter 13 allows "wage earners" to compromise their debts with creditors, Chapter 11 does the same for businesses. Chapter 11 reorganizations have been part of the bankruptcy laws for years. The revised Bankruptcy Code of 1978, however, expanded considerably on the rights of and remedies for a troubled business. As creditors are quick to complain, it can work miracles, even if those miracles come at their expense.

Al knew it could work magic for him just as it has for such corporate giants as Braniff Airlines, Daylin, W.T. Grant, Food Fair, Penn Central, and even Chase Revel, Inc., publisher of *Entrepreneur Magazine* and the guru of the "rags to riches" crowd. Chapter 11 does not discriminate between a Chrysler Corporation and the Mom and Pop grocery around the corner. Over 300,000 businesses of every size and type are alive today because their owners were smart enough to take advantage of its provisions.

As Barry Levine, a Boston bankruptcy attorney states, "Chapter 11 is fast replacing the Cadillac limousine and Lear jet as a corporate status symbol." And he's right. This year, a record 50,000 businesses will flood the bankruptcy courts seeking a fresh and healthy start. Within the next decade, the number of Chapter 11 cases will double. Once a dirty word, "bankruptcy" has become an important and positive aspect of American business.

A Quick Trip to Solvency

Let's return to Al's photofinishing plant and watch exactly how Chapter 11 helped solve its problems.

Al's problem started when several large accounts went out of business, sticking him with $60,000 in uncollectible accounts receivable. Then Al committed his own managerial sins. He neglected to check his new bookkeeper, who promptly embezzled $12,000 (Wyoming still refuses to extradite her). When his larger competitor slashed prices, Al matched them dollar for dollar until his profit margins dwindled. On top of that, Jaspen Photofinishing carried a $70,000 bank mortgage, couldn't reduce high overhead costs, and watched plummeting sales. Al's landlord handed him an eviction notice. Losses, trade liabilities and unpaid taxes began to mount. The day Al Jaspen filed for Chapter 11, his $97,000 assets were dwarfed by his aggregate $285,000 debt. The end of the road? Hardly. With the aid of Chapter 11, it was a new beginning.

Here's how he did it:

1. First, Al asked his attorney to file a petition for reorganization under Chapter 11 with the Bankruptcy Court, which is part of the Federal Court system. The moment the petition was filed, his business came under the protection of the Court, automatically restraining any further creditor action. For Al this meant:

The bank holding the mortgage could not proceed with foreclosure.

The I.R.S. was restrained from going ahead with the seizure and had to give the business back to Al.

Creditors suing the business had to forget their lawsuits. The debts owed them would have to be resolved through the Bankruptcy Court.

Other general creditors owed back debts could not seek payment. Their debts were frozen and must also be handled within the bankruptcy proceeding.

Al's landlord could no longer evict him.

As you can see, Chapter 11 *immediately* solved Al's most pressing problems. With the Chapter 11 protective net around the business, no one could legally interfere while Al tried to reorganize its financial affairs.

2. Next, Al sought new credit. With past bills frozen, creditors extending fresh credit to the corporation after the Chapter 11 filing enjoyed a priority for payment if the business did eventually fail, thus placing new creditors in an enviable position over old creditors. Voila! Credit—the lifeline of any business—was flowing again.

3. But what about those old creditors? After Al filed under Chapter 11, The Court convened a creditors' committee comprised of several of Al's

largest unsecured creditors. Their role was to act on behalf of all general creditors to negotiate a "plan of arrangement," the sort of composition discussed in Chapter 6. However, unlike many out-of-court compositions, Al could negotiate from a position of strength because the Bankruptcy Court protected him from creditor action. After several meetings, general creditors owed $200,000 agreed to accept $30,000 payable over three years in *full* settlement of the total $200,000. Given the creditors' committee recommendation to accept this plan, the majority of Al's creditors quickly approved it. Over $170,000 in past debts vanished. Al reasoned he wouldn't have any trouble paying the $30,000 over three years from future profits.

4. Because the bank was a secured creditor holding a mortgage on the business assets, Al had to handle it differently. Al was obligated to pay the bank its entire $70,000, but Chapter 11 still helped him. Since Al had missed several payments, the bank had the right to declare his note in default, but under Chapter 11, Al had the right to "cure" the default by making the payments he skipped, thereby forcing the bank to accept the payment and reinstate the loan.

5. Remember the I.R.S.? They are always a priority creditor entitled to payment before general creditors. However, under the negotiated plan of arrangement, Al agreed to pay their $15,000 bill over two years.

6. Drastically reducing debts under Chapter 11 was only part of the game plan. During the several months the company sat in Chapter 11, Al whipped his operation into line so he could start to show a profit. He cut his payroll, expanded his line, aggressively sold new accounts and even sub-let part of his space to a professional photographer who helped stimulate business. The $30,000 losses the year before turned into a projected $20,000 profit.

February 9, 1982 was an important day for Al. On that day, the Court approved his arrangement with creditors, and that was the last Al saw of the Bankruptcy Court. He'd saved his business.

Let's summarize how Chapter 11 helped Al.

- It bought time to resolve financial problems by holding creditors at bay.

- It forced the bank to reinstate a defaulted loan rather than foreclose.
- It allowed a two-year payout to the I.R.S.
- It enabled new credit.
- It afforded the right to cancel his oppressive equipment lease.
- It forced creditors to accept a three-year $30,000 note in lieu of an immediate $170,000.
- It gave breathing room for a long hard look at the overall business.

And these are just a few of the potent remedies Chapter 11 can provide to cure your sick business.

Do Al's problems sound familiar? Most businesses in trouble face similar difficulties. Your business may need Chapter 11 to stave off foreclosure. Or you may want to use it to whittle down staggering debt from general creditors. Or it might plug the drain of profits by unfavorable leases or contracts. No matter what financial problems you do face, there is a remedy under Chapter 11. Any business, large or small, incorporated or operated as an individual or partnership, can use the broad protection of Chapter 11 to seek the solutions to save a business.

Next let's examine in greater detail how a Chapter 11 can help you.

The Case of the Belligerent Bank

Al had trouble with his bank. Because he had fallen several months behind in his mortgage payments, they had the legal right to foreclose, and that, of course, would have spelled the end for Jaspen Photofinishing. Nothing but a Chapter 11 could stop it. From my experiences, over 40 percent of all businesses that seek protection under Chapter 11 file primarily to prevent a secured lender from foreclosing.

As you learned in the preceding chapter, banks and other secured lenders are increasingly reluctant to be lenient with accounts in default.

However, you have the right to file Chapter 11 any time before the bank sells your collateral, whereupon the bank must return to you possession of the collateral.

Unlike a general creditor who cannot be paid during the Chapter 11 proceeding, a secured lender can receive regular monthly installments during a Chapter 11. Oftentimes, the Court will even impose this to prevent further interest charges from piling up.

Under a Chapter 11, a secured lender has other rights, but so do you.

A secured creditor can petition the Court for permission to foreclose. Oftentimes, this becomes the Achilles heel of a Chapter 11, for if the Court believes the secured lender is not "adequately" protected, it may allow the foreclosure, bringing the Chapter 11 to a fruitless conclusion.

Frequently, secured lenders will file a petition for authority to foreclose. In determining whether the bank has "adequate protection," the Court will consider the value of the collateral against the balance due under the loan. Should the Court conclude sufficient assets exist to fully liquidate the loan if the business fails, it will usually deny the secured creditor's petition. On the other hand, if the collateral at auction would bring only $100,000 and you owe the secured creditor $100,000 or more, the Court may allow the secured creditor to foreclose. The Court may reason that if over several months of Chapter 11 proceedings the company does fail and the assets shrink from $100,000 to only $60–70,000, the secured creditor would lose $30–40,000 because it did not foreclose earlier.

Assuming the Court favors your position, you gain valuable rights.

1. If the Bankruptcy Court agrees that continuity of the loan is vital to saving your company, you can "cure" the default by forcing the bank to reinstate the loan by paying the arrears on the note.
2. You can even "cram down" or reduce the amount due secured creditors to the value of their collateral at auction or liquidation. This can be a powerful tool in saving a business because it solves the problem of secured debt exceeding asset value.

Banks (and other secured lenders) can be stubborn. There are times when they have to remember that borrowers have rights, too.

That brings us to The Case of the Belligerent Bank. I took exceptional delight with this case, because the bank president was one of those heartless souls who laughs when he forecloses. His intended victim was Lou's Lumber Yard, a client of ours who had borrowed $450,000 several years earlier and still owed $300,000 on a long-term low-interest (10 percent) loan. Month after month, my client punctually paid the loan installment. Then disaster struck when Lou's bookkeeper forgot to make a payment within the grace period.

You can visualize the scene. Since he was now loaning funds at 20 percent, the bank president prayed every morning that Lou's check wouldn't arrive in the morning mail. With the note 15 days in arrears, the bank could legally demand payment of the entire $300,000 balance, which is precisely what it did, not even bothering to send a friendly reminder notice. Nope. The form letter said, "Cough up $300,000 or we auction you off on Tuesday."

After I received a frantic phone call from Lou, I met with the bank president to explain my client's honest oversight. No dice! After two hours of pleading and begging him to reinstate the loan (it was then in default by only five days), I had his final verdict: "$300,000 by Tuesday or come and enjoy the auction." Since the first alternative was not possible and the latter unthinkable, we filed for Chapter 11.

After two months of legal maneuvering, the Court forced the bank to accept the overdue installment and reinstate the loan. Then came the fun part. We convinced the Court that the value of the collateral at auction was $180,000. Therefore, a $300,000 loan was excessive. After all, we argued, had the bank foreclosed as they insisted on doing, they would have ended up with only $180,000. Why then should my client have to pay more than $180,000? And that's just how the case ended. Our friend The Belligerent Banker pushed a bit too hard. He not only had to continue waiting for his low interest monthly payments, but his ruthless attitude cost him $120,000.

Can this same strategy work for you? Of course. Many businesses facing foreclosure can save themselves by taking advantage of Chapter 11 protection.

Even if you're not interested in saving a business, Chapter 11 can be a valuable ally. You may want to use it to control the liquidation of the business, protecting whatever stockholder surplus might come your way through an advantageous liquidation.

A case in point: a large developer of single family vacation homes on Cape Cod ran into trouble. His only creditor was the bank that held a two million dollar mortgage. Since the developer simply wanted out of the business, his only concern was to insure that the real estate sold for the best price. If the proceeds exceeded two million dollars, he would be entitled to that surplus. Conversely, if the liquidation brought less than two million, he would be personally liable to the bank for any deficiency.

To the developer's consternation, he discovered that the bank planned to auction all 50 homes in the span of three consecutive days in the dead of a Cape Cod winter. That was no way to get the best price for 50 new vacation homes.

Since the bank wouldn't agree to a rational liquidation plan designed to optimize the proceeds, we filed for Chapter 11, explaining to the Bankruptcy Court that the properties would bring only $1,500,000 if we did it the bank's way. A qualified appraiser/real estate broker confirmed to the Judge that if the same properties were sold through his brokerage office during the summer months, they might bring as much as $2,800,000. The Court agreed with the broker's logical sales plan and turned the property over to him.

In five months, the broker had sold all 50 properties for $2,750,000. After paying the broker a $175,000 commission and the bank $2,100,000 (including accrued interest), the developer walked away with an extra $475,000. Without Chapter 11 to stop a bank's foolish attempt to dump a property at auction, the developer would have owed the bank $500,000. Clearly, the Chapter 11 offered a $1,000,000 cure!

But Will They Settle for Two Cents on the Dollar?

Once you're in Chapter 11, the debts you owe general or unsecured creditors become a mere statistic. What you will eventually pay them will depend on what they would get if the business failed. Your negotiating technique is precisely the same one you saw work in "out-of-court" compositions earlier in this book.

Surrounding you at the negotiating table will be the creditors' committee representing the interests of all general creditors. As with all creditor-debtor situations, they want as much as possible–as soon as possible. You, of course, will bargain for just the opposite.

Consider again the plight of creditors who realize they'll receive nothing if your business fails, because all proceeds will go first to pay secured creditors, legal fees, back wages, and taxes. What might they be willing to accept? Check the records of many companies in Chapter 11, and you'll find that the average dividend (total payment to general creditors) is less than 20 percent. And even in these cases, the 20 percent dividend will probably be paid over 2–4 years.

But, unlike an out-of-court composition agreement, striking a deal with creditors under Chapter 11 represents only the first step toward having it finally approved.

Once the committee accepts your payment proposal, their next step is to recommend it to the other creditors. At that point, the creditors vote. To successfully conclude the Chapter 11, the debtor must obtain approval from creditors holding two-thirds of the debt and representing a simple majority in number. Simply stated, if your business has 100 general creditors whom it owes $100,000, the success of your Chapter 11 will depend on a favorable vote by at least 51 creditors who represent at least $67,000 in debt.

This underscores an important advantage of a Chapter 11 over an out-of-court composition. Under Chapter 11, a payment proposal approved by the requisite majority of creditors becomes binding on all creditors. With the out-of-court composition, any non-assenting creditor can pursue his full claim and destroy the whole process.

With the required creditor votes in hand, you face one further obstacle. The Court must be convinced that what you propose to pay your creditors is both fair and feasible.

What's "fair"? The Court tries to determine that the creditors will obtain at least as much as they would under a liquidating bankruptcy (Chapter 7). Generally it's not difficult to satisfy this criterion objectively.

Is your proposal "feasible"? That's where many Chapter 11's stumble. It's one thing to promise creditors $100,000 in dividends over five years. But can you *prove* that your company will have the profits or cash flow to pay those dividends? Under the "feasibility" test, the Court requires you to take an objective look at your future and the likelihood that your business can flourish sufficiently to honor its obligations.

Realism will make or break any settlement proposal. Too many companies file Chapter 11 to reduce debt to a workable level, then hastily promise creditors future dividends the company has no reasonable hope of paying. This is one reason why two-thirds of the firms that survive a Chapter 11 proceeding ultimately fail a year or two later. The proper goal of a reorganization is not simply to solve a temporary crisis, but to restructure the company for long term survival.

A workable settlement proposal requires intensive involvement by an accountant. It's the accountants, not the lawyers, who navigate the proper deal. Your attorney may play a negotiating role and ascertain that the proposal complies with bankruptcy guidelines. However, your accountant must determine your acceptable debt level and your firm's ability to honor the payment schedule. What role do *you* play? In most cases, the owner provides the accountant managerial insight into possible operational changes and their impact on future profits.

Striking a workable deal with your creditors under a Chapter 11 isn't easy. You encounter the same problems in "selling" a 10-cents-on-the-dollar proposal under a reorganization as in an out-of-court composition. And you'll meet the same resistance.

Time and again, I have seen creditors reject a 50 percent settlement proposal, then helplessly watch as the company is liquidated, winning them nothing. It becomes more than a matter of numbers. You're dealing with people. And handling people requires your utmost creativity.

If you can obtain creditor support for your proposal, the Court will generally adopt a passive role and approve the plan. Conversely, if the creditors do not approve the plan, you have little hope for approval. Without creditor approval, the Court has no choice but to turn your Chapter 11 into a "straight" bankruptcy and order the liquidation of the business. Sadly, many companies can't do enough to satisfy creditors.

Remember the cynic, moralist and other creditor types that you met in Chapter 6 when we discussed out-of-court settlements? They're the same crowd you'll meet on the creditors' committee under a Chapter 11. And that's what creates vulnerability for the Chapter 11 company.

Creditors may not always see things your way.

Every bankruptcy attorney has his horror stories of illogical creditors' committees rejecting logical plans of arrangement. I have plenty of my own.

Creditors of a hobby store chain turned down a 50 percent settlement offer, only to have the company liquidated and end up with 6 percent. Why? They refused to believe that the assets could bring so little at auction, foolishly figuring the assets would sell at their cost.

Personalities play a role. Sometimes they just don't like the owner. Letting their personal prejudices stand in the way of objectivity may nullify their value as a representative of *all* the creditors, but it happens.

Even with creditor committee approval, you may need an aggressive sales campaign to obtain the other necessary votes.

Chapter 11 cases always represent a challenge, because you never know what it will take to persuade your creditors until you start the negotiation process. Under Chapter 11, I have handled cases where a proposal was formulated and accepted in one meeting and others that required up to twenty meetings over two years.

My easiest case involved a small liquor retailer who owed suppliers $80,000. The attorney for the creditors' committee was an old friend and colleague who worked on many bankruptcy cases with me over the years, so I simply forwarded my client's financial statements to him early in the week and in preparation for the first creditors' committee meeting, gave him a phone call. After the usual small talk, he asked, "What kind of a plan do you see?" Now, experienced bankruptcy lawyers can glance at a debtor's financial statements and reasonably predict where the case should end up. I answered, "Henry, it looks like a 25 percent plan, payable over two years." (The creditors would receive $20,000 in full settlement payable over two years.) Henry responded, "I agree, but when you come in, let's fight a little first."

Fight we did. I pounded the table and adamantly insisted my client couldn't afford to pay more than a 15 percent dividend, payable over three years. With equal vigor, Henry threatened that unless they could receive at least 35 percent payable in the first year, the creditors would rather receive nothing and see the business liquidated. Back and forth we argued. I went up to 20 percent—he came down to 30 percent. After two hours, we happily met at 25 percent payable over two years.

My client thought I did a hell of a job working Henry down from 35 percent. Henry, on the other hand, looked like a tough negotiator as he "fought" for his client. A charade? Not really. In people-handling situations, psychology and attitude often outweigh common sense. Both parties like to feel they "negotiated."

Small cases (liabilities of less than $150–200,000) require quick resolution, because it's difficult to justify countless hours of professional or creditors' committee time negotiating a few percentage points.

But then there are the complex cases. A large corporation may go through endless meetings involving an analysis of the business, examination of books, and other investigative work before the creditors are prepared even to discuss settlement. The debtor's accountants may spend many hours with the creditors' accounting firm (creditors' committees have their own counsel, and oftentimes their own accountants—however, the debtor pays their fee). Unlike my liquor store client, Braniff Airlines may run up several million dollars in professional fees before one word is said about an agreement with creditors.

Each case presents its unique financial considerations, complexities, and politics. As one veteran bankruptcy lawyer puts it, "Creditors are not an ornery lot. They want only as much money as they can get their hands on. Unfortunately, that's seldom more than a dime on the dollar."

Cancelling Costly Contracts

So far you have seen that a Chapter 11 can:

1. Put your secured creditors on hold and even allow you to reinstate loans and reduce excessive secured debt.
2. Whittle your unsecured debt down to manageable size—and allow you to pay that reduced debt over time.

But you may have another problem. Al had leased equipment that drained $35,000 in future profits. Under his Chapter 11, he terminated the lease, escaping liability for future rent payments. Cancellation of the lease was critical for Al's future success.

Under Chapter 11, a troubled business can "reject" or cancel any lease or contract that the Court agrees is burdensome or detrimental to its financial rehabilitation. This remedy can offer one of the most important advantages of a Chapter 11, for without it, many companies could not restore the profitability so vital to a successful reorganization.

Take the case of Mammoth Mart, a large discount chain with numerous shopping center locations throughout New England. Almost half of these locations were unprofitable. If Mammoth Mart had tried to cancel these long term leases, landlord claims would be staggering, but under its Chapter 11, Mammoth Mart could decide which leases were unprofitable and cancel them. They could then reduce operations to winning locations.

Fast growth chains too frequently seek shelter under Chapter 11. Such companies may start with two or three profitable stores, and then they expand too rapidly to fifty stores. If they expanded with excessive trade credit, they'll find themselves leveraged to the hilt with accounts payable or bank financing, and they can afford few mistakes. But some of the fifty locations will inevitably turn into mistakes. Then Chapter 11 allows the company to reverse the process by cutting both debt and locations back to a solvent and profitable operation.

You may not own a high-flying chain. But you still might have the same type problem, on an appreciably smaller scale. Watch how it worked for Regal Men's Store. In business for thirty years, Regal displayed a solid financial history operating in a downtown store block. Then they made a near fatal mistake by relocating to a 6000 sq. ft. space in a suburban shopping center. Business got so bad, losses exceeded sales. The owners desperately tried to find a new tenant to "buy-out" their lease with a cash settlement to the landlord, but without success. Finally, Regal had only three options: 1) stay at the location and face inevitable bankruptcy, 2) move—and continue to pay the excessive rent which also would have destroyed the company financially, or 3) file a Chapter 11 and reject the lease.

Three days after filing Chapter 11, Regal moved back to its old location and cancelled its shopping center lease. Regal agreed to pay the shopping center developer a small dividend as a general creditor entitled to damages for breach of lease, but, as usual, the allowable claim on a rejected contract is small.

It can also work in reverse. Two years ago, I handled a Chapter 11 for a corporation that owned only one asset—an old railroad depot leased to a tenant who operated a restaurant. My client's mistake was in leasing the property for ten years at a straight annual rental of $12,000. Not only was this rental far below the value of the space, but the $12,000 didn't even cover mortgage payments on the property. When the mortgage fell several months behind, the bank initiated foreclosure, but Chapter 11 stopped the foreclosure, giving us the right to terminate the disadvantageous lease. Faced with an eviction, the tenant agreed to a new $22,000 a year lease. With the new lease in hand, the Court allowed my client to cure the mortgage default by bringing the payments current. Today, the depot generates an $11,000 rental profit, which never could have happened without Chapter 11.

Leases represent only one type of contract you can terminate under Chapter 11. You can do the same with any type agreement or contract.

Deciding to concentrate instead on leisure wear, a clothing wholesaler cancelled an order for 20,000 winter coats it agreed to purchase from a manufacturer.

An electronics firm rejected and terminated twelve costly employment contracts with its executive staff, saving over $100,000 in salaries.

An importer choosing to confine itself to mail order promotions used Chapter 11 to escape contracts with over 100 sales representatives.

An ambulance service regained profitability by cancelling unprofitable contracts with three towns—and then cancelled the leases on six ambulances used to service those towns.

Since Chapter 11 usually comes on the heels of recent losses, it's not surprising that most firms radically alter their corporate size, methods of distribution, product lines, overheads, marketing arrangements and even locations. Cancelling contracts is only part of the metamorphosis.

Shrinking Assets Can Bring Powerful Profits

Mammoth Mart shrunk to half its size and as they tell it, dramatically increased profits. Penn Central dumped millions of dollars in assets, ranging from real estate to rail lines. The expendable assets helped cut losses and created an avalanche of money to be strategically used in settling creditor claims and rehabilitating what was left of the conglomerate. Braniff Airlines reportedly (as of this writing) plans to sell off many planes and valuable air routes. They all have the same idea, to go from a money-losing monster to a money-making midget.

On a more modest scale, Carter Electrical Supply did the same. It owned three locations, but only one made money. But it couldn't close up and sell the assets of the two losing locations without the help of the Bankruptcy Court. Here's why:

Carter owed the bank $300,000 and the bank held a mortgage on all the assets of the company. Carter's owner wanted to liquidate the assets of the two unprofitable stores and figured that it would raise $100–150,000, even though the assets had a replacement value far in excess of that. Without the Chapter 11, Carter would need the bank's permission to sell, since they held the mortgage on it. Even without a mortgage, Carter would need the approval of its general creditors before it could sell the inventory out of "the ordinary course of business."

The surgery was too radical. Carter needed the Bankruptcy Court to approve the sale, decide the application of proceeds between the bank and general creditors, and see to it that everyone was treated fairly. Convinced that the assets would bring only $100,000 at auction, the Court allowed a sale at $150,000 with the bank receiving $100,000 to apply to the mortgage and $50,000 to Carter for use as badly needed working capital.

You may decide that profitability can come to your firm only by undergoing the same transformation.

Consider all your assets. Are they all profitable? Can any of the excess non-productive assets be turned into cash or used to reduce burdensome debt?

Read the auction pages of your Sunday newspaper. You'll find many Chapter 11 firms auctioning costly or excess real estate, inventory, fixtures and vehicles. No, they're not going out of business. Just the opposite is happening. They're fighting to stay in business by becoming mean and lean. Cutting costly fat from your operation can be the key to renewed profitability under a reorganization. Chapter 11 can be a marvelous diet plan.

How the Bankruptcy Court Can Help You Get Credit

This may surprise you, but most firms have an easier time obtaining credit once they're in Chapter 11 than before. In fact, many companies decide to use Chapter 11 to help open their credit lifeline.

Here's the reason: creditors know which accounts are having financial trouble. Rumors spread quickly; your financial statements point toward bankruptcy. Seldom will an existing creditor extend further credit to a troubled business. Why should they risk losing even more? Your creditors and suppliers will reason that whatever further credit they extend today may turn into a 5 or 10 percent dividend payment two or three years from now.

Put yourself in your unsecured creditor's position. If you fail or file for Chapter 11, he'll stand near the end of the line in getting paid. He also knows that if you do file Chapter 11, he cannot recover the pre-filing debt but will have to settle for a few cents on the dollar.

Debt incurred *after* you file the Chapter 11 presents another story. Suppliers extending you credit after you file sit in a considerably more comfortable position because:

1. Their bills can be paid as they fall due. In fact, the Bankruptcy Court will supervise the debtor to insure that you pay these bills.
2. Debts incurred after the filing are not discharged through the debtor's proposed settlement plan. Post-filing debts remain fully payable.
3. Should your business fail, post-filing creditors receive payment *before* general creditors holding pre-filing debt.

The case of Midland Foods, a large superette grossing $1,000,000 a year, offers some insight. After several years of operating losses, the business had $80,000 in tangible assets against $160,000 in liabilities. Seeing it in deep trouble, creditors shut off further credit. This in turn created a financial crisis, forcing Midland to 1) pay for all new merchandise C.O.D., and 2) continue to retire old payables.

Chapter 11 allowed Midland to:

1. Freeze the old debt and settle it for a fraction on the dollar.
2. Obtain new credit.

We asked the creditors to extend two-week credit terms on new purchases, producing a maximum credit level of about $30,000. How could the creditors lose? They would get $30,000 every two weeks, and even in the worst case, the failure of Midland, the $30,000 debt would win priority status and would be one of the first obligations paid. We established that the liquidation value of the assets could generate sufficient cash to cover other priority claims—and the $30,000. It was a "no lose" proposition for the creditors.

We accomplished even more, however. By extending new credit, Midland would have a better chance to survive their Chapter 11. If Midland succeeded, creditors would obtain a greater percentage on the $160,000 in old bills, while still earning profits on future sales.

If you walk into many troubled stores before they file Chapter 11, you'll see empty shelves, but several weeks later, you'll find a reasonable merchandise level.

Trade credit is only one possibility under a Chapter 11. With the assistance of the Bankruptcy Court, you may even be able to line up new bank financing.

As part of the rehabilitative process, a Court is likely to allow a debtor to obtain working capital by pledging assets. Lenders will be interested, provided the pledged assets contain sufficient collateral value.

Had Midland's creditors objected to extending further credit, we could have applied to a bank for a $30,000 loan, securing it with a mortgage on all its assets. Few banks would refuse the loan, provided they were certain they could recoup the $30,000 if Midland failed.

An interesting feature of a Chapter 11 allows the troubled business to issue new stock to raise capital, by-passing most of the registration requirements of the SEC. Of course, this will only help larger, publicly traded corporations which determine what equity capital (stockholder investment) can satisfy the financial demands of the company.

You cannot rehabilitate a company with empty shelves. A Chapter 11 can get you the needed credit or capital to keep them stocked with profitable merchandise.

Many distressed businesses by-pass the quest for new credit even when it is available. With adequate inventory levels, they continue to operate quite well, even on a C.O.D. basis.

As one owner of a Chapter 11 supermarket states, "Credit is what got me into trouble in the first place. I voluntarily went C.O.D. when I filed Chapter 11. It gave me better cash and inventory control, but it took discipline. Once I was in Chapter 11, I had no less than twelve potential suppliers trying to win my account by offering me credit. Before the Chapter 11, they wouldn't even talk to me."

The One Essential Ingredient

If you can't predict future profitability, don't waste your time with Chapter 11. Without profits, you'll just delay the inevitable.

Be realistic. A Chapter 11 can rid your company of the problems created by past losses or managerial blunders. But if you're going to repeat the same old mistakes, your company doesn't deserve to survive. You'd be better off punching a clock for your Uncle Joe. I see it all the time. Business after business seeks refuge in the Bankruptcy Court to restore solvency, but never seems concerned with profitability. It's little wonder that 70 percent of all businesses that emerge successfully from a Chapter 11 close their doors for good a year or two later.

Our firm recently represented a small pharmacy with a healthy history until a giant chain discount drugstore opened down the street. Sales plummeted 50 percent, and the owner lost $70,000 before filing under Chapter 11 two years later. I asked the owner what he expected to accomplish under Chapter 11. He said, "I want to knock down my liabilities and get my creditors off my back!" Of course, he was right— but only temporarily. Even without debt, he would have continued to lose money to his aggressive competitor. Eventually, those losses would have destroyed solvency. The only way he could save his business was to use the Chapter 11 not only to reduce debt but to cancel his lease and move the business to a location where he would have a fighting chance.

Unfortunately, he didn't see it that way. He never really thought about profits. Predictably, he ended up losing his business and now works as a staff pharmacist for his chain competitor.

What about you? In this chapter, you have seen what a Chapter 11 can do to help save your business. But notice the word "help." The Bankruptcy Court can only supply some tools to make your business profitable. You attorney can battle the creditors and guide you through the technicalities. Your accountant can skillfully navigate the numbers. But it's up to you to take a hard look at your operation and decide how your insolvent, losing enterprise can turn into a money-maker. Only then should you feed your sick business that strong medicine.

Can Chapter 11 Help You?

Take this six-part test:

1. Do you have excess debts that cannot be compromised by out-of-court settlement?
2. Are secured debts (mortgages) in default and facing possible foreclosure?
3. Does your business have unprofitable leases or contracts it must cancel to restore profitability?
4. Do you have excess assets or business locations that must be liquidated to raise cash and avoid further losses?
5. Does your business suffer from lack of credit due to its poor financial condition?
6. If the above problems can be solved—do you have the master plan to turn your company into a profitable enterprise?

Those are the questions you must consider. Chapter 11 can provide the answer.

Business As Usual: Starting Over Free and Clear

9

No law school teaches it. No bar journal discusses it. No business text mentions it. Yet each year, 300,000 businessmen allow their troubled business to fail and then buy back the assets for pennies on the dollar and start up all over again.

I call it the "dump-buy-back." The "dump" is a liquidation under an insolvency procedure. The "buy-back" simply means you set up a new corporation and have it bid to buy the assets of your old defunct company. The end result? You operate the same business at the same location with the same assets, but without the debt that caused you sleepless nights. Sound tempting?

It did to Walter. When his cosmetic distributorship went bust, he quickly paid 20 cents on the dollar to buy back all its assets. Today, Walter earns over $100,000 a year from his once-troubled firm.

Sylvia liked the idea too. Her clothing store wallowed under $300,000 in trade debt. Before long she was sick and tired of hassling with the creditors, so she threw in the towel. A week after her store went into receivership, she re-acquired its assets through a new corporation, paying only $18,000 for inventory with a wholesale value of $90,000.

Carl did it without spending a dime in the process. His furniture store owed the bank $80,000 and other trade creditors $250,000. After the bank foreclosed, Carl's corporation bought $150,000 in merchandise and fixtures for the $80,000 owed the bank, and the bank financed the entire $80,000 by simply switching the note to the new corporation. It wasn't complicated, but it did save Carl $250,000 in trade debt.

Can you do the same thing? Probably. In fact, it may be the easiest way to regain instant solvency.

Why Starting Over May Be Your Best Bet

If your firm has overwhelming debts, you have a few options. You can try an out-of-court composition or arrangement with your creditors as discussed in Chapters 6 and 7; but this requires creditor cooperation. The Chapter 11 reorganization described in Chapter 8 also requires creditor assent. Furthermore, a Chapter 11 can run up expensive legal fees, court costs and involve considerable red tape.

Large corporations, due to their complexity, diverse stockholder interest and visibility are usually limited to solving their financial problems through Chapter 11. However, the small enterprise, particularly the sole proprietorship or the closely held corporation, may find starting over a more practical solution.

Starting over offers these advantages:

1. You end up with little or no liabilities. Under a composition or Chapter 11, you still have the reduced creditor claims to contend with.
2. It is simpler and less expensive than a Chapter 11. In most cases, you can accomplish your objective with no more formality than attending an auction and negotiating terms. A Chapter 11, on the other hand, can cost $10–25,000 in legal fees, which may be prohibitive to a small firm.
3. Starting over is faster. You can be back in business in a matter of days, while your Chapter 11 could drag on for months.
4. You enjoy more control. A Chapter 11 puts your assets under the direct supervision of the Court and your creditors. If the Chapter 11 fails, you may lose control over the disposition of the assets.
5. In many instances, you can start over with little or no cash of your own.

Let me illustrate these advantages. One of my earliest cases involved a small health club that owned $10–15,000 worth of equipment on which it owed $6,000. In addition to its other small creditors, it was being sued for $100,000 by an old landlord who claimed the health club had breached its lease when it moved out. My client, Bill, claimed the landlord hadn't maintained or properly repaired the premises, but I thought the landlord had the stronger case and would eventually win. Regardless of who was right, it would cost my client $10–15,000 to fight the case. The legal fees alone could ruin his company. The practical solution? Bill liquidated his health club. The supply company holding a mortgage on the assets sent the equipment to auction. After Bill set up a new corporation, he entered the highest bid at $6,000, exactly what he owed the supply company, which readily agreed to finance the $6,000 purchase price. In reality, Bill asked the supply company only to swap the debt from the old corporation to the new corporation. Then Bill signed a new lease with his present landlord and was back in business without missing a beat. Total cost? $500 in auction costs and $300 in legal fees. His old landlord eventually won a default judgement against the original corporation, but he could more easily have squeezed blood out of a stone than money out of a corporation with no assets.

Under a Chapter 11, Bill would have had to litigate the landlord's claim. If the landlord won, Bill would have had to negotiate a settlement under Chapter 11. Legal fees of $10–20,000 coupled with a 10 percent settlement on the $100,000 would have cost my client $20–30,000. Clearly unreasonable for a business with assets of only $15,000.

Starting over isn't just for the nickel and dime operation, however. It may not save Chrysler, but it can work wonders for a business grossing even millions of dollars a year.

I remember a wall-covering manufacturing concern with annual sales of $3,000,000 and $1,000,000 in liabilities. ABC Wall Systems owed a local bank $150,000 on a first mortgage and the SBA $500,000 on a second mortgage. Other debts amounted to $350,000. The company owned manufacturing equipment that would be difficult to remove and had limited value on the open market. Inventory consisted mostly of goods in process, and since a buyer would have to complete the manufacturing process to obtain a saleable product, even the inventory had an exceptionally low auction value.

ABC consulted me about a Chapter 11. I might have reduced the SBA loan from $500,000 to $250,000 under a Chapter 11, and I might have whittled the general creditors down from $350,000 to $50,000. But my client would still owe $450,000, including the bank mortgage. Admittedly, Chapter 11 would give my client a fighting chance, but I thought we could do better by starting over, so we called in several auctioneers who verified that the assets would bring $100–150,000 at auction. I reasoned that ABC could be back in business without any debt if it could find $150,000.

That's when we approached the landlord, who sat in a dangerous position. If ABC failed, the landlord would lose a tenant who paid over $50,000 a year in rent. Who else would move into a "special use" building suitable only for a wall covering factory? The practical landlord agreed to finance my client's new corporation, XYZ Wall Systems, up to $150,000 on a secured, 22 percent interest note.

Two weeks later, the bank foreclosed (after we mailed them the keys) and auctioned the assets. XYZ ended up the high bidder at $115,000.

Look at the scorecard:

- XYZ was in business with ABC's assets, but owed only $115,000 on a long term debt.
- The landlord is collecting 22 percent on an adequately secured note and has a healthy tenant.
- The creditors? Well, a game can have only one winner.

Even when a Chapter 11 can bring about the same financial result, many business owners prefer to simply start over. A Chapter 11 can be a long and laborious process with endless court hearings and creditor negotiations. Psychologically drained from battle with creditors, few business owners relish the idea of continuing the battle in the Bankruptcy Court.

Always consider psychology. Every bankruptcy lawyer spends as much time assessing the emotional stamina of his client as he does the financial problems of the business. It makes no sense to put a client into a Chapter 11 if he's not emotionally strong enough to survive. However, that same client may be a perfect candidate for the "dump-buy-back."

I learned that lesson years ago, but the tuition was expensive—it cost my client his business. Stan owned a large gift shop that ran into the usual problems of undercapitalization and over-expansion. With a bank mortgage of $50,000 and trade debt of $90,000, Stan's business was sinking. I opted for the traditional business-saving remedy of a Chapter 11, believing we could reduce the trade debt to $15–20,000. I may have been right—but I'll never know. Stan couldn't handle it. He refused to face his creditors at a creditors' meeting, and the thought of walking into the Bankruptcy Court terrified him. Fearing a nervous breakdown, his wife forced him to quit and go back to his old job as a night watchman. He considered himself a failure, but in reality, it was my fault–not Stan's. One didn't have to take a residency in psychiatry at the Mayo Clinic to analyze Stan. He was 185 pounds of walking trauma when he dragged himself into my office. How could I expect him to stand beside me and exchange shots with his creditors?

If Stan hired me today, I'd tell the bank to foreclose. Then we'd show up at the auction and buy back his business for $20–30,000, or even the $50,000 owed the bank. Before Stan knew it, he would be back in business.

To many business owners, Chapter 11's, compositions, and other internal reorganizations spell "death on the installment plan." For a new lease on life, many of these same owners could avoid complications by simply starting over.

The Master Strategy

Keeping the assets without the liabilities always involves two steps:

1. Liquidate the business.
2. Buy back the assets for a fraction of their real value.

Sound simple? It is, if you know the "dump-buy-back" strategy:

Step 1: Liquidating the Business

You can liquidate a financially troubled business several ways. Consider your options:

1. If a creditor holds a mortgage on the assets of the business, you can simply advise him that you don't want to continue the business, thereby surrendering the collateral to him for foreclosure and subsequent sale.
2. Or you can make an Assignment for the Benefit of Creditors. Most states have passed laws that allow a debtor to assign or transfer assets to a representative of the creditors—the assignee—who then has the duty to liquidate the assets into cash, paying the proceeds to the creditors in order of priority. Generally, an assignment does not involve court proceedings. As a practical matter, most assignees are counsel to one or more creditors or independent counsels experienced in insolvency proceedings.
3. In some states, a court appointed receiver liquidates the distressed business. A debtor may have the right to petition a state court to appoint a liquidating receiver, but more frequently the receiver is appointed by a creditors' petition. Once appointed, the receiver sells the assets and distributes the proceeds just as an assignee would.
4. Finally, you might file for a "straight" or liquidatng (Chapter 7) bankruptcy, asking the Court to appoint a trustee to liquidate the business. This is the least desirable alternative, because the trustee usually has to plow through a cumbersome process to sell the assets, thus delaying the liquidation and, more importantly, the buy-back process. Such a delay can be detrimental to the continuity and good will of your business. You want the fastest possible liquidation, and a formal bankruptcy is usually the slowest.

After the first step, your business will be closed and in the hands of a secured creditor, assignee, receiver or bankruptcy trustee. Regardless of his title, we can call him the "liquidator," because he'll sell your assets as quickly as possible for the best price possible.

Step 2. Buying Back the Assets

A liquidator must sell or dispose of the assets in a commercially reasonable manner by public auction or private sale.

Of course, under a distress sale your assets will never bring more than a small fraction of their wholesale value or cost. Unless you've attended public auctions, you have little idea how small that fraction can be.

- A hardware store loaded with $100,000 in merchandise brought only $22,000 at public auction.
- A completely refurbished dry cleaning plant with $80,000 in new equipment saw its auctioneer accept a high bid of a mere $12,000.
- A restaurant grossing $800,000 a year sold its equipment under the hammer for $16,000.
- A tobacco shop with $70,000 in cigarettes and tobacco yielded only $28,000.
- A garment factory with $60,000 in equipment and raw materials barely attracted a bidder for $7,000.

It's not what you paid for your assets that counts but what someone else will pay under the auctioneer's hammer. And when you're trying to buy back your own assets, you have a distinct advantage over other bidders. As prior owner of the business, you can afford to pay a little more to start over again. You aren't looking at your assets as odd lots of merchandise to be trucked off to another location. You see them as the nucleus of a "going" business that has only been temporarily interrupted.

How high will you have to bid? That depends on many factors. Geography can be a factor. There are many more potential buyers in a metropolitan area, and such increased competition can escalate the price over what it might fetch in a rural area. The nature of the assets can govern the price. Fast moving merchandise such as cigarettes, crated foods, liquor, and certain types of clothing can yield a relatively high price. Conversely, manufacturing equipment, raw material, giftware and sundry merchandise, houseware and soft goods can sell for a depressed 10–15 cents on the dollar. The condition of the merchandise will dictate price, the mix of fast moving to slow moving inventory will play a role, and even weather conditions can control who will show up and what they're likely to bid. Demand is always a factor. I recently liquidated a printing plant's $14,000 worth of equipment for $2,000 because Boston had been hit with a glut of printing plant bankruptcies, and those that remained in business had their earlier pick of equipment.

You can obtain a fair idea of what your assets will bring by inviting a business auctioneer to give you an estimate even before you liquidate. Experienced auctioneers can predict auction values with reasonable accuracy. By obtaining a liquidation appraisal, you'll get an idea of what it will take to buy back your assets. That's an important step in your master plan. Avoid surprises.

You may even be able to buy back your assets, free and clear of liabilities, without a public auction. A liquidator can sell the assets at private sale if the price is fair to the creditors, a fair price being anything more than the creditors would receive if the assets were auctioned.

Our firm liquidates many insolvent businesses. Once the business is turned over to us, we call in an auctioneer to appraise its auction value. Oftentimes, a buyer will show up before the auction and offer more than the estimate. If so, we'd be foolish not to conduct a private sale.

Suppose a retail business faces liquidation under an insolvency proceeding, and an auctioner predicts its assets will bring $20,000 under the hammer. Along comes Buyer B, offering $24,000 under a private sale without an auctioneer. Are the creditors cheated? Of course not. The private sale will net them $4,000 more. In fact, they may come out $7–8,000 ahead because auction fees may run $3–4,000.

Few liquidators will object to a private sale—as long as they're convinced the private sale is in the creditors' best interests.

To avoid even the hint of impropriety, some liquidators will refuse to sell privately to a new corporation owned by the principal of the distressed business. That position is understandable. But many conclude that they have one obligation, to convert the assets into as much money as possible. If the prior owner has the deepest pocket, why shouldn't he be allowed to buy them back?

Though tangible assets such as inventory and equipment can be easily appraised and sold, accounts receivable present other problems. Should you repurchase your accounts receivable? If so, what's a fair price?

Many business owners repurchasing their prior assets want to buy their accounts receivable for two good reasons:

1. Customers may not be aware that the original corporation failed because they continue paying the same principals of the new corporation. This can be an important factor in maintaining good will for the successor corporation.
2. You can make a substantial profit buying back your own receivables if you can buy them for pennies on the dollar and then collect the dollar.

When C & B Distributing Company failed, its owners set up D & A Corporation and bought all the tangible assets for $60,000. However, C & B had $70,000 in good accounts receivable on the books. After some dickering with the liquidator, D & A agreed to buy the receivables for 50 cents on the dollar, or $35,000.

Everybody won. The new corporation ultimately collected over $62,000 on the receivables they purchased for $35,000, giving them a $27,000 profit. Besides, these receivables represented customers for their new corporation. Because the billing procedure remained the same, the customers weren't even aware that anything had happened to C & B. It was business as usual.

Why would the liquidator be willing to sell $70,000 in receivables for only $35,000? Liquidators know that people who owe a business money will do everything possible to avoid payment once they know a liquidator will try to collect it. Many accounts may speculate that the liquidator won't bother chasing them, or won't be able to prove the validity of the debt once in court. It happens all the time. One account says it never received the goods, another pulls the "defective" goods ploy, and others claim they paid the debt long ago. Even an aggressive liquidator (and the adjective seldom applies) may be lucky to pull in $25,000 on $70,000 in receivables. Suddenly $35,000 looks good.

You may not want the receivables, in which case you can confine your bid to only the assets you do want. That's another advantage of starting over. It gives you the opportunity to get your hands on assets your successor company needs, leaving the excess behind.

Picking Up the Pieces for Pennies

Sure you want your business back—but you want it as inexpensively as possible. To accomplish that objective, make certain you control the one item that really counts—the lease.

The strategy is simple. If another buyer can obtain the lease on your location, the value of the assets will be greatly increased because he can step in and take over a going operation. Since you are trying to do precisely that, you don't want any competition. However, if you control the lease, the liquidator will have no alternative but to sell the assets to a competing bidder on the condition that he remove them from the premises. The only way the liquidator can sell your assets as a "going" business is to sell them to you. I have seen many businesses sell for 80–90 cents on the dollar because the buyer was purchasing a going business. If the same assets had to be removed, the liquidator would have ended up with 10–20 cents on the dollar.

Put yourself in the shoes of the Sew-land Fabric Stores. Burdened with $160,000 in liabilities, Sew-land decided to start fresh, so they made an Assignment for the Benefit of Creditors, hoping to buy back their $100,000 in assets through a new corporation for perhaps $20–30,000. But they were smart. A few days before they made the assignment, their new corporation signed a brand new lease with the landlord. With the location locked up, the assignee could only inform prospective bidders that they would have to remove the assets. On a "removal" basis, the best offer was $15–20,000. The owners of Sew-land knew that many buyers would gladly pay $60–70,000 for the assets, provided they could take over the store and capitalize on its great location and $600,000 in annual sales. With the location tied up, the prior owners had the winning edge and succeeded by bidding a mere $22,000.

If your location has value, make certain you control it.

Finding Cash to Make It Happen

By now you're probably wondering how to find the money to buy back your business. Here's the good news. Almost anyone can buy a fresh start without any cash changing hands.

The O'Day brothers did it with a quick shuffle of papers. Their large mattress and bedding store had a mortgage for $50,000 and owed merchandise suppliers another $90,000. Crippled with this debt, the O'Days allowed a receiver to be appointed to liquidate their slumber shop. But the O'Days were wide awake. The next day, they set up a new corporation and quickly signed a lease for the same location. Now it was only a matter of finding the cash to buy back the inventory from the receiver.

It didn't take the receiver long to realize that the inventory would bring only $30–40,000 at auction. Since the bank held a $50,000 mortgage, it would be entitled to all proceeds up to $50,000 before other creditors saw a dime. But even the bank would wind up $10–20,000 short if the auction yielded only $30–40,000. Armed with this information, the O'Days asked the bank to loan their new corporation $50,000 to buy back the assets. Why not? It was only a paper transaction. Instead of the old corporation owing $50,000, the new corporation would owe it. Besides, with a healthy company owing the money, the bank stood a better chance of ultimately receiving the entire $50,000. The bank readily agreed.

At the auction, a competitor bid $32,000, but the O'Days generously upped the bid to $50,000—all financed by the bank. Back to business as usual!

Existing mortgage holders oftentimes agree to finance the repurchase of a troubled business. It's not philanthropy, only good business. Mortgage holders know that the liquidation of your troubled business may not cover what you owe them. By re-writing the mortgage to your new corporation, they at least have a fighting chance.

Mildred S. knew how to have her cake and eat it too. Her bakery owed a bank over $90,000, unsecured creditors another $60,000. The bankruptcy trustee figured the assets would bring only $20–30,000, which would all go to the bank. But Mildred knew how to handle the situation. She confidently went to the bank and apologized for what was certain to result in a substantial loss to them. What could the bank do but sorrowfully accept the $20–30,000 and write off the balance?

Mildred proposed a better idea. Walking into the bank president's office, she said, "If you'll re-write $45,000 of the loan to my new corporation, I'll use it to buy back my assets. That way you'll get at least $45,000 instead of $20–30,000. Of course you'll have to drop the interest a few points and extend the loan payments so I can meet my obligations." What could the president do but agree? They were coming out at least $15,000 ahead.

Beware. If you fund your re-purchase with a secured loan, be sure to limit the debt to what your business can realistically pay. It makes no sense to re-write a $100,000 loan on assets worth $30,000.

Liquidators can also finance the purchase. There's no law against it. A liquidator may find that the assets will bring $30,000 on a cash basis. But what if you offered him a premium price to finance it for you? As a liquidator faced with this situation, I would propose a nominal down payment (possibly 20 percent) on a total purchase price of $40,000. It may cost you 20–25 percent to convince me to by-pass the cash buyers, but it's worth it to you because those few extra dollars can mean the difference between being back in business or punching someone else's time clock. The liquidator can justify your plan to creditors because it will put more money in their pockets.

Don't be shy. It's only business. More often than not, liquidators will go along with a sensible financing arrangement, if you can prove the creditors will come out ahead. Even if you have to tap your personal finances for the money, this can be a shrewd investment.

Last year, we represented a discount health and beauty aid store that was about to go "belly-up" with over $150,000 in unsecured debt. Under Chapter 11 I may have been able to reduce the debt to $40,000. However, I estimated that the same assets would bring only $15–20,000 under auction. Clearly, the smarter move was to have the owner let the assets go to auction and spend $20,000 now rather than $40,000 later.

Financing a distressed business "buy-back" seldom requires the resources needed to buy a viable company. "After all," as one auctioneer aptly states it, "you're only paying a dime on the dollar."

Business as Usual at the Same Old Stand

On Monday morning, Kevin Andrews operated Andrews' Construction Corporation. On Thursday morning, all the assets of Andrews' Construction Corporation were in the hands of Kevin's Building Company. In the span of three days, he sunk his construction company and its $180,000 debt, and then he picked up the assets from a Court-appointed liquidator for only $16,000.

It's like the rise of the Phoenix from its own ashes, or as one veteran of the "dump-buy-back" puts it, "If it's not a resurrection, it's certainly a reincarnation."

But what has changed other than the fact that Kevin now enjoys a new debt-free corporation? Unfortunately, very little. As with a Chapter 11, a "dump-buy-back" won't make you profitable. It will only give you the chance to clear up your balance sheet and make the business profitable.

Credit problems? They won't go away simply because your old debt-ridden corporation vanished and you suddenly own a debt-free new one. But a healthy company can more effectively negotiate a reasonable credit line. After all, you now have a healthy balance sheet to show prospective creditors. Equally important, you won't have to waste valuable cash flow on old bills. Since you are starting clean, you should be able to stay current.

Ex-creditors may even extend credit to your new enterprise, despite the beating they took from your old corporation. Many businessmen have approached their prior creditors, explained what happened and why, then talked the old creditor into being a creditor to the new corporation. If he declines credit, he'll lose you as a customer. Then again, he may decide to throw you out his fourth floor window. That almost happened to Warren, whose Garment Company burned a fabric supplier for $60,000. Three weeks later, Warren asked the same supplier for $50,000 in credit for his newly-born ABC Garment Company. Some creditors have no sense of humor. Remember psychology.

Luckily, most customers rarely detect the game you have just played and you can keep business interruption to an absolute minimum, even using the same name and telephone number.

Ray White decided to start again by picking up the pieces of his Wholesale Auto Parts firm. How would customers react to a new company (albeit, Ray White's) suddenly appearing to service their accounts?

It didn't prove to be a problem. His attorney negotiated with the bankruptcy trustee to buy not only the inventory and equipment, but the rights to the name and telephone number as well.

His new corporation simply assumed the trade name of his old, and with the continuity of telephone service, his customers never knew the difference. Remember this important point. If you intend to continue using your old company name, and if your telephone number has value—then insist that the liquidator sell them to you as part of the deal. After all, these represent assets of your old corporation. Without their inclusion in the bill of sale, you have no rights to them. Usually, you can buy them for a nominal price, even though they may be the most important assets of all.

I recall a case in which the telephone number constituted the *only* asset worth buying, a burglar alarm company with a full page ad in the telephone directory. Even during the bankruptcy proceeding, the company's phone kept ringing off the hook with profitable service calls. when the owners of the alarm company formed a new corporation, they talked the bankruptcy trustee into selling them the telephone number for $3,500. It was a smart move. In its first year, telephone sales accounted for 70 percent of the new corporation's sales.

In other cases, the telephone number represents more of a liability than an asset. Ask anyone who has bought his or her own business back. It's not easy to explain to creditors that no—you're no longer XYZ Amalgamated, the deadbeat company that owes him $12,000. Now you're ABC Consolidated, which owes him nothing. The silence can be deadly.

Harvard, Yale, and Jail

Does my advice sound illegal? Rest assured, it's not. Smart, legitimate business people resort to these methods every day. It's the American Way. Not only do you have a right to fail, you also have a right to try and try again.

The same people who criticize the "dump-buy-back" wouldn't

hesitate to attend the auction of their own house if the price was right. Why not? Distressed assets should go to the highest bidder. The identity of the buyer is not important.

Bankruptcy courts frequently allow original owners to buy back business assets as long as they offer the highest bid. Courts worry about the creditors. If your bid gets the creditors a nickel on the dollar, while someone else's bid yields creditors only 2 cents, putting you back is in everyone's best interest.

You didn't steal the assets. You bought them fair and square from a liquidator concerned about the welfare of the creditors. Your only obligation is to strike the best deal you can, for yourself.

Make it a fair deal. Vito went first to Harvard, then to Yale, and finally to jail. He thought he could take a few short cuts to give himself a slightly better deal. Figuring his computer business would eventually go bust, he ordered $200,000 in microprocessors on credit, $150,000 of which he moved to his home basement, leaving $50,000 for the bankruptcy trustee to liquidate. Next, he bought back the $50,000 in machines for $20,000 and rejuvenated his business with the $150,000 in concealed merchandise. The last I heard, he was developing a terrific tennis backhand at the Allenwood Penetentiary.

If any cure for a sick business requires total honesty, it's the "dump-buy-back." The entire transaction will undergo close scrutiny. Don't plan to cheat the creditors. They're entitled to every cent your assets could possibly get them, even if it's only a dime on the dollar. But if you try to shrink the dime to a nickel by not playing by the rules, you'll run into trouble.

Creditors have rights too. If you ran your old company honestly (although unprofitably), and went bankrupt but bargained for the assets fairly, they may grumble, but you're still legally in business. Approach your problems with less than total honesty and you may end up playing doubles with Vito.

Here are some rules that will keep you on the right side of the law:

1. Don't build up inventory on credit once you realize your business will never make it. It's bad enough that your creditors will suffer from your honest mismanagement. Don't let them

lose more through deliberate deceit.

2. Don't move assets from the business premises. Concealing assets is illegal.
3. Don't sell or transfer goods except in the ordinary course of business. Sliding inventory out the back door is also illegal.
4. Do keep good records. Your creditors have the right to inspect your books to see what happened to *their* money. If you lack proper records, they'll never give you the benefit of the doubt.
5. Don't appoint an assignee or receiver to liquidate your business unless he can fairly and adequately represent the interests of creditors. Even if you appoint him, the liquidator's allegiance must be to the creditors. If the creditors can prove the liquidator has your interests at heart, the Court may disqualify any sale to you.
6. Don't buy any asset from a liquidator at a private sale unless you have a qualified appraisal which shows you're offering a price that exceeds what an auction can bring.
7. Don't hide your affiliation with the new corporation buying the assets. You have nothing to hide. Creditors will find out sooner or later, so why raise suspicion that you're doing something wrong?
8. Have your lawyer guide your every step. As with all insolvency matters, many technical issues will arise. What may appear harmless to you may in reality be a serious legal blunder.
9. Confront your creditors after you're back in business. An open policy is the best way to show you acted honestly and to convince creditors to continue to work with you.
10. Put yourself in your creditors' shoes. Is there any possible way they can argue they didn't get the best possible deal, even if it's under the worst possible circumstances?

Ask Vito. When creditors found out his business went bust, they just called him stupid. But when they discovered the inventory in his basement, they called him a crook. As Vito says, "It's better to be only 'stupid.' "

A failed business may indicate a lack of managerial brilliance, but does it necessarily imply stupidity? Not when you're smart enough to end up with your same business without the liabilities.

Two's Company

10

Bernie Kopel calls himself a matchmaker. He's always on the lookout for firms interested in marrying a sick business. As Bernie puts it, "They often produce profitable offspring."

Bernie recounts some of his latest corporate weddings:

Garden Chevrolet to Dwight Motor Leasing. Bernie calls it his "marriage made in heaven." The Chevrolet dealership couldn't move enough cars to stay alive, while Dwight was buying 200-250 cars annually to nourish its expanding fleet. So Dwight purchased a 50 percent interest in Garden Chevrolet, picking up its cars at a little over dealer's cost and giving Garden the volume needed to win better prices from General Motors.

Canterbury Cards and Gifts to Hutton Paper Corporation. Canterbury lay gasping in Chapter 11 without the funds to survive. But it did enjoy six valuable store leases. Hutton, always on the prowl for high traffic locations, wasted no time becoming the anxious suitor. Hutton acquired controlling interest in Canterbury, bailed it out of Chapter 11, and added six more winning locations to its fast growing chain.

Economy Wallpaper and Capital Paint made a stunning couple. Economy sat idly on one end of a busy shopping center while Capital Paint, with its dismal sales and exorbitant overhead, languished only a few stores away. The romance was inevitable. Joining forces, they found a new location on a busy thoroughfare and proudly announced the birth of Capital Paint and Wallpaper Co.

Bernie Kopel keeps busy as corporate matchmaker. He explains: "There are thousands of small firms that can't make it on their own. My job is to discover what charms they can offer to another company. If I find those hidden charms, heck, I don't even have to sell, it's love at first sight."

Should You Hear Wedding Bells?

Owners of small firms are champions of the "do or die" philosophy, fighting for survival by plundering their internal resources to achieve a turnaround. When they fail, the business dies.

Marriage to another firm can offer an effective alternative, particularly if your firm has inadequate resources to achieve its own turnaround.

Carillon Sales discovered the perfect solution to a bad problem. Carillon, a large houseware distributor, trembled when its major customer, Discount Kitchen & Appliance filed for Chapter 11. Norman C., Carillon's owner, recalls the events: "The discount chain owed us $470,000, which we soon realized we would have to write off. To make matters worse, the chain represented 68 percent of our business. We grew worried about our own survival. It was a potential 'domino effect.' We filed our own Chapter 11 to buy time to decide how to save our company. We were losing money steadily and couldn't cover current expenses. Creditors were screaming to have us liquidated before all our assets disappeared. Solutions? We knew we couldn't effectively reorganize the company, but we wondered whether our company might not seem valuable to someone. After all, we still had a warehouse full of inventory and several strong accounts. And that's what attracted Highland Housewares, our oldest competitor. They offered to buy 60 percent of Carillon's shares. Adding Carillon's sales to their own, they had a profitable sales base, and by reducing our debt to 10 cents on the dollar, they picked up our inventory at bargain basement prices. The sale to Highland turned out to be our only alternative. Though we lost controlling interest in Carillon, our shares are now worth good money.

Carillon, under Highland's control, will hit $7,000,000 this year. I stayed on to help manage Carillon for a $50,000 salary. Believe me, that's a lot better than watching Carillon liquidated and ending up with nothing but an unemployment check."

I see it everyday. Owners struggle to survive but never quite make it. When the business is finally liquidated, they lose everything. If only they would have turned to Bernie Kopel, saying, "O. K., I can't save the business, but the business must be worth something to somebody. Can you help me cut a deal that will save something for me?"

In some cases, owners choose to hunt for a mate, even though they could muster the resources to save the company themselves. "Survival doesn't prompt every marriage," insists Bernie Kopel. "Some owners decide that an affiliation with a stronger company can offer even greater profit opportunities." Several of my own cases have proven he's right.

K & C Printing crept along for years with profitless sales. Their problems weren't dramatic, but they did have excess debt they needed to compromise. After we solved that problem out of court, the crisis made the owners think of the future of the firm. They decided to merge with another small printer. Together they consolidated overhead and turned a better profit.

"Selling out was the smartest decision of my life," reports Marilyn P., an entrepreneurial maverick who started Computer Design on a shoestring. "We were undercapitalized from the first day. We had a growing company, but we couldn't finance its growth. So I sold to a publicly-traded corporation and received 10,000 of their shares worth $150,000. They had the money to exploit our ideas." Today, Computer Design enjoys $12,000,000 annual sales. With Marilyn's limited capital, it would be nothing but undeveloped potential.

Harold M. simply ran out of steam. "For 36 years, I worked day and night running Fairfax Creamery. I earned a good living, but when my employees unionized and called a labor strike, I decided to turn the company over to some 'bigger boys.' Douglas Dairies straightened out the mess, offered an attractive buy-out arrangement and kept me on as corporate Vice-President. More than their cash, I needed their management. At that time in my life, I wanted more time with my family."

Some owners, however, refuse to consider any marriage, even when it's the *only* alternative. Malcolm K. would spend every waking moment trying to figure out how to save his troubled Expo Health Food chain. To bail it out, Malcolm needed $200,000 in fresh capital, but Malcolm couldn't even afford the lease payments on his Honda Civic. I tried to help him before he lost everything.

I proposed:

A health food manufacturer who would pay Malcolm $175,000 for his interest in Expo. But Malcolm wouldn't even consider the deal. Expo was his baby, "Not for sale," was his lullaby.

A vitamin manufacturer who would loan Expo $200,000 and acquire a 40 percent stock interest in Expo for an additional $50,000. The vitamin manufacturer was lured by the idea that Expo could sell tons of the manufacturer's vitamin line.

Malcolm remained the unwilling bride. He didn't want to hear about my "deals." He was "hanging tough" and didn't need help from "outsiders."

On June 27, 1981 when Malcolm watched us auction off his pride and joy, the vitamin manufacturer stood first in line and picked up the entire chain for $80,000. Only two weeks earlier, Malcolm could have been handed a quarter of a million dollars from the same buyer and would still own most of the company. Some people don't know when it's time to consider a marriage proposal.

The right company can bail you out, if it provides:
1. Capital or financing you can't find internally.
2. Inventory or product lines unavailable through conventional suppliers.
3. Added income or distribution to achieve profitable sales.
4. Management to help you through the turnaround and make your business grow.

It boils down to letting someone else help you when you can't help yourself.

Spot Your Hidden Charms

Why would another company be interested in you? Simple. Hidden under your mountain of debts lie invisible assets that can be valuable to someone else, but you must learn how to spot and use those assets as bargaining chips.

Let's uncover some of those assets and watch how others have employed them to maximum advantage.

1. Leases: Your company may hold valuable leases that could motivate another company to write out healthy checks.

Remember Canterbury Cards and Gifts? When Canterbury filed for Chapter 11, it had inventory and fixtures valued at $300,000. Liabilities, however, exceeded $800,000. Ed C., Canterbury's owner, didn't think his debt-ridden company would be worth much to someone else, and he certainly couldn't finance the reorganization, but he was sitting on a hidden gold mine. Canterbury held six favorable long term leases in the best shopping malls. Canterbury was paying annual rents averaging only $10,000 per location. Today, the landlords would demand over $25,000 for the same locations. Each lease represented a savings of $15,000 per year. Rent savings for the duration of the six leases would amount to a whopping $850,000, a powerful bargaining chip.

Hutton Paper Corporation wanted those bargain leases and agreed to purchase Ed's Canterbury shares for $400,000. Hutton took over, helped Canterbury through its Chapter 11 by agreeing to pay creditors $250,000 on their $800,000 in claims and went on to build a healthy company. For Hutton it was a smart move. They ended up with $300,000 in tangible assets and leases worth another $850,000 by paying out a total of only $650,000.

Ed was amazed. He never thought about his leases. As he will tell you, "Without Hutton, Canterbury would have folded. The creditors would have ended up with the auction proceeds, and I certainly wouldn't be wealthier today. My lease put $400,000 in my pocket!"

Homan's Candy Shops used their lease to a $168,000 advantage. Homan's held a lease on a retail store in a high traffic waterfront mall. Homan's wasn't insolvent, but neither was it profitable. It decided to pull out, liquidate its fixtures and call it quits. However, one of Boston's busiest restaurants stood adjacent to Homan's. I calculated the restaurant would pay handsomely to take over Homan's lease so they could expand. We approached the restaurant owner, told him Homan's was about to sell out to another candy chain but wanted to give them first crack at the space. They jumped at it, agreeing to pay Homan's $168,000 in four annual installments. Had the restaurant declined the deal, they could have waited three weeks for Homan's to move out and picked up Homan's space for nothing by writing a new lease directly with the landlord. But how could they know we didn't have a buyer in the wings?

Whenever Bill Homan thinks about the deal he pulled off, he says, "I never could understand why owners close up shop and abandon valuable locations without first trying to parlay those leases into some cash for themselves. All you have to do is look around and decide who would pay you for the chance to take over the location."

Look over your lease. You may be standing on your best bargaining chip.

2. Customers always have value. And you may be able to channel your customers to another company in exchange for an interesting proposition.

When Harry A.'s Chilton Meat Supply began to fail due to undercapitalization and poor sales, Harry decided to liquidate by throwing his company into bankruptcy. But why let competitors grab 400 retail accounts for nothing? Harry approached Puritan Food, one of his larger competitors, and negotiated a deal to turn his customers over to Puritan. Harry would aggressively follow up on the accounts to make certain they joined Puritan's, provided Puritan paid him 3 percent of sales on his former accounts. Last year's sales to his prior customers amounted to $2,000,000, so Harry picked up $60,000 in commissions. "It's like an annuity," says Harry. "Besides, it's more money than I made owning Chilton."

What are 600 landscaping accounts worth? Apex Landscaping Service will soon find out. Gino, its owner, recently decided to shed the business' landscaping service and focus instead on its failing garden supply outlet. Our best offer so far is $60,000. Gino figures he'll eventually find a buyer who'll pay over $100,000. I hope he's right. He needs the capital to pay Apex creditors and add inventory to his garden shop.

Ever hear of the Body Works? Maryville town fathers took a dim view of the controversial massage parlor and with bureaucratic predictability decided to drum it out of business. Undaunted, Mike C., its flamboyant owner, sat down to strike a clever bargain with Sunset Massage, a massage salon in an adjacent and more liberal town. Mike would send his customers over in return for a 30 percent ownership in Sunset. It made sense. Sunset recently expanded to handle Body Works' 500 steady customers.

Calculate what your customers generate in annual sales. How profitable would those accounts be to another company? They *can* continue to be profitable to you if you handle them right.

3. Franchise and Distributorship rights can attract money-rich companies like magnets. They certainly drew cash to Richmond Wholesalers, a growing baby goods wholesaler whose mainstay was its valuable Johnson and Johnson distributorship granting Richmond exclusive sales rights to the area's department and discount outlets. The Clancy brothers, Richmond's owners, built the firm into a profitable enterprise but ran into serious cash flow problems. The banks wouldn't consider further loans.

Monarch Merchandising rushed to the rescue. They were well entrenched in the discount trade as children's wear wholesalers. But they could see instant value in Richmond's customer base and its exclusive Johnson Products line. For Monarch, it was a logical route for expansion.

Monarch initially bargained for a total takeover. However, the Clancys shunned a complete sale and instead negotiated to sell a 49 percent interest. The marriage worked. Last year, Richmond's sales doubled to over $3,000,000, and the Clancys expect to double sales again in the next two years. "When we sold 49 percent interest in Richmond," states Jim Clancy, "we were able to demand top price and a commitment for all future expansion capital. Our Johnson Products distributorship sealed the deal. Without it, we would be just another starving wholesaler, and would have eventually given the company away for a few dollars."

4. Channels of Distribution can catch interest. Many firms will buy into or develop business-saving relationships with companies that can offer sales velocity for their products. Here's how a few of these deals worked:

> Putnam Mills constantly searches for floundering retail men's clothing outlets, looking for stores that can feature its lines and effectively operate on a low-overhead discount basis. Putnam finances the turnaround, inventories the store on consignment and even provides management assistance. In return, Putnam demands token ownership in the retailer and 10 percent of sales. But what they're really interested in is an opportunity to sell their goods. Some of their affiliated stores have quadrupled their former sales and many unprofitable retailers have begun to show a 10–15 percent profit under Putnam's umbrella.
>
> A drug wholesaler recently acquired a 70 percent interest in a small drug chain, injecting a survival dose of inventory and cash. The wholesaler expects the chain to produce a profit, but the wholesaler also expects to sell its new subsidiary over $3,000,000 in products this year.
>
> Reston Stereo, a seven-store stereo discounter, on the financial ropes with $300,000 in debt, couldn't raise the capital to pacify creditors or re-merchandise the business. They found a Hong Kong stereo manufacturer who agreed to invest $500,000 in the struggling chain, $300,000 in the form of long-term debt and $200,000 for 40 percent of the shares. The manufacturer expects Reston to retail over $2,000,000 worth of its stereo equipment annually.
>
> Bernie Kopel loves to match the business that can provide sales to the business that needs a sales vehicle. "Don't make a mistake," counsels Bernie, "when you reach out in desperation for a marriage partner, don't just look horizontally to others in your business. Sure, they're your best bet, but companies that can flow their merchandise through your business can work wonders, too."

5. Tax Losses can offer tax savings for a profitable company which buys you out and applies your prior tax loss against their future taxable profits. Your $200,000 tax loss may mean $100,000 in tax savings to the acquiring company in the 50 percent bracket.

Recent tax changes have made the tax loss less attractive. Complicated limitations control tax benefits, and the IRS prescribes a long list of regulations one must follow to take advantage of tax loss benefits. Your accountant or tax counsel can analyze your situation to see if your company can offer big tax benefits to a buyer.

A word of caution. Companies seldom buy or merge with another company on the strength of the tax benefits alone. The successful marriage depends on more than wedding gifts from Uncle Sam.

In some cases, a deal will come together for other reasons. If you have special expertise, *you* may represent the most valuable asset. Some buyers want to buy management, and the only way they can get it is to by someone's company in the process.

Your business name and its good will may attract buyers. We recently convinced a large mail order firm to acquire a financially distressed small promotional outfit on the strength of its solid reputation. The promotional outfit had operated for years, and its name enjoys considerably greater recognition than the buyer's.

Don't overlook the economics of the situation. Many buyers will agree to a deal if they can acquire your assets at considerably less than fair market value. In itself, this won't motivate buyers, but it certainly becomes a strong inducement when the buyer planned to acquire such assets elsewhere.

Highland Supermarket presents a perfect example. It had amassed a $200,000 inventory and fixtures one couldn't replace for less than $50,000. Unfortunately, debts exceeded $300,000. Highland's owner, Mark B., didn't relish the hassle of returning Highland to solvency. More accurately, future profitability bothered Mark the most. Highland hadn't shown a profit for years, and Mark didn't have the blueprint for future profits.

Why throw Highland into a liquidating bankruptcy? That certainly wouldn't benefit Mark. Did the business own something that would entice a buyer?

A small supermarket chain showed mild interest in Highland. They saw it as a borderline situation. Perhaps they could make Highland profitable, perhaps not. The solution was to give them a "no risk" deal. Here's how it came together:

Mark would turn ownership of Highland over to the chain on a "no cash down" basis. Under the chain's ownership, Highland would file for a Chapter 11 reorganization to cut the $300,000 debt down to a manageable size. The chain agreed that Highland's assets had a fair market value of $250,000. Our proposition was simple. Mark would get 25 percent of every dollar by which Highland reduced its debts below $250,000. What could the chain lose? In the worst case, the reorganization would fail. The chain could walk away and would have lost only time and effort. Fortunately, the Chapter 11 worked. The creditors, convinced that the assets would bring only $100,000 at auction, agreed to settle all claims for $120,000. With a fair market asset value of $250,000, Highland had an immediate "paper" gain of $130,000. Mark picked up $32,500 or 25 percent of that gain. It was better than throwing the keys to the creditors. As it turned out, Highland didn't prove to be a moneymaker for the chain either. However, that didn't bother them. They simply trucked Highland's inventory and fixtures to their other stores. As the chain figured it, the $250,000 in assets cost them only $152,000, including payment to Mark.

The opportunity to acquire assets at far below replacement cost can be attractive to a buyer. When you couple it with a "no risk" proposition, it becomes a powerful motivator. This double feature has loads of charm!

The New Math: 2 + 2 = 5

Mergers do not just benefit larger corporations, the fast-growth, publicly-traded firms scrambling to build conglomerates on pieces of paper.

Even the smallest firms can merge to create a stronger enterprise than individual companies standing alone. In fact, mergers between the smallest firms can produce some real moneymakers. I call it "The New Math," joining together of two struggling firms so the total effect is greater than the sum of each.

Teaming up worked for:

Academy Printers. It ran into trouble shortly after starting its business. Saddled with $50,000 in new equipment, Academy couldn't generate the business to meet its stiff monthly obligations. They found the perfect marriage partner, a local newspaper publisher who couldn't get the service it needed from other printers. By joining forces with Academy, the newspaper could rely on "in-house" production. Academy, in turn, could keep its press constantly humming with newspaper printing. After reviewing the economics of the deal, the printer and publisher decided to combine the two businesses into one on a 50/50 basis. The equally matched firms could capitalize on each other's strengths.

Huron Cheese and Wine did it differently. Operating a beautiful store with the latest fixtures and decor, Huron nevertheless faced two problems. First, the store was overspaced and suffering needlessly high rent. Further, Huron stayed open 80 hours a week and owner Joan T. always had trouble finding reliable employees to manage the store in her absence.

A small meat market occupied a location on a nearby side street. The elderly gentleman who owned it wanted to work several more years but didn't want the continued problems of running his own business. So, Huron purchased the meat shop's equipment and inventory and moved it into Huron's excess space as a new department. The meat store owner stayed on as manager of the department and became that reliable second person Joan needed to oversee the entire business during her absence. The gourmet meat department created more sales than ever and both operations prospered.

Prentice Drug was limping along on $240,000 sales and losing $10–12,000 annually. They retained us to clear up their debts, but that wouldn't give Prentice the long-term profitability it needed. It would continue to suffer from a fatal combination of poor sales and excessive overhead. Checking further, we found that Prentice had only one other competitor in town, Harbor Pharmacy, which also struggled to stay afloat. It appeared their competition would extend to seeing who hit the bankruptcy court first.

Were two small stores trying to divide a pie only big enough to satisfy one hungry appetite? "Let's clean up the creditors of both stores," I said. "Combine the assets of Prentice and Harbor, making them equal partners in a new operation and relocate to a dynamite location, a nearby shopping center recently vacated by a small supermarket."

In three months, it all came together with the birth of Banner Pharmacy, grossing $800,000 annually with profits over $50,000. As Prentice's Sharon T. will tell you, "The merger allowed us to duplicate overhead, payroll, rents and utilities. By combining our inventories, we had more to work with and could strengthen our buying and merchandising. The best part? Banner could set high prices because it was the only pharmacy around."

Common sense? Of course. That's what makes all mini-mergers work. It's not a matter of high finance. Such exploits won't appear within the pages of the *Harvard Business Review*, but they can save businesses.

How to Structure the Deal to Work for You

How can your company join forces with another to achieve *your* objectives? Unfortunately, no simple formula exists. Some mergers are extremely simple, others highly complex. Every successful marriage, however, demands a formula that satisfies everyone's objectives and fits economic realities.

The Outright Takeover: Over 60 percent of the small companies follow this route to the perfect "bail out." The outright sale is simple, and it's considerably easier to find a buyer to take over completely rather than bargain for a more complex partnership.

When a large corporation buys a smaller one, it will commonly resist anything less than a total takeover. To do otherwise would violate its own corporate structure.

Troubled owners sometimes make the mistake of believing they must retain some ownership interest in the business to make it all worthwhile, but they frequently come out ahead by agreeing to a complete sale rather than a partnership interest.

When Canterbury Cards and Gifts began its search for a cash rich company, Ed C., Canterbury's owner, wanted to keep at least 50 percent of his company. It wasn't in the cards. The one or two partial investors who knocked on his door weren't suitable marriage partners. Hutton Paper Corporaton, a corporation closely held by the Hutton family, wanted compete ownership of its subsidiaries. There was no room for Ed as a partner.

However, Ed wanted to own card and gift stores. If he couldn't do it through a partnership interest in Canterbury, at least he could get $400,000 from the sale of Canterbury and strike out again on his own, which is precisely what he did. Today Ed owns two healthy gift shops, both made possible by turning over the keys to Canterbury before it was too late.

That's how to look at the outright sale. You may no longer be part of your troubled business, but you can get capital to start again.

Partnership Deals: Countless combinations exist. In many cases, the acquiring company will agree to invest the necessary funds to keep your business afloat in return for a percentage of shares in your corporation. But what division of stock is fair? Investing companies usually bargain for a majority interest and control. Ending up a minority stockholder in your own corporation may be better than nothing, but as Harold M. of Fairfax Creamery explains it, it isn't the perfect solution. "To bring in the turnaround financing, I had to sell out 80 pecent of the company. As a 20 percent stockholder, I had little to say about anything. I was only one notch higher than an employee."

From my own experience, I usually try to avoid the deal that provides my client a minority stock interest. It's usually better to sell out completely for whatever cash one can obtain and then start over on a smaller scale with total ownership.

In the big league mergers and takeovers, stock swaps provide the foundation for the takeover. The acquiring company pays for the takeover by issuing some of its own shares to stockholders of the acquired company. That's how Marilyn P. for Computer Design sold out. She gave up complete stock ownership in Computer Design for 10,000 shares of the acquiring company's publicly traded shares. To Marilyn, that was money in the bank. She could sell the shares the next day.

Stock/Loan Combinations: These are popular. The acquiring company capitalizes the turnaround by loaning the troubled company a specified amount of cash and paying more for a percentage of shares. That was how I tried to peddle Macolm K.'s Expo Health Foods. The interested vitamin manufacturer proposed the $250,000 bail out transfusion, $200,000 as a direct loan, and $50,000 more in exchange for 40 percent of its shares. True, the business eventually would have to repay the $200,000, but under this formula, Malcolm would have retained 60 percent ownership of the company. Malcolm would have gone along with the deal if the investor agreed to pay $250,000 cash for 40 percent of the shares, but that defied economic reality. The business was insolvent and couldn't justify the price.

Most "partnership" transactions involve a combination of stock and loan. From my viewpoint, it's far better to retain a controlling stock interest by agreeing to a loan than to insist on a straight partnership deal where you'd have to bargain away controlling interest. Once the business repays the debt, you are back in the driver's seat with your controlling interest.

Faced with a stock/debt deal, bargain to sell as little stock as possible and allocate as much as possible to the loan. Make certain you can handle the resultant debt. Agreeing to an unrealistic debt level can be self-defeating. One beleaguered company obtained $200,000 in needed capital by agreeing to a $180,000 three-year secured loan, with the remaining $20,000 for 30 percent ownership in the company. Two months later, the loan went into default. The investor/lender simply foreclosed on its mortgage and now owns the entire company.

Pooling Interest: Two or more companies merge by combining their assets into either one surviving company (a merger), or they set up a new corporation with the collective assets of the existing companies (a consolidation).

This approach lends itself to merging companies which enjoy a certain parity in size and value and can make nearly equal contributions to the new enterprise. That allows the participants equal ownership which usually provides the most stable and equitable arrangement.

Seldom, however, do the merging firms share identical values. When one company provides more than another, it's best to equalize values by adjusting debt, while the owners still retain equal ownership.

When Prentice Drug and Harbor Pharmacy joined forces, their owners each ended up with 50 percent ownership in the successor Banner Drug. Although Prentice and Harbor were nearly equal in value, Harbor had more assets and fewer liabilities. We agreed that Harbor was worth about $30,000 more than Prentice, so Banner equalized the contributions with notes worth $30,000.

Joint Ventures: Oftentimes you can affiliate with another company which can provide you the tools to "bail out" your firm without either a sale or partnership arrangement. You retain full ownership of your firm and enter into a functional alliance or affiliation.

This works best when you can offer distribution opportunities to another firm. Remember Putnam Mills? Two other companies joined forces to sell only Putnam's lines. Putnam gave them survival strength through strong merchandising, promotional "know-how" and managerial assistance. Putnam didn't demand an ownership interest either. They're happy moving their lines through the stores and collecting an additional 10 percent over-ride on sales.

The well-designed affiliation takes on the characteristics of a franchise. It can provide the best of both worlds, the strength of a large company coupled with the motivation that comes from running your own show.

What Are You Really Worth?

Let me shoot straight. Throw away your notions about what your business is worth. And forget textbook formulas that place values on companies. Why? You aren't selling or dealing with a solvent, profitable enterprise. You're on the ropes. You know it, and prospective buyers know it. You're talking to outsiders because you want to save what you can as a last ditch effort before the business collapses, leaving you with nothing. Yours is not a normal sale. It's the final straw.

I have cemented deals for over 600 troubled companies, and I always saw the same bottom line: *the best deal we could get.* Sometimes it was far better than we hoped, in other instances it was far worse.

However, in every case, we beat the bushes for every possible buyer we could find, presented our case, aggressively listened to the best offers and tried to boost them through last minute negotiations. When the final offers lay on the table, we looked them over and chose the one that best satisfied the owner's objectives. They seldom *matched* expectations, but at least one offer came closest. Often we've had few deals from which to choose, so the picking was easy.

That doesn't mean you're at the total mercy of the buyer. After all, you have something of value to him and he's not the only buyer who may be bidding. You can substantially improve your bargaining position if you follow the:

Thirteen Ways to Get Your Best Deal

1. Define your objectives. Do you need an outside company to help you achieve profitability, solvency, or both? It will help you define the companies which can fulfill those needs.

2. If your problem is lack of profitability, then resolve any insolvency problems on your own before you go on the market. You'll be in a much stronger bargaining position with a financially sound business.

3. Start early if you see your business slipping into insolvency and realize you'll need another company to help bail it out. You can get considerably more for your company during the initial stages of insolvency than in the terminal stage, when buyers develop the killer instinct.

4. Add up your selling points. What does your company have to offer? Translate it into terms a buyer can appreciate. You have to convince him he can make money with your business and you have to show him how.

5. Know your objectives. Do you prefer a complete sale or do you want to remain affiliated with the company as a partner or employee? Match your objectives to the reality of the situation and the companies you are seeking out.

6. Solicit proposals aggressively. Contact every company which might possibly be interested in your firm and satisfy your objectives. In many of my cases, we had to contact hundreds of firms before we landed a "no nonsense" deal. You don't have time to play the field. You need as many offers as you can obtain and you need them in a hurry.

7. Stay flexible. The deal you think you want may be entirely different from the deal you'll be offered. And what you're offered may be the better deal. Let the buyer give you his ideas. It may be an exciting proposition.

8. Don't fall for "pie-in-the-sky" deals. You're usually better off with hard cash than soft promises. Many troubled firms are handed over on the basis of "future profits" or other speculative contingency. It can be a mistake.

9. If you are to retain an interest in the company, then define the buyer's expectations for the company. It's the same as any other partnership. You must share objectives for the firm and how you expect it to reach them.

10. Watch for the "bail out." Many firms will invest in a troubled company and then close or pull out of the business when the business doesn't quickly achieve expectations. The buyer's commitment to give the business a reasonable chance is an important ingredient.

11. Consider personalities as much as finances. Most business marriages end in divorce, not due to business reasons but personality clashes. To rebuild your company, you need a solid working relationship with your new partners. Once conflict occurs, you'll probably fall victim to the acquiring company which may have the upper hand.

12. Look like a survivor. The buyer knows you're in trouble, but don't let him think time is running out for you. If he believes you can make it without him, you can bargain at his level, and you won't have to listen to any last minute "take it or leave it" ultimatums.

13. Use some "phantom" buyers. Don't let him think he's the only interested buyer, even if he is. He needs competition if you're to get a reasonable deal and that can happen only when he is forced to "outbid" other prospects.

Two Blunders to Avoid

Just as there are points to follow, conversely there are costly mistakes you can make. Here are two of the most common, and often fatal errors:

1. The Vulture Syndrome:

Here's a bleak fact of life. About 50 percent of your prospective buyers have no inclination to cut a deal with you. They're playing the "vulture" game, hovering around you to see what they can pick up once your business goes under. They may be after your location, customers, employees, or whatever other benefit they can derive by staying close to you, pretending to be interested in buying. Competitors are always likely suspects, for they are in the best position to exploit the benefits of your bankruptcy.

The vulture isn't always easy to spot, but there are some telltale signs. Watch for the buyer who seems overly preoccupied with only one phase of your operation. Delayed, protracted negotiations are another clue. Often they'll keep lulling you with increasingly better offers, hoping you'll turn your back on sincere buyers and extend yourself beyond the point of no return. Then they can watch your business crumble and be on standby to pick it up for pennies. It's a common ploy. Don't fall victim to it. Your only defense is to stay with my earlier advice. Watch your cut-off date and cement the deal in writing with all the legal safeguards so the buyer can't slip away. If your buyer isn't inclined to close the deal within your time requirements and after he has had a reasonable opportunity to negotiate, you probably are playing with a vulture.

2. The "Deal Around The Corner":

Every owner thinks he'll find a better deal the next week or the next month. Why not? If your company is worth so much to Company X, then who's to say there isn't a Company Y lurking around the corner who will offer you more? There may be, but from my experiences, it's not probable.

What routinely happens is that owners take their search beyond the point of no return only to find they've lost the solid deal they had and that other bird in the bush was only a mirage.

That's why I define a cut-off date to solidify a deal. You should beat every bush before then to find interested companies, and simultaneously negotiate with as many companies as possible until that date, but don't go beyond it looking for other deals.

Bernie Kopel adds to this final point, "You can tell when the deal is right. The two companies can immediately see how they can fulfill each other's needs. But the real key in making it work is the attitude. The owners have to see this not as an opportunity to exploit, or even as a marriage of convenience. It has to be a marriage of opportunity."

He's right. But then again, that's what the successful turnaround is about, an opportunity to make your business what you always dreamed it could be.

Putting It All Together

11

Talk to a criminal lawyer, and he'll fascinate you with his court battles. Lend your ear to a divorce attorney, if you want it filled with details of gossipy marital squabbles. Negligence lawyers can boast of their $1,000,000 malpractice verdicts.

An insolvency lawyer has his own brand of story to tell. You won't see these stories in the headlines, but you will see them dotting every city and town—businesses everywhere that wouldn't be alive today but for that careful blend of ingredients that can turn an enterprise from a failure to success.

You'll see some of those stories come to life in this chapter. Strategies of the earlier chapters come together to breathe new life into companies that thumbed their nose at the odds.

I selected these particular cases from my files because they display a wide range of problems and solutions for troubled businesses.

Not every story ends in success. Many do fall by the wayside. Yet failure can be a great teacher.

As each story unfolds, analyze how the prescription for profitability was designed. Examine the tactics used to clear operational hurdles and finally regain solvency.

Meet these owners and learn from their experience. They have some interesting stories to tell.

A Case of Indigestion (Kendall Electronics)

In 1977, President James K. conceived Kendall Electronics as a specialized importer of low-priced consumer electronic items he could profitably sell through an aggressive mail order program.

The young company grew steadily between 1977 and 1979. First year's sales exceeded $1,200,000, then climbed to $1,800,000 in 1979. Although the company lost $40,000 during its first year of operations due to extensive start-up costs, profits for 1978 and 1979 held steady at 7 percent of sales. Solid and steady was the only way to describe the company as it avoided swings in profitability and cash flow by ordering pre-determined quantities of watches, radios, and portable stereos from its Taiwanese supplier, all timed to arrive when the demand created by its national advertising campaign peaked.

By 1979, assets, primarily inventory, had shot to $180,000. Liabilities totalled $96,000 ($65,000 owed a bank on letter of credit financing and $31,000 due on accrued accounts and expenses payable). The constant flow of profits improved the financial position of the company, and the firm was beginning to take on the glow of the successful start-up enterprise.

Then James K. decided to strike out for "bigger bucks" by manufacturing his own electronics. "Why buy, when we can make the same product ourselves?" he reasoned. Flushed with his earlier success, Kendall found a likely small manufacturing firm in Edison, New Jersey. Aberdeen Components looked like a good deal to Jim. Its sales exceeded $2,000,000 annually and it generated an average annual profit of $120,000 over three prior years. Best of all, Kendall could pick up the manufacturing plant for only $700,000, financed with $100,000 down and the balance paid through the assumption of $200,000 in existing debt and $400,000 on a five-year secured note guaranteed by Kendall.

As Jim recalls, "It was a case of creative financing. We scrounged together the $100,000 by mortgaging our home for $40,000 and having Kendall borrow $60,000 against its assets. I should have realized I was in over my head when my banker started throwing big words at me like 'Amortization, adjusted pay-back, net-cash flow.' Hell, the largest word in my vocabulary was 'mayonnaise'!"

Aberdeen Components became Kendall's manufacturing subsidiary in 1980. Could the combination succeed? Only if both Kendall and Aberdeen continued on a straight course of profitability. But that happens only in textbooks. It was a perfect example of a house of cards built on quicksand.

Less than a month after Jim wrapped up the acquisition, Lady Luck turned her back on Aberdeen.

First came a labor strike that knocked the plant out of commission for sixty days. Next, a large Aberdeen account declared bankruptcy, stiffing Aberdeen for $70,000. The *coup de grace?* Kendall found that it was costing more to produce their own electronics with Aberdeen than to buy from its original Taiwan supplier. To add insult to injury, if Kendall didn't buy through its own subsidiary, the sales of Aberdeen would drop and further drain the parent firm. If Kendall did buy Aberdeen's products, profitability would suffer. The house of cards was beginning to crumble.

Jim fell behind on his notes to Aberdeen's prior owners, who threatened to foreclose. Kendall's bank could see the crisis looming on the horizon and was ready to pounce on its own $60,000 mortgage.

Cash flow reversed. Kendall continued to pump working capital into Aberdeen to keep it afloat. But Kendall's own financial problems soon stopped that. Aberdeen's labor problems slowed the flow of new products to Kendall, costing it over $200,000 in lost sales during the first three months of 1980.

The scoreboard for the first three months of 1980? Kendall lost $240,000, Aberdeen $168,000. The secured creditors smelled blood, and it looked like the end of Jim's fledgling empire.

Did it come together again? Let's see:

1. Prescription for Profitability

After analyzing both Kendall and Aberdeen, we quickly decided that Kendall could once again be profitable if it returned to its prior proven formula. We would return to the Taiwanese supplier and concentrate on marketing.

Aberdeen could have become a profitable operation too, but the $300,000 needed to finance it until it regained profitabilility lay beyond Kendall's financial resources. Survival required us to focus all our energies on Kendall while cutting Aberdeen loose.

2. Operational Hurdles

Cash posed a problem for Kendall, which needed $100,000 to stay afloat. $50,000 came from merchandise prepayments following a special ad campaign and another $50,000 from a combination of employee loans and the sale of excess office equipment.

The major operational problem was inventory. The Taiwanese supplier would ship only on a bank letter of credit, but getting that letter of credit was not easy. The supplier would ship the needed $100,000 in goods without a letter of credit only if we could find another way to secure their inventory. We proposed that the supplier ship the goods to a local warehouse and retain title to them. On a weekly basis, Kendall would draw on the inventory to fill orders for the prior week, paying for the inventory when they picked it up. Weekly cash payments wouldn't be a problem, because Kendall's own customers pre-paid through the mailorder campaign.

The combination of cash and inventory availability restored Kendall's former operational approach.

3. Solvency

Kendall's return to solvency depended on our ability to extricate it from the debts and obligations created by the Aberdeen acquisition.

The problem was the $400,000 guaranteed note Kendall owed Aberdeen's previous owner. If we liquidated Aberdeen and gave the prior owner less than $400,000, he would come after Kendall for the difference. Should that happen, we could either try to compromise the debt or seek protection for Kendall under a Chapter 11 reorganization. We made an interesting proposition. We would give the prior owner his company back, and Kendall would agree to pay $50,000 over five years in exchange for a release on its guarantee. The prior owner agreed because it was a smart move. He knew that if he foreclosed, he'd never see his $400,000, but Aberdeen could eventually return even more than that in profits.

By December 1981, Kendall had recovered from surgery. Weekly sales were back to $40,000, the bank was again issuing letters of credit, and inventory was flowing through its front door. Profits returned.

Jim will tell you, "We still have our scars. The Aberdeen folly almost cost us our business. We had to cut overhead and even my own salary to pay the bank the $100,000 used for Aberdeen's down payment. Legal fees, operational losses during the turmoil, and that damn $10,000 a year to Aberdeen's prior owner made life miserable. But we desperately wanted to survive. Biting off more than you can chew can cause indigestion."

Why Fight City Hall? (Bigelow Nursing Homes)

Certified mail always brings trouble. The letter bearing the official state emblem brought plenty of trouble for Bigelow Nursing Homes.

Hy C. recalls the day. "The letter gave me a shock. The State Medicaid Department was demanding $450,000 from us. After a spot audit on its medicaid billings, it discovered a few overcharges and assumed all my past billings were wrong. Boy, was the letter sinister. If I didn't remit the $450,000 in seven days, they would recoup it from my future medicaid billings and throw me out of the medicaid program if I gave them any trouble."

For Bigelow it was a dangerous situation. Hy knew the state was arbitrary and not entitled to $450,000. But, the Medicaid Department turned a deaf ear to all complaints. The courts? They wouldn't hear the case for months. Bigelow would be bankrupt by then. They certainly couldn't pay the $450,000, especially if the state shut off their cash flow by grabbing all the receivables from future billings. With Medicaid accounting for 75 percent of Bigelow's business, weekly cash flow would drop from $20,000 to $5,000.

Hy understood the crisis. "You think you own a profitable, healthy business and suddenly—with one letter—you are staring disaster in the face."

First, we reviewed the balance sheet. Bigelow had $12,000 in cash, $38,000 in receivables (other than the Medicaid we couldn't collect) and furniture and equipment worth $65,000. On the liability side, we could only find $35,000 due trade creditors and on current expenses. The $450,000 state claim would, we hoped, be only a statistic once we performed surgery.

Since the nursing home was a constant money-maker, profitability wasn't the problem.

Operational hurdles? The possible disappearance of 75 percent of cash flow threw up more than a hurdle. It was a minefield created by bumbling bureaucrats.

Solvency was tied into cash flow. If the state eventually prevailed on its $450,000 claim, the business would sink. Whether the state eventually won or lost, the case was academic. Bigelow would be out of business by the time the case came to court.

We batted around the idea of a Chapter 11, thinking maybe a bankruptcy court would require the state to continue payments until it heard the case. But we abandoned the idea. First, it would take the Court 3-4 weeks to provide relief. Bigelow couldn't wait that long. A larger reason loomed. There clearly were some overcharges to the state. Bigelow didn't owe it $450,000 from padded billings, but the state could ultimately claim some violation of the billing regulations and disqualify Bigelow from the Medicaid program. If the state threw Bigelow out of the program, the nursing home would be out of business even if we dramatically reduced the $450,000. Luckily, the "dump-buy-back" was tailor-made for Bigelow.

Here's how the story unfolded:

Bigelow leased the building which housed its facility. The real estate was owned by the home's prior owner, who retained the real estate while selling Bigelow only the business. The landlord sympathized with the problem and went along with the idea of Hy setting up a brand new corporation to take over the lease.

With the lease for the new corporation in hand, Bigelow made an assignment for the benefit of creditors. The assignee took over all assets in order to liquidate the furniture and fixtures. A week later, the assets went up for public auction. Hy relished it. "It was fascinating! The assignee and auctioneer were trying to sell off used nursing home beds and a collection of metal furniture. There was only one problem. The beds had patients in them. Who would bid for a used bed and throw an old, feeble patient into the street? The scene bordered on the ridiculous. I had no trouble outbidding everyone else. They had all gone home!

The assignee agreed to sell Bigelow's furniture and equipment to my newly formed corporation, Skyview Nursing Home, for $25,000 payable over two years. The patients didn't even know what was going on. One minute they were Bigelow patients, then with the drop of the auctioneer's hammer, they became Skyview patients. The employees? They enjoyed the show, knowing we were doing an 'end run' on the bumbling bureaucrats."

So, Hy was back in business. Actually he was never out of business. The assignee, of course, operated the home until Skyview took over.

Working capital presented a bit of a problem. Skyview started to generate its own accounts receivable once it took over, but it would take time to turn them into cash. Hy threw $10,000 into the business, and the old suppliers of Bigelow understood the situation and agreed to grant credit to Skyview until the receivables flowed through the pipeline. Even the employees cooperated, deferring salaries for two weeks.

Lets examine the scorecard:

1. Hy came out on top doing business at the same old stand. Skyview Nursing Home grosses $1,200,000 annually and is debt free.

2. Bigelow's old creditors? They'll get most of what Bigelow owed from the assignee, because the assignee ended up with $24,000 in cash and collected receivables, plus Skyview's $25,000 note for the purchase of the furniture. Hy assured them that if they didn't get paid in full from the assignee, Skyview would make up the difference.

3. The state? They're still chasing Bigelow, a defunct paper corporation. As Hy puts it, "Maybe some day the bumbling bureaucrats will wake up and realize they're chasing their tail. But let them chase, they can't touch Skyview because it's a separate corporation. Now when I see a state envelope, I smile. I know I'll find a Medicaid check inside. But do you know when I'll really laugh?" asks Hy. "The day I open the envelope announcing that they've thrown Bigelow out of the Medicaid program."

The Case of the Corporate Eunuch (Weyland Textile)

The Harvard Business School towers as the citadel of training for corporate America. But they too can make mistakes. One of them is a recent graduate, Peter T.

When Peter took over his father's Weyland Textile, a small but healthy stocking manufacturing firm with steady sales in the $2,000,000 range, everybody assumed that young Peter's high powered education would really make things happen. His father, retired in Florida, said, "Harvard cost me $30,000 in tuition. I figured once I turned the helm over to Peter, I could sit back and watch him build it into a Fortune-500 conglomerate."

But Peter headed in another direction, to Boston's waterfront district where he could prominently park his shiny new DeLorean and spend the afternoons cavorting in one of its fancy French cafes. Peter said he was "maintaining corporate visibility."

Peter's father Hal, unaware of it all, happily collected his weekly check and continued to soak up the Florida sun. However, one day Hal was served a lawsuit by the bank which had loaned $100,000 to Weyland on Hal's personal guarantee. The loan was in default and the bank was going after Hal for its money. Hal got on the next plane for Boston.

Here's what he found when he stormed into the office the next day:

A $38,000 loss for 1979, outclassed by the 1980 losses of $74,000.

Sales down from $2,000,000 to $1,000,000.

Liabilities up to $240,000 due trade creditors on top of the defaulted $100,000 bank note.

Productivity? It was difficult for the employees to even shake Hal's hand when he made his grand entrance. It's always difficult when your right hand is holding a beer can. The business was floundering. The employees knew it, the creditors knew it, the customers knew it, and now Hal knew it. Peter? He was so busy playing "executive," he didn't even know Hal was back in town.

We needed a sudden game plan. After first plugging the holes through which Weyland's lifeblood was draining, we needed drastic surgery to regain profitability. This required a two-pronged approach:

Sales had to shoot back to $2,000,000, while costs and expenses had to decline $60,000. Pumping up sales proved difficult. Lost accounts weren't excited about coming back into the fold. They had plenty of legitimate complaints: Late deliveries, incorrect billings, lack of personal attention. Fortunately, old customers had enjoyed a strong relationship with Hal. Gradually, the lost accounts began to return. So did sales.

Cutting costs proved easier. Hal enjoyed it. Turning first to Peter, he demoted his son to the shipping dock, slashing his pay from $45,000 to $15,000. Hal justified his benevolence this way: "My first inclination was to murder him, but I figured that would needlessly disrupt my retirement in the Florida sun. My second thought was to fire him. But Peter would only haunt me for spending money to pump gas into his damned sports car. So, I figured, why not give him a good dirty job lugging cartons?" Further reductions came through employee lay-offs, reduced fringe benefits and even a small savings on rent from a sympathetic landlord who wanted to keep Weyland on the premises. The bottom line was beginning to look good. Hal slashed not $60,000 but $85,000 in expenses.

Operational problems? They also required a two-fold program.

Weyland sold two delivery trucks for $30,000 to raise cash and turned deliveries over to a delivery firm.

Cash flow increased dramatically when Weyland offered accounts a 5 percent discount for payment within ten days. Several long outstanding receivables were collected in light of a one time only 20 percent "discount" on their bills.

Payments to creditors halted. Weyland adopted a strict C.O.D. buying program. Hal's philosophy was to buy "only what you need, only when you need it." Not only did he freeze payment on old bills, but he increased liquidity by turning excess inventory into sales.

Solvency? The bank Weyland owed $100,000 held a mortgage on the company's assets. They continued to get paid, but I was curious. I asked the bank's attorney why he sued Hal. "Why didn't you foreclose on the business and recoup your loan that way?" The lawyer was truthful. "The bank instructed me not to. They could see Peter killing the business and simply wanted Hal to know about it. We could have phoned Hal down in Florida, but the bank didn't want to come between father and son. We figured Hal would get the message once we slapped him with the lawsuit."

Trade creditors had to be dealt with. Weyland temporarily froze their past debts of $240,000. We calculated that if the business failed, the trade creditors would see perhaps 20–30 cents on the dollar after the bank got its $100,000. Hal convened a meeting of his largest creditors and told them the full story. The story wasn't necessary. The creditors had suffered enough dealings with Peter to understand the problem. Hal explained that the business could generate only $35–40,000 annually to pay off trade debts, and offered to pay this amount for four years if the creditors agreed to reduce the total from $240,000 to $150,000. The smaller creditors held out for full payment. Since it would cost Weyland a mere $10–15,000 to settle with the small nuisance creditors, Hal reasoned paying them would be cheaper than throwing the company into Chapter 11.

A month after Hal's return, the company was regaining its fiscal health.

The business was operating at close to its break-even point, but it was heading toward renewed profitability.

The balance sheet fell into line. The bank was collecting its monthly payments after reinstating the loan, and the trade debt was cut to $160,000 payable in monthly installments of $3,200. Weyland could handle them.

But the best was yet to come. Hal had no intention of spending the rest of his life navigating Weyland. He was pushing 70 and wanted to return to the golf links down South. Who would manage the business? Hal decided to sell out.

A large conglomerate saw potential with Weyland. It agreed to acquire Hal's shares for $300,000 in cash and $200,000 in its publicly-traded stock.

With his pockets bulging with cash and negotiable securities, Hal was on his way back to Florida. But first he had some parting advice for the president of the conglomerate. "Why don't you let my son Peter run things for awhile. He's brilliant and comes complete with a Harvard MBA." I detected a very wry smile on Hal's face as he left the building.

The Case of Contaminated Chow Mein
(China City Restaurant)

Can a few microscopic organisms swimming in an otherwise delicious bowl of Chow Mein destroy a prosperous purveyor of oriental delicacies?

The first signs of trouble for China City came when a fat, middle-aged female patron began to experience gastric distress after devouring her third helping of chow mein. The Chen brothers, always the polite hosts, called an ambulance.

Unfortunately, the Chens' graciousness did not conciliate matters. Two weeks later, they faced a $500,000 lawsuit arising from "contaminated chow mein."

By itself, the suit didn't worry us. After all, the business was insured, and who could prove the lady hadn't gotten sick on something she'd eaten somewhere else?

The newspapers had a field day with the story. The Town Crier broadcast the lawsuit in banner headlines. "$500,000 LAWSUIT FROM CONTAMINATED CHOW MEIN AT CHINA CITY." The story gave all the gory details.

China City operated in a small town where everyone read the local paper, which can make or break a business. China City broke. Before the story had splashed onto the front page, China City enjoyed profitable sales of $6–8,000 a week. The day following the story, the cash registers rang up a paltry $137. The Chens' few customers were either illiterate or tourists passing through.

China City couldn't survive long without customers. Saving their business meant finding a way to get the cash registers ringing again, and they had to ring rapidly to cover mounting expenses.

A phone call from Chen's accountant brought me into the case. One month after the unfortunate newspaper story, nary a bowl of chow mein had been served. Cash reserves dwindled to nothing, as the Chens continued to meet their $2,700 weekly payroll. $2,500 for next month's rent and the usual array of overhead costs drained yet more cash.

Initially, our role in the case was limited to negotiating a rent extension with the landlord, but from our box seats we watched a spectacle unfold. Either the Chens would find a way to bring back the customers, or they'd have to close their doors forever. It was time for a game plan.

The Chens started an advertising campaign. Every promotional gimmick was employed. But the Chens discovered that good advertising can't counteract bad P.R. Not when the bad P.R. involves botulism.

The accountant offered a crazy idea. He wanted to convert the place to an Italian restaurant under the name "Little Italy." He argued that the tainted food reputation of China City would vanish with its sign. The Chens were't impressed. As Yu Chen would say, "If we didn't have notoriety before, can you imagine what the town will say when we start dishing out Italian food? Before it was contaminated chow mein, now it will be fetid fettucini."

Our wheels were spinning, but the customers still stayed away in droves.

I had my own idea. Pick up shop and transport it to another nearby town where perhaps the saga of China City was unknown. Cooler heads prevailed. One hint to the local newspaper, and we'd be back to where we started.

Selling the business? We doubted whether we could find a buyer with that perfect combination of stupidity and money.

We had run out of time and ideas. To complicate matters, the landlord wouldn't extend the rent. He had a limited vocabulary: "Pay up or get out." Time was running out.

Business is largely a matter of timing sprinkled with a seasoning of luck. The newspaper that carried the article about the botulism soon printed a story on the last page about the "victim of the contaminated chow mein." It seems she had mysteriously developed food poisoning from seven other restaurants. A neighboring state had even indicted her for false claims.

The Chens were ecstatic. Here was their vindication. But what good was the truth if we couldn't bring it to the eyes of the same 200,000 people who read about the original poisoning?

We promptly sued the rip-off artist for defamation and a variety of other charges. Though we figured we wouldn't collect a dime in damages, we could safely spread the word about our lawsuit. We designed a magnificent publicity campaign. The newspaper played it up, the Chens plastered the clippings in their window and even threw a party for the press and city dignitaries, which produced some great pictures. There beamed the Mayor and all the other top brass of the bureaucracy enjoying the Chens' famous chow mein.

The customers came back, slowly at first, but with an increasing pace, until the Chens were back in business. As Yu Chen will tell you, "Some people have been declared dead and mysteriously come back to life. That's what happened to our business."

Prescription for a Dying Drugstore (Dunhill Pharmacy)

Insolvency strategy demands the correct medicine. It's like compounding a prescription.

Dunhill Pharmacy occupied a 3000 sq. ft. store in a large shopping center. A giant discount store anchored one end of the center, a supermarket the other. In between nestled twenty small tenants feeding off the customer traffic created by the "anchor" tenants.

Dunhill's future looked reasonably prosperous. Sales were slowly climbing and had recently passed the $400,000 mark. Profits were small, but it was enough for owner Dick C. to pay his bills and take home a comfortable salary.

All that changed in May, 1979, the day the giant discount store closed its doors under bankruptcy.

Without the discount store to draw customers, the shopping center's tenants were in dire straits. Dick painted a bleak picture. "Even on Saturday, you could use the mall for a bowling alley." Dunhill's cash register tapes confirmed it. Sales dropped from $1,100–1,200 a day to $300–400, until the pharmacy was operating with sales two-thirds below its break-even point. Of course, the other tenants were in the same predicament. I almost expected them to ask for a group rate on their collective bankruptcies.

Dunhill couldn't survive long without a new "anchor" tenant alongside. Though the landlord kept hunting for a new "anchor," most chains were consolidating rather than expanding.

For Dunhill, things could hardly get worse. Dick fell $18,000 behind on his rent and several thousand dollars behind on his bank note. After sixty days, his suppliers stopped further credit.

At that point, Dick's concern was no longer saving the business. He wanted only to save himself. He had personally guaranteed the lease which stood $18,000 in arrears, and he had many more months to go. The bank held a mortgage on Dick's house to collateralize the mortgage on the store. If the business failed, the bank wouldn't get all its money from the proceeds of an auction, so Dick faced eventual loss of his house.

We quickly dispelled any thoughts of a Chapter 11, out-of-court compositions or even a "dump-buy-back." Those would yield temporary solvency, but the business would still leak money through a sieve.

We defined our obejctive: To bail Dick out of his personal obligations.

We reasoned that the landlord, without the rents from the discount store, must be suffering his own cash flow problems. Checking the registry of deeds, we found our assumptions to be correct. The insurance company holding the mortgage on the shopping center had started foreclosure. That was our bargaining chip. We were fighting for survival, and so was the landlord. We would help him survive, if he helped Dick survive.

First, we convened a meeting of the twenty remaining tenants. They all teetered on the edge of their own disasters. Other than the supermarket, Dunhill was now the largest tenant. If we moved out, how many other stores would follow? Sixteen admitted they would have no choice but to quit. Without Dunhill, the shopping center would see even fewer customers. I had my ammunition. Armed with the fact that Dunhill's decision to stay or leave would prompt the same decision from sixteen other tenants, we approached the landlord and slapped our cards on the table.

1. Dunhill was closing up. Dick couldn't afford to cover its losses and he couldn't sell its business.
2. When Dunhill moves, sixteen other tenants will move with it.
3. After the mass exodus, the shopping center will have only four tenants.

As I talked, the landlord could see his shopping center vanish. It's difficult to pay a mortgage with no rents coming in.

We launched into Act II, proposing an alternative that could save everyone's business. Dunhill and its sixteen faithful followers would stay if the landlord agreed to:

1. Cancel the back rent owed.
2. Release Dick as a guarantor of Dunhill's lease.
3. Cut the $2,000 monthly rent to $750 until a discount store opened up.
4. Loan Dunhill up to $25,000 as needed to cover continuing losses.
5. Pay any deficiency due Dunhill's bank should Dunhill fail and the bank not get all its money from the business assets. (This proviso would save Dick's house.)

A hard bargain? Sure, but it would give the landlord a chance to stabilize the center and give it a fighting chance to survive.

The landlord wasn't thrilled, but he got the message. And a week later we had it all in writing.

Two months went by, during which Dick exhausted the $25,000 loan, and still no discount store tenant showed up. The landlord, fearing we'd soon be back to the well for more concessions, came to us with his own proposition. He'd buy the drugstore, by paying off all debts and handing Dick $100,000.

The result? Dick now manages a pharmacy for a large drug chain. But he enjoys counting the interest on the $100,000 he has salted away in the money market.

The landlord still owns the pharmacy and most of the other tenants remained. It paid off! Six months later, a new discount chain tenant signed up and the shopping center is thriving.

I enjoy thinking about the Dunhill case. My approach to saving Dunhill indirectly saved an entire shopping center and sixteen other tenants. But I'm not all smiles. I collected only one fee.

A Final Act (Tip Top Toys)

Scene: A four-store toy chain, owned by four partners.

Players: Ben — Store 1
Steve — Store 2
Art — Store 3
Corey — Store 4

Plot: A grand scheme to see who could milk the most out of the business, undetected by the other three.

Climax: Ben — $ 60,000 richer
Steve — $ 45,000 healthier
Art — $ 49,000 wealthier
Corey — $ 57,000 happier
Creditors — $200,000 poorer

The first four acts must have been fascinating, but I came in only after the final curtain. The shelves were empty, creditors were hovering around like a swarm of hysterical hornets. Tip Top Toys was not in tip top shape.

One of my clients, Henry P., agreed to buy all the shares of the crumbled company from its four, feuding partners for the grand sum of $1,000. Henry even offered to pay them each a $5,000 bonus if the business stayed alive five years. The partners liked the deal because it gave them some travelling money and the chance for even more based on Henry's turnaround ability. At worst, the partners could console themselves with the thought that Henry, not they, would captain the sinking ship.

Henry reasoned that it was a chance to turnaround and gain from a troubled company with little risk. Everybody signed the contract with a smile on his face.

With Tip Top Toys in Henry's hand, the curtain began to rise once again.

Assessing the business was difficult. We could tabulate $200,000 in inventory and fixtures for four stores. Liabilities included a secured bank note for $120,000, back taxes of $16,000 and $400,000 in unsecured trade debts.

Profitability was impossible to predict. The books were a shambles and substantial sums had mysteriously by-passed the cash registers on their way into hungry pockets. Henry concluded that past profitability would tell him nothing. Since the chain no longer stocked the inventory to adequately run each store, and since Henry detested absentee ownership, he consolidated the inventory, narrowed the operation to one store, discounted the toys, and slashed expenses. Discounting made a lot of sense, because Henry didn't have any fast-moving inventory on hand, just the slow movers. He adopted the approach of a "close out" store.

Two weeks later, Henry negotiated a lease on an abandoned supermarket, cannibalized fixtures from the four locations and relocated the inventory to its new home. Tip Top Toys became "Toy Bargains," with discounts as big as 50 percent. A few hard hitting newspaper ads later and the new business began to hum. Sales crept from $6,000 a week to $8,000 and within a month roared to $12,000. It delighted Henry, who knew it would take only $7,000 in weekly sales to break even.

Of course, turnarounds don't provide the convenience of fighting one battle at a time. Operational problems abound, and you can't ignore the clamor of creditors.

Henry immediately threw Tip Top into Chapter 11. This chilled any further creditor action and gave Henry time to build the business and navigate the maze of operational problems.

Cash wasn't a major problem. "The store operated on a cash and carry basis, and we had $200,000 in saleable products. We operated with a positive cash flow from the first day," recalls Henry.

"Inventory replacement was our key problem. Since we were in Chapter 11, we had virtually no credit. But even that was only part of the problem. To discount 50 percent, we needed close-out inventory we could buy at knock-down prices." Henry pounded the sidewalks of Manhattan, scouting toy dealers who would take a chance on him. He sold himself by displaying his track record and the fact that he was the White Knight. The prior owners, not he, had run Tip Top into the shoals. Gradually, goods began to appear. $3,000 from one supplier, $5,000 from another. And Henry followed through with timely payments. The merchandise lifeline began to flow.

Regaining solvency posed the third problem. The bank wanted to foreclose on its $100,000 mortgage. Henry dissuaded them, offering to personally guarantee $15,000 on the note if the bank reinstated it. Henry added "sweetener." The business was depositing over $16,000 a week with the bank. By year's end, the bank would enjoy a $1,000,000 depositor.

Seven of the largest creditors formed the creditors' committee, and they were howling mad. But not at Henry. He had established credibility. He came in to rescue the company. Emotions slowly subsided, until the committee was willing to consider hard numbers.

The numbers confirmed that if the company were liquidated, the assets would bring $150,000. Before general creditors could see a dime, priority creditors would get:

- $100,000 due the bank as secured creditor
- $ 16,000 due on back taxes
- $ 20,000 due creditors who shipped after the Chapter 11 filing
- $ 15,000 for legal fees

It was a dismal picture. If general creditors voted to liquidate, they'd wind up with nothing. After several negotiating sessions, the committee agreed to accept $50,000 payable over five years. The other creditors voted to accept the plan, and almost three months from the day Henry took over, the company emerged solvent from the Bankruptcy Court.

Today, Toy Bargains grosses $3,000,000 annually and has cautiously expanded to a second location and may soon open a third. Henry turned down an offer to buy Toy Bargains that would have netted him $300,000. Not a bad return on a $1,000 investment. But Henry's holding out for the day he can sell for a cool $1,000,000 profit.

Ask Henry about business turnaround. He puts it all in perspective. "Years ago, I invested $30,000 from my savings to buy a furniture business. I lost that business. I constantly think about that defeat and now realize why I couldn't save it. I had the wrong attitude, thinking about the business I was *losing*. It puts you on the defensive emotionally. Now when I see a troubled business, I look at it as something that's already lost. It's the creditors' business. They're handing me the keys and saying 'If you can do something with it, it's yours.' It allows me to think and act positively because I can only *win*."

Henry has the right attitude. He didn't look at the business as a pack of trouble. No, he saw it as his pile of opportunity. And your business represents that same opportunity.

Will you achieve your goals? I think so, and I'll tell you why. I know nothing about your business, but I do know something about you. You aren't going to call it quits, and you won't give up without a fight. You want to save your business and are willing to find solutions and do what's necessary to accomplish your goal. How do I know? Simple. Why else would you be reading this book?

And I hope it helps you.

Bibliography

Altman, Edward I. *Corporate Bankruptcy in America* (Heath-Lexington, 1971)

Argenti, John. *Corporate Collapse* (Wiley, 1976)

Barmash, Isadore. *Great Business Disasters* (Ballantine, 1973)

Bibeault, Donald B. *Corporate Turnaround* (McGraw Hill, 1982)

Burger, Robert E. and **Slavicek, Jan J.** *The Layman's Guide to Bankruptcy* (Van Nostrand Reinhold, 1971)

Druker, Peter. *Managing in Turbulent Times* (Harper & Row, 1980)

Eisenberg, Joseph. *Turnaround Management* (McGraw Hill, 1972)

Groupe, Leonard M. *Going Broke and How to Avoid It* (Thomas Y. Crowell Co., 1972)

Myers, Jerome I. *Wipe Out Your Debts and Make a Fresh Start* (Chancellor Press, 1973)

Mishkin, William S. *Techniques in Corporate Reorganization* (President Publishing House, 1972)

Nicholas, Ted. *How to Get Out of Debt* (Enterprise Publishing Co., 1980)

Ross, Joel E. and **Kami, Michael J.** *Management in Crisis* (Simon & Schuster, 1973)

Rutberg, Sidney. *Ten Cents on the Dollar* (Simon & Schuster, 1973)

Sloma, Richard S. *No Nonsense Management* (MacMillan, 1977)

Smith, R.A. *Corporations in Crisis* (Doubleday, 1966)

Index

A

absentee ownership, 73–74
Absolute Moralist, 27
accountants, 18, 38, 43–45
accounts payable, 6, 210
accounts receivable, 62, 63, 90–91
assets, 3, 8, 13, 14, 89, 165, 176
attorneys, 39–43
auctions, 8
Avenger, 116

B

Buck Passer, 29
business broker, 6

C

capital gain, 5
capital loss, 5
Certified Management Accountants, 45
Chapter 7, 39, 151
Chapter 11, 10, 38, 42, 76, 151–169, 175, 225
collateral, 12, 96, 130, 133, 142, 143, 155–156
combat fatigue, 22

competition, 3
competitors, 21, 66, 68, 86, 181
comptrollers, 44–45
Confirmed Optimist, 26
consignment goods, 97
consultants, 38, 40, 45–51
corporate tax returns, 4
corporations, 4–5, 7, 8, 15
credit associations, 41
credit rating, 12
customer relations, 105–106
cynic, 115

D

defining objectives, 19–21, 204
divorce, 25
dreamers, 2, 3, 4, 29
dump-buy-back, 171–187

E

employee loans, 92
employees, 85, 102–105
expenses, 65

F

failure, preparation for, 1–15
financial controls, 75
financing, 6, 7, 11, 92, 132, 134
flight syndrome, 21

G

gross profit, 65
guarantees, 11, 12, 13
guarantor, 13

H

homestead exemption, 14

I

incorporation, 4–5
inventory, 61, 63, 77, 86, 87, 88–89, 94, 185, 212
IRS, 5, 13, 43, 151

J

judgment proofing, 13, 14, 15

L

lawsuits, 13
loan defaults, 62

M

management action plan, 81–82
management mentality, 30–36
marital problems, 25
merchandising, 70
mergers, 189–207
mini-holding company, 10–11
Moralist, 116

N

National Bankruptcy Reporter, 2
negotiating, 113–127, 154
Nervous Nellie, 27

O

objectives, defining, 19–21, 204
Ostrich, 26
overexpansion, 33–34, 74–75
overhead, 70

P

partnerships, 55, 145, 201
peer pressure, 122
Perennial Pessimist, 28
Peter Principle, 34
Pirate, 28
pricing, 72
profit planning, 78–81
problem solving planning guide, 106–108
proprietary rights, 94
purchase money mortgages, 97

R

real estate, 9
risk, 2, 4, 7

S

salaries, 69, 127
sale/leaseback, 90
sales trends, 64
SBA, 52, 129, 130, 131, 134
SCORE, 52
Section 1244, 5
shrinkage, 46–47
starting smart, 3–22
State Bar Association, 41

T
team effort, 37–57

U
undercapitalization, 7

W
warning signals, 60–62